The Predicament of the Individual in the Middle East

The Predicament of the Individual
in the Middle East

Edited by
Hazim Saghie

Saqi Books

British Library Cataloguing-in-Publication Data
A catalogue record for this book is available from the
British Library

ISBN 0 86356 053 9 (hb)

This edition first published 2001

Saqi Books
26 Westbourne Grove
London W2 5RH
www.saqibooks.com

Contents

Introduction

Are advancement and progress feasible nowadays for a nation, any nation on our planet, without a parallel development in individualism?

The answer is definitely: no.

In our epoch individualism[1] has permeated each and every domain of life in the advanced societies of the west. 'Difference' is the key demand of rapidly increasing numbers of individuals.

For economies and markets to function well, computers must lead and information must spread everywhere. This trend will empower citizens at the same time as it eradicates barriers and state control. Tolerating individual choices and political freedoms will become, sooner or later, a precondition for wealth.

This applies to economies in general but also to the development of their ingredients, especially the services whose role is growing daily all over the world. Services, seen today as the modern sector of any economy, in some countries already account for a larger share of jobs than any other sector. The figures range now from 60 percent in Japan to about 75 percent in America. But the nature of those services has changed. *The Economist* described this process as follows: 'A century ago, most of them involved a direct personal service: being a servant, in other words. Now, most are indirect and concerned with information: education, accountancy, government, communication and so on.

'So the rich today have far less direct command over people – fewer servants, fewer exclusive services – even though they have far more command over things. Household tasks have become increasingly mechanized, through washing machines, vacuum cleaners, dishwashers and so on, and food production more industrialized, reducing the time devoted to cooking at home. That means far fewer women are employed as cooks and maids, but many more are able to go out to work.'[2]

A new economy that is based on technology and information relies to a large extent on personal initiative and innovation. The Asian experience, which combined economic liberalism and political patriarchy, became very difficult to sustain as such, and even more difficult to imitate or duplicate.

Those culturally 'distinctive' communal institutions, such as lifelong employment in Japan, the *chaebol* or family-based business in Korea, and the networks built on kinship lines among the Chinese of South-East Asia are being challenged to change, either directly from the IMF and the World Bank or indirectly through competition in a globalized economy. In the near future Japan and similar societies in Asia will be left with such a shortage of labour that women en masse will have to work, shaking to its roots the traditional division of labour within the family and the recessive stability that arises from it.

Asian societies in China, Korea and India have to face the problem of modernity and tradition on different levels. Increased longevity, for instance, is imposing tremendous stress on the Confucian duty to take care of parents. Sooner or later, they all have to face reconciling communal values with the changing technological and economic environment caused by the introduction of modern capitalism.

The Internet, by extending its control qualitatively over the public aspects of our lives, has given us 'a greater degree of personal autonomy than ever before'. And by subverting the national boundaries and the power of the nation-state, the worldwide web is permitting 'the reconfiguration of human communities in line with individually chosen grounds'.[3]

The merger between America Online and Time-Warner, for example, says a lot about the age in which we live. It proves that, in order to reach us, the material and the data, which it is the job of Time-Warner to collect, need the access, which is provided by American Online. This access is supplied exclusively by the Internet because, among other things, the individual, who is the hero of the Internet, is taking the precedence over the family, which is the 'natural' audience of television.

This same phenomenon occurs in different spheres and walks of life. Take fashion, for example. Alicia Drake, a fashion and style writer based in Paris, could not have chosen a better title than 'The Quest for Individuality' for an article in which she surveyed new clothes and new tendencies in design.[4]

In offices, things are changing in a similar direction. Some very 'respectable' companies and institutions have relinquished the old habit of imposing a uniform on their staff. The necktie, for example, is no longer a must.

Political ideologies are not so different. Gone are the days when the west used to support and uplift any Chilean dictator or Afghani fundamentalist who could, and who wanted to, combat communism. It is common knowledge in our post-cold war era that only societies that are familiar with liberalism and individualism can fight totalitarianism without harming progress or hindering the prospects of democracy.

Nevertheless, this burning need is still very tentative in the non-European world, to which the Middle East belongs. Commenting on a visit to Cairo, Thomas L. Friedman wrote: 'One of the most important things these [globalization, Internet, etc.] do is increase individual choices. At their best they empower and emancipate the individual. But for traditional societies, such as Egypt, the collective, the group, is much more important than the individual, and empowering the individual is equated with dividing the society.'[5]

In fact individuals have always existed in the Middle East as elsewhere on our planet. Those who are familiar with Arab history and literature know about the pre-Islamic marginal poets known as *sa'aliq*. These poets held some opinions, or did some deeds, that were totally rejected by their tribes and communities. They had to flee their homes and kin and live as exiles in a no man's land in the desert.[6]

What did not exist, however, was individualism, for that exists only together with and because of modernity. But a society in which individuals exist and the concept of individualism does not is one lacking in choice and freedom. Individuals are likely to be looked at as unpredictable, lunatic or, at best, extravagant persons. They are liable to be sacrificed for no reason. Their suppressed individualism finds few outlets for self-expression. Its easiest refuge is in some odd bodily gestures or some funny behaviour, or, as in the case of the *sa'aliq*, some poetry that is 'strange', either in its vocabulary or in its content.

In this regard no coherent attitudes can be ascribed to these individuals. They cannot develop an individualist discourse concerning life and death, love and hatred, politics and culture.

Owing to the weakness of individualism and its tradition in these societies, any trace of individuality is commonly confused with selfishness and anti-social behaviour. On the other hand, all sorts of inflated and paranoid egos can flourish in such a social environment as a result of repression from within and from outside.

Computers and portable telephones are undoubtedly used very widely nowadays in many Middle Eastern countries, but internalizing individualism entails more than importing some of the technological means. It rather has to do with prevailing cultures, norms and value systems.

Some writers have argued, moreover, that the material conditions that are so vital in explaining the nature of a certain culture and civilization (for example, the Indian caste system, which resulted from the need to bind scarce labour to the land in a country without a strong central government) cannot by themselves explain the rise of our modern economic world.[7]

This thesis suggests that undergoing a deep process of westernization is a precondition of becoming modern. According to the same thesis, all the Asian civilizations (Hindu, Chinese, Islamic and Orthodox) were unable to go beyond what Deepak Lal has called 'Smithean' gains from trade: India during its Mauryan period, China in the Song Dynasty and Islamic peoples under the Abbasids were hampered in this way. The Christian west, on the other hand, was the only civilization that succeeded in attaining 'Promethean' growth rooted in the security of long-term advances in technology and means of production. This difference derives mainly from reasons related to cultural tradition and a cosmological set of beliefs.

Here, we cannot overlook the thoughts and influence of Max Weber.

The idea that only in the Christian west could a culture of authentic individualism develop, where belief in a transcendent God encouraged individuals to defy the authority of the social structures surrounding them (the family, the Church and the state) is implicit in the Weberian theoretical scheme. Such a universal God not only prevented the secular authority from ascribing sacredness to itself, but also assured people that nature was subject to hidden, universal laws, and thus facilitated the discovery of modern natural science. And exactly because this individualism could liberate the Christian peoples from the bondage of inherited structures and tradition, innovation became possible and modern capitalist society was subsequently identified with the technical mastery of the world.

Nevertheless, when it comes to exact dates, Deepak Lal differs from Weber. Modern individualism, for him, was the offspring of a European family structure, the result of a process that began more than ten centuries ago. Contrary to common belief, the nuclear family was not a by-product of industrialization, but in fact predated industrial society by centuries and, in a sense, helped to bring it to life. Its roots can be traced to Pope Gregory I and the seventh-century Church, which, because of its greed for money, discouraged certain marriages in a way that kept private property within close-knit family groups. This, in its turn, benefited the Church while giving individuals a material basis for independence from the large, tight kin groups such as persisted in the east.

This process was, on a grass-roots level, the forerunner of industrialization. The distinctions Lal makes throughout his book are based on what he sees as a qualitative difference between 'shame' and 'guilt' cultures. In the civilizations of the east, shame is the cornerstone of moral behaviour, which means that manners or habits are enforced by external social pressure.[8] By contrast, in Christianity, which is a guilt culture, morality rose over an inner state of intentionality and found its endorsement in the individual's belief that God, and only God, can know and judge that inner state.

This analysis might hold water, if only in general and historical terms, but this does not make it absolute in any sense. No one can say that the battle for individualism, which became an utmost necessity, as I mentioned earlier, is totally won in the west itself. Tibor R. Machan warns of communitarianism in the United States, of the tendency not to recognize the role played by individualism in the most individualistic society, and by the continuous celebration of the family instead.[9]

Furthermore, no one can rule out the possibility of a reactionary backlash, highly unlikely though it may be, in this post-industrial country or that. On the other hand it is quite legitimate to doubt the influence of Christianity, even as a background, on many social activities in Europe and elsewhere in the 'world of Christendom'.

But when it comes to the developing countries, we should be more vigilant. True modernization is not internalized yet, but there are plenty of reasons to suppose that in the globalized era the elites have to unify with their colleagues in the advanced societies. The sooner and faster they do it, the better. Otherwise a civilizational, rather an existential, impasse lies ahead for all of us.

A globalized west, in turn, cannot for long tolerate the continuation of the schism that existed and was acceptable when the world was based on the west–east fragmentation, on nation-states and the seclusion they imply.

Two theoretical points may be raised here.

Without any doubt, 'old' loyalties (kinship, ethnic, local and religious ties) will die very hard, and for an unknown period of time they will continue to challenge and hinder the introduction of individualism. The latter cannot prosper fully in the context of outright confrontation with these loyalties, rather it has to reach a certain modus vivendi that combines criticism and understanding, advancement and assimilation. In this way, individualism may avoid the severe ruptures that can produce dictatorships, destroy the present reality in a single strike and exaggerate its quasi-prophetic mission of salvation.

Among other virtues embodied in this gradual evolution, the link with society may be kept alive instead of offering blind support to authoritarian regimes that repress individuality and/or 'modernize' it in a very superficial and violent way. It may be appropriate, in such situations, to envisage the creation of a temporary parallel means of representation, or a combination between what is modern and individualistic on the one hand, where merit is the key to any role in the public sphere, and what is sectarian, ethnic or religious on the other. Such an arrangement would respond to the immediate present without sacrificing the secular future, which should be based on popular will in politics and on rational criteria in civil service.

Individualism in 'non-European' societies such as ours should not necessarily be accompanied by a Jacobean and instant secularization imposed from above. But, when long-term strategies are being set, a lot of attention should be given to what is global and common. In other words, the 'specific' should not be repressed, but neither should it be enforced, appeased or over-represented. It should be used as a means to facilitate the transition to modernity and make it smoother and less violent. Otherwise we will end up sanctioning what is backward and surrendering ourselves to everyday political tactics that lead nowhere.

The challenge is how to respond democratically to the immediate while simultaneously building for the future. But it seems that what used to take ages before can nowadays be accomplished quite quickly.

In this regard India may be the best example, not only because it preserved democracy without engaging in revolutionary upheavals, but also because it could, within the context of this experiment, enter the new technological era, which it owes to the individual talents of its population. The country now churns out 115,000 engineering graduates every year, many of them English-speaking specialists in computer programming, whom the United States and Europe compete to attract.

Another issue that deserves attention and obliges a nuanced approach is the economic side of individualism in a poor region such as ours. Hayekian liberalism, or rather neo-liberalism, has assumed the role of guardian and corollary of individualism. Margaret Thatcher caught this mood when she stated that 'there is no such thing as society. There are individual men and women, and there are families.'[10] This is a very extreme point of view, which negates one factor in order to stress another and fails to deal with all the factors in their totality and the interaction between them. It is, furthermore, reactionary in the sense that it fails to see the constraints that families place on individualism. In this sense what Thatcher preached is a revolutionary approach in a conservative direction.

It is obvious that individualism is related to a minimalist state and minimalist intervention. But in the developing world, poverty, if left unchecked in spite of the welfare programmes designed to eradicate it, will only help to strengthen collective loyalties and consciousness. In this context Durkheimian mechanical solidarity will completely obliterate the organic and modern solidarities and prevent their development.

Here to we are compelled to betray orthodoxy and try to be a bit imaginative. Individualism in the developing world amounts not only to asking the government to smooth out some of the rough edges of life, to cut taxes and to establish individual social-security accounts on terms that reward the most successful. It implies, as well, a minimal communal vision in which the government sets national economic goals and then individuals are rewarded when they help achieve these goals besides their own. In other words, the elites of most of the countries in the region may face, in this globalized era, a delicate, if not partially contradictory, task: how to weaken the state's propensity for oppression and supervision without weakening its parallel capacity to act as a social safety valve for the poverty-ridden?

The essays in this book examine, in different styles, genres and approaches, the politics and culture of individualism in different countries of the Middle East. The goal throughout is to stress the shortcomings of society in these various countries, the gradual social progress that is occurring and the burning necessity for more radical development.

Ramin Jahanbegloo traces the beginning of individualistic culture in Iran as represented by its three pioneers, Amir Kabir, Malkum Khan and Furughi. Khaled Mustafa discusses the modern history of Sudan from the angle of the collective versus the individual. Yaron Ezrahi explains how a brand of secular individualism, or rather secular singlehood, evolved in Israel resulting from the fragmentation of collective frames of meaning. Murat Belge, whose contribution focuses on the development of individualism in Turkey, pays special attention to both political history as reflected in the state and to the role of the intellectuals. Hussein Ahmad Amin, using a civilizational approach, studies the dialectics of individual versus authority in Egypt. Saleh Bechir tells us that, in the Arab Maghreb, the individual will not necessarily emerge from within the political sphere but rather from society itself and as a result of grass-roots changes. Sami Shourush studies the obstacles to individualism in the experience of the Kurds, drawing attention to the tribal fabric of society and the violence, whether at local or state level, that is inherent in it.

Iliya Harik, in contrast to his co-authors in this book, defends communalism, as distinct from collectivization, which looks to him, especially in the Lebanese experience, more likely to be able to guarantee democracy and pluralism.

Heavy emphasis is laid on developments in the field of culture and artistic representation. Els Van der Plas, commenting on the work of the Iranian artist Shirin Neshat, addresses the theoretical question of the individual as artist and the artist as a part of history. War and death in Israel are the themes on which Emmanuel Sivan concentrates, highlighting how civil society uses history as a weapon to confront the state and what is communal. Gadi Taub draws a line of demarcation between the individual and the collective in Israeli culture and discusses how this line developed. Muhammad Abi Samra's view is that individualism is arrested in contemporary Arab culture. He goes on to lament the fact that Arab experiences of life are still outside the range of writing and recording. Ibrahim al-Aris goes back to the 1950s to document the first manifestations of individualism in the Arab film industry. Mai Ghoussoub, mixing testimony with analysis, narrates the story of some individual routes in their relation to gender.

Taken together, these essays paint a portrait of a region undergoing change and suffering traumas as it faces fundamental and existential questions.

Thanks are due to friends and colleagues who helped in different ways: Fred Halliday, Moris Farhi, Kanan Makiya, Eberhard Kienle, Sami Zubaida, Emma Sinclair-Webb, Yucel Terzibasoglu, François Zabbal, Roger Hardy and Haleh Esfandiari among others. Emmanuel Sivan, in addition to his important contribution, accompanied the project from the beginning and gave much advice. The patience of André Gaspard and Sarah al-Hamad from Saqi Books was crucial for this book to materialize.

Hazim Saghie

Notes

1. For a history of individualism in western thought, from Enlightenment to the late twentieth century, see: Lorenzo Infantino, *Individualism in Modern Thought from Adam Smith to Hayek*, London, Routledge, 1998.
2. *The Economist*, 11 September 1999, p. 12.
3. Gordon Graham, *The Internet: A Philosophical Inquiry*, London, Routledge, 1999, pp. 37–8.
4. *International Herald Tribune*, 6 October 1999.
5. *International Herald Tribune*, 29–30 January 2000.
6. Interestingly enough, the early communist translators of *The Communist Manifesto* arabized the term 'proletariat' as *sa'aliq*. Thus the famous slogan 'workers of the world unite' became in Arabic translation '*sa'aliq* of the world unite'.
7. See as an example: Deepak Lal, *Unintended Consequences: The Impact of Factor Endowments, Culture and Politics on Long-run Economic Performance*, MIT, 1999. Lal is, however, critical of the western version of modernity.
8. Very far from being an individualist, the French sociologist Emile Durkheim asserted in his concept of the division of labour that there is a collective consciousness that is both 'coercive' and 'exterior'. For him, coercion implied that the individual in a society whose solidarity is 'mechanical' cannot dissent from the norm, and that the reaction against such dissent is, by definition, a social punishment. Exteriority, on the other hand, means that the social phenomenon exists outside the individual and independently from him and is produced by the collective totality.
9. See: Tibor R. Machan, *Classical Individualism: The Supreme Importance of Each Human Being*, London, Routledge, 1998.
10. Interview in *Woman's Own*, October 1987.

PART ONE

Politics and Society

CHAPTER ONE

Iranian Intellectuals and Democratic Individualism

Ramin Jahanbegloo

Modern individualism and democratic individuality

Modern individualism emerged from a complex of social processes, which taken as a whole is understood as the process of modernization. According to Marcel Mauss and his successor Louis Dumont, who both conceive the 'individual' as a concept of a unique and indivisible unity, the historical process of the west from Antiquity to Christianity and from there to modern times demonstrates a constant transition of the awareness of the self 'from a simple masquerade to the mask, from a 'role' (personage) to a 'person' (person), to a name, to an individual; from the latter to a being possessing metaphysical and moral value; from a moral consciousness to a sacred being; from the latter to a fundamental form of thought and action'.[1] Therefore when we study the concepts of individual and individualism we have to take into account the moral and the political dimensions of the individual. As the history of modern western civilization witnesses, the concept of 'individual' is interconnected with the two concepts of 'rationality' and 'autonomy'. According to Dumont the individual, as found in modern ideology of man and society, is 'the independent, autonomous and thus (essentially) nonsocial moral being' and 'the rational being' who is 'the subject of the institutions'.[2] In other words, modern individualism not only promotes 'disenchantment of the world', as discussed by Max Weber, but also involves an aspiration towards an autonomous self and a democratic society. Individualism, particularly a rights-based individualism, is imposed on the modern self as a requisite for the maintenance of modern society. Modern life then creates the kind of individual necessary for the maintenance of its institutions. Therefore, modernity and modernization call forth the democratic, individuated personality, which is fundamental to a liberal society that tries to affirm the individualistic configuration of ideas and values against the holistic view of the 'collective individual'. In sum, the individualist spirit of modernity, with its concern for human dignity, is strenuously at odds with 'holism' and with the desire to see others as a part of a collective order rather than as equal individuals. Unlike modern society, a traditional society is characterized generally by a culture that sacrifices the rights of the individuals. As a result, rights-based individualism prepares the social and political way for constitutional democracy. In turn, the practice of 'democratic individualism' prepares, guards and fulfils rights-based individualism.

As this article suggests, the idea of democratic individuality is a complex subject to map in modern Iranian history. It is as complex as the thoughts and actions of its principal animators, Amir Kabir, Malkum Khan and Furughi. The division of the concept of 'Iranian individualism' into three aspects of individuality may not be tactful or philosophically subtle. I may be too eager to bring historical facts into political philosophy but to ignore these is to ignore the best conception of Iranian individualism.

Amir Kabir and Dar-ol Fonun

Iran entered the twentieth century as a backward country, whose sovereigns had lost their moral faith and political authority to rule it. In 1896, the year of the assassination of Nasseredin Shah, Iran was economically bankrupt and endangered by internal social chaos. The weaknesses of the regime also manifested themselves through an administration untouched by modernity. The Qajar bureaucracy was characterized by functional confusion, in which no specific or technical knowledge was required for most of the positions. The personalization of the Qajar bureaucracy was a direct result of personalized politics, which brought about a great deal of conflict in the system. This total absence of legal and political rationality led to a state of paralysis of the system.

As a result, a quest for order and organization became a serious need among Iranian reformers. The central role was given to the intellectuals, who were not only consumers of modern values and ideas but also their promoters among the leading political class of Iranian society. These were mostly western-educated men and greatly influenced by European liberalism and ideas of social equality.

Hand in hand with this need for rationalization and progress came an interest in a new interpretation of the world, bringing about a new horizon of significance of the self, one that advocated a rights-based individualism. Europe, they reasoned, had advanced by virtue of being governed by an instrumental rationality that allowed the modern self to evolve. Even though they considered that the adoption of material aspects of western civilization was an important step towards progress, they argued that the modern conception of the individual, insofar as he is the bearer of values in modern society, had still not being grasped. To that end, they decided to defend the idea of an independent and autonomous self, as found primarily in the modern view of the world, by rejecting first and foremost the ontological and epistemological foundations of Iranian holism that had long been accepted by political and religious traditions in Iran. Knowing that they needed power to defend the new concept of 'individualism' against the religious tradition of 'holism' (crystallized by the close relationship between the ulama and the throne), they conceived of the notion that they may slowly mould reality by establishing a relationship with the imperial power. By reawakening the dormant interests of the king and the aristocracy in the splendours of the west, they tried to find a way to impose their blueprints for reform. Although their roles as advisers to men of power often brought them some success in influencing the path of 'democratic individualism', their relationship with the imperial power usually proved highly unstable. Sooner or later most of them were forced into retirement and exile or put to death. In this respect, three intellectual statesmen, Amir Kabir, Malkum Khan and Furughi, may be considered ideal proponents and representatives of 'democratic individualism'.

Mirza Taqi Khan Farahani, better known as Amir Kabir, was a nineteenth-century Iranian prime minister renowned for his far-reaching reforms during the first few years of Nasseredin Shah's reign (1848–96). His aim was to limit foreign interference in Iran's domestic affairs by increasing Iran's potential for self-sufficiency. Amir Kabir believed that the success of such a reform necessitated regularization and centralization of the government and the adoption of European technology. Robert Grant Watson, a European who was in Iran at that time, described Amir Kabir's programme as endeavouring 'to erect his country into a powerful and firmly established monarchy upon the basis of law and justice'.[3] For Amir Kabir the first step was to increase the awareness of Iranian officials of the importance of modern developments in the west. In order to consolidate his reforms he published the first official newspaper in Iran, called the *Ruznameh-ye Vaqaye-e Ettefaqiyeh*. The purpose of the newspaper was that 'the people of this exalted country become more informed, aware and insightful'.[4] Its content included domestic news, foreign news and articles on modern science. Amir Kabir had named an Englishman, Edward Burgess, as the head of his translation bureau, whose duty it was to translate articles from foreign newspapers. Burgess was also the editor-in-chief of another gazette, which was deigned only for the shah and the members of the government.

The keystone of Amir Kabir's reforms was the establishment of a European-style educational institution in Iran, called the Dar-ol Fonun. This institution was supposed to train students to form a government cadre capable of instituting reform measures. Furthermore, Amir Kabir preferred not to follow the policy of previous Qajar king of sending selected groups of students abroad. According to Comte Gobineau, Amir Kabir: 'did not look favourably on Europeans, and, desirous of keeping them at a distance, he wanted, on the other hand, to borrow from them military knowledge and some other industrial skills'.[5] Amir Kabir was aware of the great importance of establishing the Dar-ol Fonun and adopting European technological advances. In a letter to Nasseredin Shah he wrote: ' In the matter of the school, great precision is necessary. It requires very reasonable and dignified men who are skilled in everything European and Iranian.'[6]

This letter shows that for Amir Kabir the only right way of pursuing his 'democratic individualism' agenda was to mount a professional challenge to the traditionally structured educational and judicial systems, which were largely the prerogative of the clergy. Amir Kabir's dilemma of modernizing Iran while preventing it from becoming Europeanized was solved by his decision to recruit Austrian instructors instead of asking for the help of the British or Russians. Under to the contract between the foreign instructors and the Iranian government, signed on August 10th 1851, the foreign instructors agreed not to involve their diplomatic representatives in their business. According to one of the medical instructors, Dr Polak, 'It was Amir Kabir's intention to have the teachers that had been engaged isolated from the politics of the country so that they would devote themselves to their teaching duties with undivided attention'.[7]

As the result of Amir Kabir's modernizing efforts, Dar-ol Fonun became the first European-structured educational institution in Iran, but, despite its many achievements, it failed to emerge as a catalyst for further substantive reforms. The association of Dar-ol Fonun with western culture constituted a real threat to the institutional power of the ulama, who rejected any kind of knowledge that was transmitted to the students outside the *madreseh* system. Therefore, the Dar-ol Fonun appeared as a symbol of social and political change promoting a 'democratic individualistic' structure. Despite his awareness of Iran's social and technological weaknesses vis-à-vis the west, Nasseredin Shah failed both to support the efforts of Amir Kabir and to enforce reform measures effectively. Faced by the high level of opposition from the ulama to Amir Kabir's reforms, Nasseredin Shah dismissed him from office only a few days before the inauguration of the Dar-ol Fonun. Opposition was led against Amir Kabir by all those who considered the prime minister's attempts to establish the primary structures of 'democratic individualism' in Iran as a danger for the existing holistic system of privileges and inequalities. These included the courtiers, the ulama and the Queen Mother, who planned the assassination of Amir Kabir.[8] The Shah himself took political measures to stop the process of 'democratic individualism' in Iran by putting a ban on the European-structured institutions. One of the major examples of this was the closure of the Faramushkhaneh in 1861, which was created by Mirza Malkum Khan in a form imitative of French Freemasonry.

Mirza Malkum Khan and the Faramushkhaneh

The term *Faramushkhaneh* (House of Oblivion) has been associated with a secret society established in Tehran in 1858. Mirza Malkum Khan was an Armenian of Julfa converted to Islam. He was the first Iranian who was interested in Freemasonry and who considered the Masonic lodge as a basis for the promotion and political implementation of 'democratic individualism' in Iran. Malkum, who had spent some time in Paris, had a sceptical and utilitarian mind and was fully convinced of the absolute superiority of modern civilization. This positive attitude to modern values made Malkum Khan one of the most coherent advocates of western 'democratic individualism' as opposed to 'Asiatic holism'. As Hamid Algar clearly explains: 'Malkum subscribes to the nineteenth-century concept of "Asia" as the antithesis of the materially active west, the inexhaustible breeding ground of religions and speculative philosophies, and of the "Asiatic", an irrational individual firmly caught in a mesh of lifeless and stultifying traditions'.[9] Malkum's involvement in Iranian political and social affairs made of him one of the key figures of reform during the Nasseredin Shah period. On his return from Paris to Iran in 1852, Malkum joined the newly established Dar-ol Fonun as an interpreter for foreign instructors and as a teacher of such subjects as natural sciences and geography. By introducing the Iranian students of Dar-ol Fonun to modern sciences he drew their attention to western civilization and they ended up by joining the Faramushkhaneh. The aim of this secret society was to integrate the political tradition of modern Europe and the ideals of the French Revolution into Iranian society by preparing for their implementation in the Qajar administration. The principles of Malkum's secret society, as mentioned in the course of his conversations with Fath Ali Akhundzadeh, were: 'to shun evil, to strive to do good, to fight against oppression, to live peacefully with one's fellows, to seek learning, to diffuse learning and as far as is possible to strive to maintain harmony among one's compatriots and fellows'.[10]

What is clear from Malkum's writings is that he believed sincerely in the triumph of science over superstition, but he did not consider the essence of Islam to be superstition. Accordingly he wished to maintain the essence of religiosity, but by reforming Islam. In a treatise written by Malkum in defence of the Faramushkhaneh, he refuted the accusation that he was trying to introduce innovations in matters of faith (bid'at) by claiming that all the prophets and saints were aware of the secret revealed by Freemasonry. 'Because of their perfect wisdom,' proclaimed Malkum, 'the prophets did not wish to disclose in their own age the totality of hidden knowledge, and thus they made no pronouncement concerning the telegraph, the camera, the New World, or a thousand other truths.'[11] In so saying, Malkum was expressing his belief that the purpose of the Faramushkhaneh was to propagate universal truth, which was conceived as an esoteric truth. His invocation of the principle of secrecy suggests that Malkum had an accurate knowledge of the history of secret societies inside and outside Iran and of mechanisms through which he could apply the concept of 'democratic individualism' to the structure of Iranian society.

Alarmed by the leading ulama of Tehran, who accused Malkum of propagating heretical ideas and anti-royalist principles, Nasseredin Shah began to take action against the Faramushkhaneh by publishing the following decree in the official gazette on October 18th 1861: 'It has recently come to our knowledge that certain of the lowly ruffians of the city have spoken of founding and organizing European houses of oblivion, and expressed a desire to establish such. Therefore a clear imperial decree is issued that if henceforth anyone utter the expression and phrase "house of oblivion", let alone attempt to establish such, he will be subject to the full wrath and chastisement of the state. Let use of this word be completely abandoned, and let none concern himself with these absurdities, for he shall without doubt receive thoroughgoing punishment'.[12] As a result of this decree, the Faramushkhaneh was dissolved and punitive action was taken against its members. Malkum himself continued to propagate his ideas and even to maintain in secret another organization called Jame-ye-Adamiyat (The Society of Humanity). But, accused of irreligion, heresy and conspiracy against the Shah, he was exiled to Baghdad.

Inevitably, one of the suspicions raised against Malkum was that of republicanism. It appears that Malkum's intention was to reform the holistic structure of Iranian monarchy and clergy through a political and economic reorganization of the society according to European models. A contemporary of Malkum affirms that 'He used to say that a republican regime should be established in accordance with the system prevailing in most European states, and that individual citizens should participate in the allotment of posts and the assignment of functions in the affairs of the country and the matters of the state.'[13] Yet, as has been mentioned above, the projected reforms by Malkum based on the ideals of the French Revolution were represented as being consonant with a 'religion of humanity'.[14] W. S. Blunt in his *Secret History of the English Occupation of Egypt* reproduces a lecture delivered by Malkum in London in 1891, in which he proclaimed that there was no essential difference between the Qur'an and the principles of Christianity. Blunt also states that Malkum claimed to have produced a Bible of his creed.[15]

In the final analysis, the influence of Mirza Malkum Khan in contributing to the principles of 'democratic individualism', which led to the Constitutional Revolution of 1906–7, should not be underestimated. Probably the Faramushkhaneh was of great importance as an example of an institution for the transmission of modern western ideas in Iran. It was followed and its work pursued by other secret societies and intellectual circles of the constitutional period. The modernization/westernization dilemma mirrored by Malkum in his writings was taken up by other reform-minded intellectuals who advocated the adoption of the principles of 'democratic individualism' in Iran. Among these Muhammad Ali Furughi played an important part in Iranian politics and culture during the first half of the twentieth century.

Furughi and modern liberal institutions

Furughi belonged to the second generation of modern Iranian intellectuals, who, thanks to the Constitutional Revolution of 1906, were able to participate more actively in the political life of the country. The goal and hope of Furughi (as of Amir Kabir and Malkum Khan) was to create suitable conditions for the implementation of democratic individualistic principles in Iran, by concentrating his efforts on 'reforms from above'. In order to achieve these goals Furughi attempted to influence not only the political actions of Reza Shah (1921–42), by involving himself in the different branches of government, but also by introducing modern ideas to Iranians through translations, speeches and writings. The reign of Reza Shah was marked by a series of cataclysmic changes in Iran. The western influences that had been filtering into Iran through the Qajar political and cultural elites finally gained ascendancy in the efforts of men like Furughi. These efforts were of sufficient magnitude to be qualified as revolutionary changes. The ideal underlying these revolutionary changes was complete dedication to the principle of 'democratic individualism' through a breakdown of the holistic power of religion and a rapid adoption of technical rationality. Furughi's acceptance of democratic individualistic ideals was accompanied by a deep belief in the cultural and spiritual values of Iran. His aim was to create a strong, centralized government able to resist foreign domination and to modernize Iranian society.

Like most of the intellectuals of his generation, Furughi considered Reza Shah as the charismatic leader who could put an end to the chaotic situation of Iran of the early 1920s. To realize such an aim, Furughi supported the extensive programme of reform instituted by Reza Shah during his two premierships, and he was the major force behind Muhammad Reza Shah's accession to the throne in 1942 following his father's abdication. Yet Furughi's political career started many years before Reza Shah's rise to power, with the foundation in 1908 of the first official Freemasons' lodge in Iran, called 'Le Réveil de l'Iran' ('The Awakening of Iran'), where he held the rank of Grand Master. For Furughi as for Malkum Khan before him the Freemasonry was an institution dedicated to striving to spread ideals of 'democratic individualism' in Iran through universalization and promotion of western principles of freedom, education and secularism.

Furughi continued his task of enlightening others as a professor and later as director of the Political College in 1908–10. His writings and translations of this period were mainly discussions of the fundamental rules of constitutionality in western European countries. As a follower of the principles of the French Enlightenment, Furughi insisted on the idea of separation of the different branches of government. As he wrote:

> The duty of government is to be the protector of the rights of the people, that is, to be the keeper of justice. The government will not be

able to undertake its duty unless it acts according to laws. The existence of laws will not be realized except by two means: first, through making laws, and second, through execution of laws. Therefore the government has two powers: first, the making of laws, and second, the execution of laws. If the powers of legislation and execution remain in the hands of a single person or a single group, the conduct of government will result in despotism . . . Therefore, government is constitutional only when it has separated these two powers from each other and invested them in two separate groups.[16]

These ideas and concepts of Furughi on constitutionalism, freedom and equality played a significant role in familiarizing Iranians with the principles of 'democratic individualism'. Furughi continued this task by secularizing the Iranian courts along the lines of those in European countries during his incumbency as the first head of the High Court of Appeals in 1912. This was the way in which the holistic structure of the Iranian judicial system, which was controlled by the ulama and regulated by the Shari'a, could be replaced with the modern codes of procedure based on democratic individualistic principles.

Knowing that the cultural system was under the virtually exclusive control of the clergy, Furughi founded the Iranian Academy (Farhangstan) in May 1935. He served in the Academy as a regular member and as its first president, during the time when he also held the post of prime minister. In a message addressed to the Academy, Furughi affirmed that this institution had to take an active role in directing the process of reform by familiarizing Iranians with the works of their great writers, as well as by asking people who had a good knowledge of foreign languages and an excellent command of Persian to translate the classical works of European civilization. It is worth mentioning here that Furughi had a special interest in western philosophy, in particular with the teachings of Plato and Descartes. In 1918 he published his first philosophical work, entitled *The Philosophy of Socrates by Plato* (*Hekmat-e Soqrat be Qalam-e Aflatun*). Later in 1922 he translated the *Discours de la méthode* by Descartes and added a long introduction to it entitled 'The Course of Philosophy in Europe' ('Sayr-e Hekmat dar Urupa'), in which he briefly discussed the historical development of philosophy in the west. This book could be considered a philosophical foundation for Furughi's democratic individualistic principles in Iranian politics. In 1927, while serving as Iran's ambassador to Kemalist Turkey, Furughi published his *Distant and Lengthy Thought* (*Andishey-e Dur va Deraz*), a short treatise on future advances in science and technology. According to Furughi, the ultimate result of this evolution would be that 'the distances and barriers that today exist between people and their goals would no longer exist . . . Their souls would be united; the childish desires of today would be abandoned; man's knowledge of the world of creation would become more perfect and his benefits from it would be increased. In short, he would be a step closer to God'.[17]

It is clear that Furughi's main goal in writing such a treatise was to 'educate the youth and to make them think'. In fact, it seems that intellectuals such as Furughi hoped to bring about the necessary reforms in Iran by educating Iranian youth to the philosophical outlook of 'democratic individualism' founded on a wide range of knowledge on politics, science and culture. There is also another dimension in the work of Furughi, which is complementary to that of Amir Kabir and Malkum, namely the influence of the liberal style in Iranian politics. Even if he found little opportunity to put his liberalism into action during the Pahlavi era, he played a significant role in promoting democratic individualistic ideals by practising a policy of transparency in Iranian society during his two-term premiership. He allowed the press to publish freely, freed political prisoners and allowed women to decide for themselves whether or not they wanted to wear the veil. The versatile career of Furughi appears as the turning point in a long period of conflict between religious and autocratic 'holistic' ideas and the principles of 'democratic individualism' in Iran. This conflict was perhaps inevitable, given the functions assigned by Iranian society to the royal power and the clergy. Moreover, Iran's contact with modernity gave rise to intellectual changes and the emergence of a secular-minded, politically engaged intelligentsia, who, although in conflict with the holistic philosophy of their time, played an important role in creating among Iranian-educated citizens a sense of the urgency of implementing democratic individualistic ideals.

In conclusion, we can say that both the achievements and the failures of the reformist ideas of Amir Kabir, Malkum Khan and Furughi in the pre-constitutional period and the Pahlavi era provided an important philosophical and political background for the later introduction and implementation of some of the principles of 'democratic individualism' in Iran. These three men were the first to identify the obstacles to the implementation of democratic individualistic ideas in Iran. Their failures therefore served as a poignant experience for future generations of Iranian intellectuals who were confronted with the dilemma of 'holism' and 'democratic individualism' in the decades before and after the Revolution of 1979.

Notes

1. Marcel Mauss, 'A Category of the Human Mind: the Notion of Person, the Notion of the Self', in Carrithers, Collins and Lukes (eds), *The Category of Person*, 1985, p. 3.
2. Louis Dumont, *Essays on Individualism*, Chicago, University of Chicago Press, 1992, p. 62.
3. Robert Grant Watson, *A History of Persia from the Beginning of the 19th Century to the Year 1858*, London, Smith, Elder and Co, 1866, pp. 381–2.
4. See F. Adamiyat, *Fekre-Azadi va Moqadameh ye Nehzate-Mashrutiyat dar Iran*, Tehran, 1340 solar, p. 45.
5. J. A. Gobineau, *Trois ans en Asie*, Paris. 1859, p. 240.
6. See F. Adamiyat, *Amir Kabir va Iran*, Tehran, 1334 solar, p. 190.
7. J. E. Polak: *Persien, das Land und seine Bewohner*, vol. 1, Leipzig, 1865, pp. 297–8.
8. See Abbas Amanat, *Pivot of the Universe: Nasir al-Din Shah Qajar and the Iranian Monarchy*, Berkeley, University of California Press, 1977.
9. See Hamid Algar, *Mirza Malkum Khan*, Berkeley, University of California Press, 1973, p. 18.
10. F. A. Akhundzadeh, *Alifba-yi Jadid va Maktubat*, Baku, 1963, pp. 294–5, quoted by H. Algar, op. cit., p. 38.
11. Ismail Ra'in, *Faramushkhaneh va Framasonri dar Iran*, Tehran, 1969, I, p. 546, quoted by H. Algar, op. cit., p. 39.
12. Quoted by H. Algar, op. cit., pp. 48–9.
13. Quoted by H. Algar, op. cit., p. 47.
14. See F. Adamiyat, 1340 solar, p. 103.
15. W. S. Blunt, *Secret History of the English Occupation of Egypt* , London, 1903, pp. 82–4.
16. Muhammad Ali Furughi, *Huquq-e Asasi Ya'ni Adab-e Mashrutiyat*, Tehran, 1907, p. 19.
17. Muhammad Ali Furughi, *Andishey-e Dur va Deraz*, Istanbul, Ahmadi Matba Ashi, 1927, p. 32.

CHAPTER TWO

Individualism and Collectivism in Israel

Yaron Ezrahi

Bhikho Parekh in an essay on 'the cultural particularity of liberal democracy'[1] argues that, as a political system, liberal democracy is a dialectical welding of two not fully compatible elements, of which liberalism is less universalist, less well received and less deployable than democracy. The claim that the individual is primary while the community is derivative is more controversial than the value or the application of democratic procedures such as free elections. In every society there is a different balance between the liberal and the democratic components, the rights and powers of citizens as individuals or members of minority groups, and the rights and powers of the state and the majority that controls the instruments of government.

During the last two and a half centuries the encounter between liberalism and nationalism or clericalism has found the Jews mostly on the liberal side as articulate protagonists of individual freedoms and minority rights. The affinities of Jewish intellectuals to cosmopolitan enlightenment ideas had come to be regarded as a special characteristic of Jewish secular culture and of the Jewish intelligentsia.[2]

This record has raised expectations that a Jewish polity will rest on liberal principles and uphold the fundamental commitments to a bill of rights and principles of equality. In the light of such expectations, how can we account for the fact that Israel, the 'Jewish state', has no constitution, no bill of rights, a dismal record of discrimination against the non-Jewish minorities (particularly Arabs and Druses) and finally a hegemonic religion, an established church, with the political power to divert massive public resources to support sectarian religious education and limit civic education in the Israeli school system? How can we account for the weakness of the liberal component in Israeli democracy, the death of the Israeli liberal party, the loneliness of the Israeli Supreme Court as the custodian of individual rights, and the feeble checks on arbitrary uses of state powers vis-à-vis Jews and non-Jews alike?

This state of affairs is not only at odds with Jewish liberalism in the Diaspora but also with powerful liberal ideas, which can be found in classical Hebrew texts. The present alliance between both orthodox and ultra-orthodox Jewish establishments and the nationalist block obscures other, currently neglected strains of Jewish religious culture. Several scholars, including, most recently, Aviezer Ravitzky and Menahem Loberbaum, have shown the depth and the richness of the rabbinical traditions generally espousing secularized conceptions of politics. Maimonedes, Adret and Gerondi, for instance, stressed the limits of the Torah in guiding the handling of ordinary affairs, thereby allowing a considerable freedom for pragmatic flexibility.[3] Moshe Idel insists that the rabbinical rationalist individualist strain in Judaism is marginal in relation to the mythological, mystical and irrational components of the Jewish religious world view and practice. This in itself, however, need not rule out circumstances or historical forces that can select and elevate the marginal over the mainstream. Those therefore who seek support for liberal individualism in Jewish classical texts and Jewish general culture need not despair. Some sources seem even to anticipate specific liberal ideas such as the primacy of the individual. Shalom Albeck argues, for instance, that according to Alfasi (1013–1103), his student Ibn Migas (1077–1141) and later Meir Abulafia (1170–1244), 'the community is not a legal persona distinct from its members but rather a partnership of individuals'.[4]

Despite the persistent power of the idea of the 'people', the Jewish collective, in Judaism, tensions between individual and community are present in various spheres of Jewish culture. The absence of a powerful liberal-individualistic component in what emerged as the modern Jewish state cannot be accounted for by the absence of religious, cultural or historical resources that could be relied upon and developed to support it. While I do not wish to belittle the power of collectivism in Judaism both as religion and as culture, the explanation for the weakness of the liberal element in the modern Jewish state seems to lie elsewhere.

In some of the great liberal traditions of western Europe, like the English or the French, the liberal impulse to protect individual citizens against arbitrary use of coercive state power grew largely from a history of domestic conflicts and civil wars between governors and their own subjects, citizens and their own state. Jews were vulnerable, of course, to such abusive state powers but not from their own state. Their enemies were not their own governors. The history of Jewish powerlessness has, therefore, encouraged romantic and even mystical notions of Jewish military force, notions blind to the dangers inherent in such force in a Jewish polity. Instead, Israeli and many Diaspora Jews have come to view the power of the state as the actual or symbolic embodiment of their freedom, not a potential threat to their liberties. For decades, Israeli secret services have kindled the enthusiasm and fantasies of millions of Jews in Israel and around the world. This was only one symptom of a more general celebratory romantic orientation towards Jewish power and its agents. Israelis were unable, in this climate, to develop the vital liberal culture of ambivalence and guardedness towards the power of their own state; the very kinds of ambivalence and suspicion that in other societies have encouraged the internal evolution of constitutional constraints on the uses of state powers.

Until very recently, the editors of Israeli daily newspapers collaborated with the state in practising voluntary self-censorship. For years, the focus on the use of force vis-à-vis non-Jews outside and inside Israel retarded the development of liberal sensibilities and internal legal, institutional and ethical limits on the uses of state powers.

In the absence of a socio-political support system, Israel developed as a lean procedural-institutional democracy. The fragility of the Israeli liberal-constitutional structure was revealed, even before the assassination of Prime Minister Yitzhak Rabin in November 1995 and the events that led to it, by the frivolous tinkering with the electoral law introducing a clause for the direct elections of the prime minister, which put Israel on a par with Latin-American regimes. In May 1996, with the first direct election of its prime minister, Israel stopped being a parliamentary democracy. I would like to suggest that in this context, without constitutional checks and balances, the introduction of a majority rule or a mass vote, which limits the scope and authority of proportional representation, was a dangerous victory of anti-parliamentary, populist politics over the liberal element in Israeli politics. In a country where the organic notion of peoplehood is so deeply rooted, majoritarianism, combined with ethnic religious communitarianism, could pose a direct threat to such vital institutions as the Supreme Court.[5]

Another factor contributing to the weakness of the liberal element in the

Israeli polity is the obvious fact that Zionist enterprise was developed historically as a national liberation project, in the context of which the emancipation of the Jew as an individual was a derivative idea and for a long time a practical impossibility. The stress on the return and liberation of the Jewish people in their homeland actually turned the individual into a missionary of the group. Settlement, conquest, war, the development military ethos, nation building and the like are not typical liberal objectives, nor are they the kind of projects that reinforce commitment to liberal values or the cultivation of liberal sensibilities. Communitarianism was much more effective and functional than liberalism in supporting the extractive policies of the state in the decades of nation building. Liberalism has been more relevant as an ideological and political resource in the more limited context of evolving a modern legal framework for the new state, which claimed a place in the family of enlightened modern democracies. The primary preoccupation of the new immigrant society of Israel before the establishment of the state on May 1948, and even more so since, was with the means of developing and legitimizing sufficiently effective physical force to uphold the founding and survival of the new state. Here socialism and nationalism were, of course, much more relevant frames.

Inspired by the Russian Revolution, socialist-Zionists from eastern Europe were the carriers of a tradition that rested on ethical justifications for the use of force in the pursuit of an ideal society. In the context of Zionism, socialism had a special appeal in providing, among other things, a universalist-ethical rationale for the use of force in the service of pragmatic nationalism. On the other side of the political spectrum, nationalist-Zionists evolved a Jewish version of the particularistic rationale of violence as a means of group survival. Drawing on Darwin, Spencer and Realpolitik doctrines, nationalist Jewish intellectuals such as Jabotinsky laid the foundations for the idealization of the Jewish army as means of survival and liberation. The Holocaust, by dramatically internationalizing the tragedy of Jewish victimhood, in fact expanded, if not fully universalized, the justification of Jewish national aspirations and the nationalist rationale for the use of violence. With its establishment in May 1948, the state of Israel was presented and perceived as a state of former victims with a mandate to redress a historical injustice to the Jewish people. Since 1948 the Israeli Leviathan has turned out to be one of the most demanding and extractive states in modern times relying on the radical sacrifices of blood, sweat and money from its tiny population. Liberal ideas and practices, which were imported to Israel by Jewish immigrants from Germany, western Europe and other countries, did not survive for long although some did find enduring expression in the tradition of the Israeli Supreme Court and in the development of financial and commercial institutions.

In the atmosphere of nation building, the absorption of mass immigration (mostly from poor countries) and the state of almost permanent war with the Arabs, liberal individualism could be neither attractive nor feasible. It was identified with the negative values that appeared opposed to Israeli communal idealism. As against Israeli patriotism, asceticism, self-sacrifice, military prowess, group solidarity, Aliya and the like, individualism came to represent self-indulgent hedonism, egoistic materialism, legal formalism and migration to such affluent societies as the United States and Canada. Perhaps more important still was the fact that, in the context of a Jewish state directed by a Jewish majority, Jews lost the political motive to seek emancipation as individuals or to nourish their liberalism in societies hostile to the development of their collective ethnic, religious and cultural identities. In the Israeli context, classical liberal ideas of individual and minority rights appeared to serve the claims of non-Jewish minorities and therefore to provide rationales for limiting the powers of the Jewish majority. Thus within Israeli politics liberalism often came to rival nationalism.

In retrospect, it is clear now that Israeli-Zionist collectivism rested on very fragile foundations. Zionism was essentially a syncretic movement based on a temporary truce between socialist, nationalist, liberal, religious and secular Zionists, and between western and eastern cultural outlooks. During the first decades of statehood this pluralism was restrained by the enormity of the tasks of survival and nation building. But with the consolidation of Israeli security and economy, the stabilization of its place among the nations and the necessity of facing hard choices with respect to the Palestinians, the surface consensus started rapidly to erode. Israel's public life has come to centre on a series of controversies about wars that appeared unnecessary, an occupation that appeared to an increasing number of Israelis to be corruptive and untenable, failed leaders who encouraged the spread of distrust in the government, the assassination of a prime minister, the issue of the peace with the Palestinians, the place of religion and religious authority in the state of Israel and the widening of the gap between rich and poor. These developments and particularly the breakdown of the thin consensus among the secular Left and the secular Right on issues of war, territories and peace opened the political system for the ascent of the religious parties and their ability to translate their political power into an effective assault on civic education and secular culture as well as the bastion of Israeli liberal values, the Supreme Court. At present the great-grandchildren of the early secular Zionists who rebelled against traditional religious culture are waging a defensive cultural and institutional battle against a powerful front consisting of the descendants of the Jewish fundamentalist reaction against Zionism and their right-wing Zionist allies.

Israel has evolved a brand of secular individualism, or rather secular singlehood, which, unlike the richer and deeper forms of liberal selfhood that evolve slowly from an internal culture of spiritual, ethical and intellectual individualism, results from the collapse and fragmentation of collective frames of meaning. In this Israeli universe the individual is more a survivor of a collective that lost its force, a fragment of a former whole, than a rich, albeit small, whole unto itself. This is not yet the kind of liberal individualism that can uphold a liberal society and liberal democratic institutions or generate the sensibilities and cultural forms of a universe that is nourished by forces unleashed by newly acquired freedoms. This is not yet the kind of pluralistic, internally open, mobile and tolerant individualism that is upheld in a liberal-democratic state by a culture of inherently unsettled meaning, a culture that rests on a dynamic core of what William Connolly has aptly called 'productive ambiguity'. This is a condition that literally disempowers the state in its attempts to ground power and authority in a hegemonic, institutionalized, cultural and normative frame.[6] Despite these limitations, however, along with the sectoral consolidation of a new Israeli fundamentalist identity, the most significant force working within and reshaping Israeli culture today, amidst the ruins of broken collectivist utopias, is the increasingly articulate expressions of individualism.

In the early decades of statehood sporadic expressions of individuality were bound to emerge through friction with collective expectations and trigger pressures for group conformity. But with the relaxation of such external communal sanctions in recent years, the focus seems to have been gradually shifting to more internal domains expressing the urge to escape the oppressive gaze of the collective.

At present the new Israeli self seems at a loss to marshal the strength and the skills to transcend one-dimensional singlehood of the kind that is produced by fragmentation of collectives and to evolve an internally cultivated and therefore more attractive normative individualism.

Decades of redemptive epic politics of sacrifice and normative Zionist collectivism have created in Israel generations of Jews cut off from what Michel Foucault aptly called 'technologies of the self', the tools and strategies that have been developing for centuries, especially in western societies, to form selves that are differentiated from collective, often hidden, clusters of communal consciousness and power, individuals free from fantasies of spontaneous holistic social harmonies.

Without such techniques and without visions of selfhood as a positive programme (not just the relic of a ruined community), Israeli or, for that matter, any democracy cannot flourish. Even if we acknowledge with Emil Durkheim that individualism depends on socially generated structures of significance that repudiate the idea of essentialist liberal individualism, liberal individualism remains a potent political strategy of democratization. The question that remains, however, is: from where could Israeli individuals draw the models, the motives and the strength to assume responsibility for fixing the meaning of individual life, the courage to engage in self-narration rather than be attached to precast frames of life? A viable Israeli individualism that can generate or uphold commitments to democratic civil society and yet hold its own in the face of the pressures of coercive communitarian norms cannot be imported. Nor can it be sustained on the basis of a culturally impoverished economic egoism. Like English, French and American individualism, so too Israeli individualism must be forged from local materials within its own particular society. For the Israeli individual cannot escape the arduous tasks of negotiating the cultural, psychological, political, legal and spiritual spaces within which it can define itself and develop. Israeli individualism cannot evolve without reckoning with constraints such as the Israeli-Jewish essentialist or organic conception of peoplehood, the rejection of the liberal democratic notion of majority as an aggregate of all individual citizens and therefore inclusive of non-Jews, the influence of the Israeli military ethos, or the political chains that arrest changes in Israeli education. Its future will depend largely on its capacity to draw upon indigenous Israeli cultural materials such as Hebrew poetry, art, progressive religious thinkers, etc.

Such Israeli individualism may have first to go through a phase of flat individualism, what I called before the democratization of Israeli singlehood, before it can go on to the richer phase based on the democratization of uniqueness and pluralistic selfhood. The earlier expectations that liberal individualism will evolve and spread as a universal phenomenon, a logically necessary phase in the process of modernization, were based on false enlightenment conceptions of politics and history. Many intellectual historians and political theorists have regarded individualism as a necessary or, at least, probable development concomitant with the transition from *Gemeinschaft* to *Gesellschaft*, traditional community to society, an aspect of modernization as a universal process of rationalization of culture, society and politics. We understand better today that the intellectual history of complex processes such as the genealogy of individualism is too narrow and incomplete without, say, the history of group emotions and their social expressions. Israel may be a case in point. When the history of Israeli individualism comes to be written at some future date, I trust that the development as well as the changing expressions of pain and emotional ambivalence in relation to the price of the Zionist project, the split between those Israelis who could entertain the dual narratives of liberation and conquest and those who could see only liberation or only conquest, will be a very central chapter.

In the epic universe of monumental history, ambivalence is either absent or rare and pain, if it is articulated at all, tends to be an abstract category. Pain denotes a different experience when it develops in conjunction with the emergence of an individualism that redefines the loss of each individual life as irremediable.

A community that is conceived as the voluntary creation of discrete individuals develops a different notion of death and mourning from that of a community conceived as an organic whole in which individuals can be regarded as interchangeable extensions of the collective. The multiplicity of heterogeneous individual perspectives, and the erosion of shared understandings of death in action raise the frightening possibility of meaningless death, meaningless pain. Nothing seems to limit the capacity of the state to mobilize its citizens and to convince them to risk their lives for the collective more than the fear that the meaning of sacrifice, which appears glorious today, will be debased tomorrow; that those who died yesterday in a war of liberation will be remembered in the future as soldiers who died in a colonial war; or that the heroes who died in the last war will be remembered as victims or victimizers. When the structures of communal meaning attached to the goals of power and the sacrifices of the citizens are unstable, a war can be defended only on the much less culturally or religiously rich grounds of minimal security requirements.

Such a condition increases the burden of the state to provide acceptable justifications for risking the lives of its citizens in the battlefield. It is instructive to examine the shift in attitude that has occurred recently, marked for instance in the letters sent to bereaved families on Memorial Day by Begin, 1981, and Rabin, 1987.[7] Begin wrote: 'On this Memorial Day all of us invoke the eternal memory of our heroes, those who redeemed Jerusalem.' Rabin's language is very different. In 1987 he wrote: 'I have no words to console you, to remedy your pain. I know that there are no words that can fill the emptiness created at your home . . .' Rabin's letter is responsive to a deep process of individualization of pain in the course of the 1980s.

In the late 1990s there was a widening rupture between the two outlooks on community pain and death, between mostly (but not only) religious Israeli youth, who are highly motivated to fight and risk their lives for a communal notion of the land of Israel and a restored Jewish sovereignty, and other young Israelis, who are much more sceptical and ambivalent with respect to this project and the anticipated costs in lives and suffering. The former seem to ally collectivism, patriotism, high fighting spirit, nationalism, religious outlook and the willingness to overcome individual losses and pain. The latter seem to link individualism, a commitment to a peace settlement based on territorial compromises, liberal values, secular outlook and an unwillingness to suffer or inflict the losses and the pain involved. In a sense, one sign of the times has been the politicization of pain. While for one group the pain and suffering in the conflict have been enlisted in defence of a more vigorous use of force, for the other individualization of pain and bereavement has evolved as a part of a process of distancing the individual from the community and questioning the costly missions of the state. While such differences in outlook and orientation do not warrant simple dichotomies and the spectrum of attitudes is certainly much more complex than we can describe, here these distinctions are sufficiently significant to warrant close examination.

Among many types of illustrations and evidence one can find these two outlooks compellingly articulated and juxtaposed in two photographs by Adi Nes shown in exhibitions of contemporary Israeli art at the Israel Museum in Jerusalem and the Jewish Museum in New York (1998–9). One photograph depicts a yarmulke-wearing Israeli soldier, apparently of Oriental background, flexing his muscles. In the picture the exposed part of his body seems to identify fully with the uniform. The other photograph shows a group of soldiers, who look like Ashkenazi, apparently clapping somewhat hesitantly for an unseen subject. They wear their uniforms loosely and one of them allows his white T-shirt to show beneath his unbuttoned army shirt. A one-armed soldier who cannot clap his hands is sitting like a living statue in their midst wearing only his army trousers and an undershirt. The undershirts seem to challenge the uniform, just as the private person within resists the soldier without. Together the two photographs seem to convey the widening gulf between ambivalent and unambivalent attitudes towards the use of military force in contemporary Israel. Jonathan Mandell, who reviewed the exhibition, which is significantly entitled 'After Rabin,' reports for *Newsday*[8] that when Avi Nes's religious soldier was shown at the Israel museum in Jerusalem, several American tourists asked whether they could get a postcard of it 'mistaking it for an unironic symbol of a New Israel'. The power of irony and ambivalence to expose the uncertain relations between death and meaning is, of course, one of the most subversive strategies of art as political criticism. It reveals the very gaps that often undermine the power of the state to mobilize the sacrifices of its citizens. In Israel, where religion and ideology have competed for long on the sacralization of all aspects of society, Israeli artists have been evolving a profane emotional aesthetic culture of irony and ambivalence in which the Israeli self can increasingly discover the rich options between messianic enthusiasm and melancholy. Such ambiguities, the under-determinism of meaning, which is inseparable from the rise of modern and, even more, post-modern individualism, often appear threatening to conservatives like Michel Sandel. They worry about 'the drift to formless Protean storyless selves, unable to weave the various strands of their identity into a coherent whole'.[9] But at this time Israeli artists see the breakdown of such a coherent whole as opening the way for emancipation into a new kind of freedom.

Larry Abramson, an Israeli painter, has perhaps captured the particular mood of contemporary Israelis who try to write poetry, paint or compose, standing in what looks like a junkyard of broken utopias. 'The family cell of Israeli art,' he observed, 'the family parented by both Zionism and modernism has long disintegrated. We Israeli artists are orphans, we have no family, no name, no home, no purpose . . . [we] learn to grow up alone and take full responsibility for our lives. The abandoned children are condemned to make meaning from scratch, from nothing, and form a critical voluntary community out of a haphazard assortment of the homeless. Eventually, everyone will discover that he or she is an orphan . . . The citizens will lift off the burdens of pre-cast truths and will turn to the artist-orphans for guidance. The future belongs to the orphans.'[10]

Abramson's imprinting of oil paintings on newspaper is suggestive of the dialectics of effacement and creation, concealment and expression of the Israeli experience.

If Abramson dwells upon the ironies of the dualism between seeing and not seeing, painting and effacing, another leading Israeli artist, Nurit David, explores the deepest personal sources of subjectivity by focusing on being and disappearing. In her paintings almost everything occurs in the stair-room in what she says is 'not a real place but a surfing site, an experience of constant fluctuations between appearance and disappearance'.[11]

At the moment, to be an Israeli Jew has become very much like moving up and down the stairs in this mediating space in which nothing is settled or predictable. To be an Israeli is, at least for secular Israelis, increasingly an act of improvisation, of trying, exploring, experimenting and moving between several possible spaces and identities. It is hardly conceivable, nor even desirable, of course, that liberal individualism or its post-modern mutations could ever become a total alternative to Israeli collectivisms. The question is more whether Israel can grow to accommodate individualism, which is grounded in a rich culture of the self, a universe of diverse and assertive subjectivities that can provide a normative base for individualism as a check on coercive statist and communitarian powers and authority. At present, the incipient Israeli individualism coexists tensely with fundamentalist Jewish identities for whom Israel as a place is a primordial given and Jewish fate is inescapable. But the future will belong neither to the orphans nor to the children of Israel. It will largely consist of what the children of Israel who declare themselves orphans and those who worship their fathers will do or not do to negotiate the terms of their coexistence. At the moment, however, the stair-room does not connect to the apartments and those locked up safely in their apartments do not open their doors to the stair-room.

Theoretically, one of the most potent liberal critiques of nationalism is that the very act of creating state power precedes the expression of the very will that can legitimate it. It is, therefore, a case of power that fixes and protects the very system of meaning that in turn legitimates it. The only defence against arbitrary power, in the liberal view, is, therefore, to dismantle the encompassing social structure of significance that legitimates power, to disrupt the tyranny of supposedly shared meaning and divide and subdivide power. David Quint, in his brilliant *Epic and Empire*,[12] refers to the role of power in the selection and shaping of the narratives of communal lives in his discussion of Virgil's *Aeneid*. While empires have, according to Quint, the power to narrate history as an epic, minor power and losers must accommodate contingencies. Unlike the defeated, victors experience history as a coherent story directed by collective will. Liberals might reverse this order, making the real winners all the citizens who are freed from experiencing history as a coherent, single, celebratory master narrative.

Notes

1. Bhikhu Parekh, 'The Cultural Particularity of Liberal Democracy', in David Held (ed.), *Prospects for Democracy*, Cambridge, Polity Press, 1993.
2. Yaron Ezrahi, *Rubber Bullets: Power and Conscience in Modern Israel*, New York, Farrar, Straus and Giroux, 1997.
3. Menachem Loberbaum, *Secularizing Politics in Medieval Jewish Thought* (forthcoming).
4. ibid.
5. Attempts to repeal or modify the law that introduced the direct election of the prime minister in Israel are continuing all the time.
6. William E. Connolly, *Identity-Difference: Democratic Negotiations of Political Paradox*, Ithaca and London, Cornell University Press, 1991, chapter 7.
7. I draw here on an unpublished study by Shaul Shenhav.
8. *Newsday*, 11 September 1998.
9. Michael J. Sandel, *Democracy's Discontent*, Cambridge, MA, The Belknap Press of Harvard University Press, 1966, pp. 350–1.
10. *Studio Art Magazine* (in Hebrew), 94, June–July 1998, pp. 16–19.
11. ibid., pp. 21–30.
12. David Quint, *Epic and Empire*, Princeton, Princeton University Press, 1993.

CHAPTER THREE

Individualism in the Turkish Context

Murat Belge

Individualism is a product of western history. In this article, focused on the development of individualism in Turkey, we need not, indeed should not, try to go into all the complex forces and mechanisms in western history that contributed to the birth and the subsequent growth of the individual. The victory that Plato presented to Socrates over the Sophists and their *homo mensura* was endorsed by Europe throughout the Middle Ages. But when Descartes said *cogito ergo sum* or when Luther insisted on the individual character of grace or when the novel became the most popular form of literature (in conditions as described by Ian Watt), the triumph of individualism became the foundation stone of western culture. As Braudel says, 'Since the development of Greek thought . . . the tendency of western civilization has been towards rationalism and hence away from religious life . . . With very few exceptions . . . no such marked turning away from religion is to be found in the history of the world outside the west.' Rationalism and secularism in the west naturally went hand in hand with individualism. In some way, and for a variety of reasons, individualism became the 'ideology' (it is actually both more and less than 'ideology', rather like the 'vessel' in which 'ideology' is put and is then shaped by it) most compatible with the social forms and institutions created by western development. As I do not believe in teleology, I do not see this process as inevitable in any way. Protagoras and his fellows might have remained as a group of eccentric thinkers of antiquarian interest. But as history, unwittingly, in its totally impartial progress, bent the dial in a certain direction, they, also unwittingly, found themselves – or, we found them – in the honourable position of precocious prophets of what was to become a global development.

The Renaissance was another, perhaps the most glorious, step towards the maturation of the individual. In Japanese painting parallel lines do not converge at the horizon and this is in accordance with objective reality. But Renaissance painters had the audacity to depict forms as they were perceived by the senses of the individual observer. Both methods contrast with the Middle Eastern miniature tradition, where the spiritual eminence of the figure in life and his place in the social hierarchy largely determined his 'size' in the picture, irrespective of perspective or anything else.

All that happened in the west legitimized in some way the right of the individual to define and describe life as he/she perceived it without consulting the explanation provided by traditional authority about that particular area or aspect. The ultimate reason why such a thing was possible is that, under the general conditions of existence in the tiny bit of the world that we call western Europe, this method was able to prove its relevance – it had, in other, more contemporary words, 'market value'.

Copernicus made his personal observations and then, with considerable timidity, made them public. These public observations, together with others added to them later (such as the personal observations of Brahe, Kepler, etc.) proved to be much more valuable, because they were more practically useful, than the explanations of Ptolemy, despite the veneration that traditional authority had piled on them.

The Chinese also had an immense knowledge of the stars, but it was their ideology that determined their understanding of the order of things and the phenomena of space, and it did not allow them to diverge from traditional authority, which emphasized the virtues of 'stasis'. Consequently, the only explanation they could supply for the obvious movement of the planets was that 'even some stars can behave in an erratic way'.

At one level, this is a much more commonsensical and comfortable way of understanding the world. At that point it was the west that had the problem – not 'the rest': in western history life was unable to go on peacefully in accordance and in conformity with the norms of traditional (inevitably religious) authority.

I believe that all human beings share an equal potential for individualistic development. What varies is the conjecture of objective conditions that will activate or curb, hasten or slow down the working out of that potential. Here, at this point, there is a sharp contrast between the history of the west and human experience in the rest of the world.

The Ottoman Empire was geographically and spiritually located in that part of the non-western world that was closest to the west. It was perhaps the first society in history to try what was later generally called 'westernization', before 'modernization' became more fashionable. Actually, Ottoman westernization largely coincides with that of Russia under Peter the Great. Though both societies, with their physical borders touching the west on more or less the same longitudes, embarked on this adventure at more or less the same time (mainly, the first decades of the eighteenth century), there was a major difference between them, which determined the general character of the effort to a very considerable extent. Russia had been growing and expanding almost continuously and had reached a point that may be defined as a threshold on the way to becoming a world power; now it was in need of westernization to gain the power to fulfil this promise. Ottoman society, on the other hand, had already had its golden age and was now in a process of decline. It had to 'westernize' merely to survive! Its glorious past, however, was its chief handicap in the new effort. History seemed so full of valuable things to preserve.

And so authority weighed heavy in the Ottoman attempt. At that stage no one, including Europeans, had a clear notion of the human causes of the material superiority of Europe, and no one can blame the Ottomans for failing to recognize the importance of individual enterprise in general in creating a powerful society. Everything in their ideology pointed in the opposite direction. They were much more reluctant than Russia to seek personal physical contact with the west. It is said that Peter sent thousands of Russian students to acquire know-how in many arts and crafts in Europe. By contrast, the Ottomans were able to send only about a hundred students during the reign of the most radically westernizing Sultan, Mahmud II, a hundred years later.

There is an inherent paradox in this kind of education, which we have encountered in all experiments in westernization ever since. In this 'confrontation of civilizations', the westernizing state, inevitably paternalistic in its attitude towards its society, sends out students who are expected to learn western ways and mentality, while remaining absolutely loyal to their 'father' state at the same time. Often this creates an insurmountable difficulty for the students. Some may shift completely to the 'other side'; but more often, having entered the enterprise with patriotic feelings, their initial commitment to their society remains while their loyalty to their state is shaken, and thus they end up as 'oppositional intellectuals'. This stance changes their relationship with their state in a radical way – how radical depends on political developments.

In Russia, the intelligentsia that were ultimately behind the 1917 Revolution evolved from this process and the much more conservative Ottoman intellectuals also contributed to a more western-oriented pattern of legal-political change in Turkey.

If I may make yet another dangerous generalization, I will say that this tension, as it was lived in Russia, created a socio-political polarity with an irreconcilable clash between the opposing sides. The tension made moderation itself difficult, if not impossible. Consequently we have figures such as Dostoevsky, who go from one extreme to another, demonstrating that both attitudes cannot coexist peacefully within the mind or the psyche of the same individual.

In the Ottoman case the individual intellectual's mind became the site where the drama of the tension was acted out. A polarization such as existed in Russia would have exploded that mind – any individual mind. Consequently, in Turkey the terms of the conflict were much more diluted. The ideal, from the beginning, was reconciliation. This does not mean that there was no division in society, no opposing intellectual/ ideological camps. They certainly existed, but the edges were never as sharp. The same phenomenon can be observed on another level, on that of the political parties. The Union and Progress Party (UPP) of the Ottoman era and the People's Republican Party (PRP) of the Republic are the two ruling (and westernizing) parties of Turkish history. There was constant opposition to them, but this opposition was not always organized in the form of a political party. On the other hand, the main party was never ideologically homogeneous; it always included shades and nuances of political opinion, moderate forms of liberalism, socialism, even religious conservatism, thus carrying its opposition within itself. This is why the PRP is defined as the 'father of all political parties in the country' (the same can be said, and has been said, of the UPP). To have included Stolypin and Nechayev in the same party would have been impossible in Russia. In Turkey their radicalism and determination would have made it hard for them to survive at all, but highly moderated counterparts would coexist as representatives of the different branches of the one and only ideology, Turkish nationalism!

To say that the individual mind is the site of the civilizational polarity seems to suggest an infinite potential for individualism to develop there, but this is not the case. That legitimation of the individual way of seeing, understanding, formulating things never took place in the Ottoman/ Turkish instance. That is to say, the legitimacy of the individual was not acknowledged in the public sphere. It did not, could not, become a social/cultural force. In the private sphere it no doubt thrived, as it received much interesting nourishment from the intellectual climate, with every private individual trying to effect his/her own balance or synthesis between the civilizational poles. Thus all westernizing Ottoman writers write novels (the mere fact of 'writing a novel' is enough to place one in the westernizing camp) criticizing young men who slavishly copy western modes of conduct, thus squandering their inheritance, which symbolizes their 'betrayal of the father'!

Namik Kemal, the most prominent intellectual and writer of the Tanzimat period (the Ottoman version of *perestroika*, perhaps), wrote a play, a tragedy, criticizing marriage arranged by parents. But since a young woman who defies her father is not only unacceptable but also unthinkable, even in 'westernized Ottoman' morality, our heroine has to sacrifice her love and submit to her father. Consequently, the plot, to qualify as the 'tragedy' it was meant to be, has to condemn the young couple to tuberculosis and suicide, thus ending on a 'pitiful' note and avoiding a clash of values between the generations. It is up to the father to understand and regret his mistake.

When traditional authority weighs so heavily, it is not easy for individualism to liberate itself. Disallowed in the public sphere, individualism had to follow two subterranean courses in Turkish history: either i) as the personal idiosyncrasies of an individual, or ii) in the economic sphere, as individual economic enterprise. This latter includes all the rapacity and egotism necessary for bourgeois primitive accumulation, without the intellectual/cultural courage, originality or creativity of the bourgeois individual so active in western civilization.

This was inevitably so in the last days of the Ottoman Empire. However, here we have to make room for a very significant exception.

Looking back over the history of Turkish thought during the Republican Age, one is struck by a certain fact: in almost every specific area of thought there is a pioneer whose intellect was formed just before the proclamation of the Republic. The father of modern Turkish historiography, for instance, was Fuat Köprülü (1890–1966); the first outstanding literary critic and historian was Ahmet Hamdi Tanpinar (1901–62); Nurullah Ataç (1898–1957) was another outstanding critic, cultural revolutionary and essayist; Ahmet Hamdi Başar (1897–1971) was an important economic thinker and an early proponent of liberalism; Şevket Süreyya Aydemir (1897–1976), a Communist Party member in the Soviet Union as a young man, later became an influential ideologue and interpreter of Kemalism as a Third World alternative to socialism; Ömer Lütfi Barkan (1902–79) was the most important economic historian; Besim Darkot (1903–90) pioneered in geography while Arif Müfit Mansel (1905–75) carried out the first scientific archaeological excavations.

In literature and arts, Yakup Kadri Karaosmano lu (1889–1974) is considered to be the finest novelist of the early generation of Turkish writers of the Republican period; Nazim Hikmet (1902–63) was, and to a considerable extent still is, the first Turkish poet of international renown; Nusret Hizir (1899–1980) was the first major philosopher; in music, the greatest name is Mesut Cemil (1902–63).

More names could be added, though not too many. The oldest birth date here is 1889 and the latest 1905. Together they make an extraordinary list, more brilliant than any generation that precedes or follows it by many years. They were all founders of a discipline or school of thought that was new in the country and they have not been surpassed yet.

In comparison, the Republican output is not so spectacular. Why?

There cannot be a simple explanation; but I shall try to put down a few reasons that appear most cogent to me.

The generation I referred to above were born and brought up under conditions of catastrophe in which there was nevertheless the feeling that something could still be achieved to turn the tide. The bankruptcy of the Ottoman system in general taught them that they would have to stand on their own feet. The tragedy of the collapse of the Ottoman state was not too crushing as it was immediately followed by the happy foundation of a professedly secular Republic in which there was abundant challenge and probably many rewards for the intellectual work of which society was in such dire need. The last tottering period of the long-lived Ottoman state was rich in culture, weak in ideology. This contrast made it easier for the individuals enumerated above to move around a truly international world of ideas and ideologies, theories and methodologies, and make their own personal appropriation of them. The nation-state of the Republic immediately created the usual overpowering imperatives of the national cause and reversed the ratio of culture and ideology in intellectual life: strong ideology, weak culture. Just as the fledgling 'national industry' had to be protected behind walls of high tariff, so the purity of the national mind had to be safeguarded against 'foreign' ideologies.

Westernization was relaunched with renewed vigour during the Republican era, despite this fear of the 'foreign'. Modernization necessitated the creation of the nation-state and here again the western model was all-important. The western experience, however, in which 'nation' and 'state' came together spontaneously and smoothly, was impossible to emulate even in Central Europe, in Italy and Germany, where it gave rise to so much pain before, but especially after, the creation of the nation-state. The rest of the world had to pay for the lateness of the unification of Germany in particular. Further east the challenge was much more difficult, if not impossible.

In the form in which this 'wedding' was adopted, or had to be adopted, by the non-western world, the 'state' forms itself with relative ease and tries to become the Pygmalion of the 'nation-to-be'. The problem is the incongruity of the art of sculpture, whose product is static by definition, as model for a society, which has to move, grow, change, etc. All these activities may seem obnoxious, impertinent or ungrateful to the 'sculptor', or the 'social engineer' or 'founding father'. Nor is the 'child' ('nation'), at any point in history, allowed to become the 'father of man' ('state').

The severity of this patriarchal figure deterred the development or the maturation of the 'individual' in the Republican era. The loyalty that the new nation-state demanded of its individual citizens, its intellectuals and so on, was greater than that expected by the dwindling Ottoman state and was far more internalized – the sacrifice of individuality to the 'greater community' being of paramount importance in all such ideologies. Of course, the demands were stricter on elites of all kinds, in that social stratum where individualism and individuality are most likely to flourish. Feelings, as well as ideas, had to be correct.

Yakup Kadri, the novelist, once said that Proust was the writer he would have aspired to emulate though the circumstances of his country forced him to adopt the realism of Balzac. Many intellectuals of the early Republican era felt a similar 'call of duty' in their careers, to which they felt they had to give a positive response, no matter how constricting they found it. The process of the formation of the nation-state, to which they were totally committed, forced them to identify themselves with the 'nation' and to submit to the imperatives of the state.

The bureaucratic character of the Turkish 'modernization' is another factor to be taken into consideration in this context. Experience on a wider scale shows that this is quite inevitable in cases where modernization is imposed by a small elite minority from above on a society that is largely the passive and usually reluctant recipient of social change. Not getting a sufficient contribution of energy from society and unable after a certain time to reproduce its zeal for transformation, such an elite becomes the prisoner of the ossified rules and conventions that it has itself created. In the Turkish case, Atatürk, the great hero who founded the Republic, is venerated, if not worshipped, by generation after generation, who believe that he cannot be surpassed or even equalled. Leaders, civilians or military, make the same speeches with the same rhetorical devices every year on the occasion of every national anniversary. Teachers at school harangue their students with the same discourse. The media adopt the same language. The little that can be novel in this general discourse is immediately noticed and imitated if it is not against the norms of correctness. Consequently, imitation rather than creativity becomes the safe way to success.

However, this is not the entire picture. Although this ossification is very much present even today, especially where official ideology is dominant, there have been and still are countercurrents in society since the mid-century. As Turkey emerged from the single-party regime in the aftermath of the Second World War, and as the gradual development of capitalism created new jobs and forms of livelihood other than that of utter dependence on state salaries, variation in all spheres of life, including the intellectual, became visible. The political regime and the ideology that dominated political life have always been inflexible and strong. The paradox here is that the rival ideologies of the oppositional political movements, themselves inevitably modelled on state ideological practice, have aspired to be equally strong and inflexible and consequently quite intolerant of any individual expression within their own 'monopoly of truth'.

But once a society is set on a path, progress along which will eventually create the conditions for producing, reproducing and supporting social diversification and cultural variety, it is next to impossible for an authoritarian state or rival authoritarian political movements to apply the spiritual straitjacket with any guarantee of success. Turkey has been on such a path of development since the 1960s. The percentage of the urban population has for some time been higher than the rural one. Several million Turks have been or still are resident workers in European countries. The numbers of people who have a chance to climb on the ladder of education to a certain (of course, varying) level is slowly but steadily increasing – though the quality of education is decreasing at perhaps a faster rate. More and more of the educated young people are finding their way on the Internet. Concepts that begin with such prefixes as 'mono-' or 'uni-' are still valued highly in official ideology and its political rival movements, but what is taking place in daily life in society is quite different. In such a diversified society even these highly monistic ideologies have to coexist without being able to eliminate one another.

The individual, much more than individualism, is difficult to pin down. One could walk along a train in Britain and observe perhaps six young women reading a magazine called *Me* in each compartment. To my way of thinking, this is the ultimate in individualism, in the aspiration to be different from anyone else, and entirely characteristic of the so-called 'me age'. Yet how similar all these young women are – the way they dress, their make-up, their expression. And how could it be otherwise, since the insipidity of this particular magazine is designed to satisfy about forty thousand 'individuals'?

The counterpart in Turkey would be a magazine named *Us*, if not *Solidarity*, read by probably the same number of people who are very different in their social and ethnic backgrounds, their aspirations, their religious tendencies, their political convictions etc, though all united in the firm and comforting belief that they share the same national and moral code.

CHAPTER FOUR

Individualism in the Arab Middle East: An Overview

Hazim Saghie

I shall start with a personal story. When I was a kid my grandmother used to tell me every time I wanted to go out: 'Don't speak to this or that person if you meet him, because our family are not friends with him'. When I asked her why she would tell me that this person had had an argument with my father or my grandfather, or that his father or grandfather wasn't on good terms with my family. Some of the events my grandmother mentioned had occurred many decades before I was born. Nevertheless, I had to abide by the strict laws of a familial history to which I hadn't contributed. Whether I had or had not been born at the time was a mere footnote in this epic of hatred and animosity.

Everyone who has read the Albanian Ismael Kadare's *Broken April* will be familiar with the feuds in a non-modern, non-European society. Feuds like these can last a long time. They can last as long as the individual does not replace the inherited social formations, be they religious, sectarian, tribal or ethnic. They can dehistoricize any society or culture that suffers them. In the Arab Middle East these formations were, and still are, so overwhelming that little room was left for the individual. Criticizing the Middle East does not imply, in this regard, any exclusivity. What is true for the Middle East is true, to a greater or lesser extent, for the entire non-

European world. Even modern Europe itself was not immune. In the not very distant past it witnessed a horrible form of tribal and collectivist resurgence in the form of Fascism. Nevertheless, in the Arab Middle East the tribal tradition that predates Islam was one of the origins of our collectivist tendency. Transmitted to us by poetry, and 'reinvented' in a very authoritarian setting, it helped to cement our self-consciousness as groups.

A very well-known line of poetry, which goes back to the pre-Islamic period and which has been recited again and again, reads as follows: 'I am but a member of [the tribe] Ghuzayyat. If the Ghuzayyat go to war, I go. If they turn to moderation, I moderate.' Other poets of the same period stressed this point very clearly. One of them, Amru bin Kulthum, who was a Christian Arab, wrote a poem that can be described as a paradigm of tribal pride, setting out everything that 'we', the Taghlib tribe, can do and everything that the others can't do to 'us'. The pre-Islamic poet was rightly portrayed as 'the lawyer of his tribe'. He was its spokesman and defender, justifying its actions and accusing its enemies and critics. Islam altered this relationship but it did not abolish it or defeat it entirely. The change it brought about was thus quantitative not qualitative.

A new group came to light, a group of believers, encompassing an unsettled balance among tribes and families. The Islamic state, because it was born as a sacred one, left little room for the non-political sphere, while politics was to a large extent identified with religion.

A very important development occurred with the advent of the new religion, which helped to perpetuate this stagnation. This was the concept of the holy wars (*jihad*) against enemies both within the Arabian peninsula and outside it, which reinforced the fundamental centrality of the 'group' and of consensus. The Muslims had been ordered to 'find refuge in the rope of God and not to scatter'.

In addition to this 'ideological' background, everyday life under Islam facilitated the politicization of many levels of human activity, but fell short of encouraging the rise of a political society in which people are treated as citizens and individuals. Though blood in the modern racist sense was totally alien to the culture of Islam, Islamic civilizations labelled their citizens as permanent and separate closed groups. The stratification was kept rigorously and tightly. Under the Umayyads, it was the Arabs versus the non-Arabs. Under the Abbasids it was the Muslims versus the non-Muslims. During the Ottoman era we had both: the Muslims versus the non-Muslims, and then the Turks versus the non-Turks.

Ibn Khaldoun, the great Muslim historian and the forefather of modern sociology, in his *Muqaddamah*, interpreted the history of Muslim societies and the rise and decline of states and civilizations according to *asabiyah*, or solidarity through blood.

Bernard Lewis, in his study of 'the political language of Islam', observed that

> Indeed, the term 'citizen', with its connotation of the right to participate in the formation and conduct of government, and with its origins going back from the French and American revolutions to the city-states of ancient Greece, was totally outside the Muslim political experience and, therefore, unknown to Islamic political language. When ancient Greek political writings were translated into Arabic in the high Middle Ages, and served as the basis of a new and original political literature in Arabic, there was an equivalent for the city; there was none for the citizen.[1]

Against this background, it becomes clear that there was only a small chance for the birth of an individualist tradition. The early expressions of individuality in the Arab heritage revealed, above all, an inflated egoism, which had been accentuated by poetry as a medium of expression.

Al-Mutanabbi, the Abbasid poet who was well known for his *fakhr* (self-pride), wrote that he looked down on all the people whom God created and whom he himself did not create 'as if they were but one of the hairs in my parting'. In his poetry, al-Mutanabbi did not ascribe to himself the qualities of an individual, but rather the qualities that more usually associated with collective bodies or acts of nature. He thought of himself as not merely different from others but superior to them.

In the modern age, after what came to be termed the impact of Europe, modernity meant, to most of the Arabs and, for that matter, to many non-European civilizations, importing the means to acquire material power. When Mohammad Ali Pasha, the ruler of Egypt in the early nineteenth century, set out to Europeanize his country, he concentrated on introducing those elements that had made the European states militarily able. Discovering the 'secret' behind European supremacy was overwhelming, but the human face and legal aspects of modernity were not internalized within society in this experiment.

Nevertheless, history often evolves in a contradictory way. In this part of the world some glimpses of European life in the nineteenth Century had been conveyed into Arabic by Rifa'a Rafi' al-Tahtawi, who was sent as imam of a regiment in the new Egyptian army, and who was the imam of the first substantial mission sent by Mohammad Ali to study in Paris.

Al-Tahtawi kept his ambivalence towards the symptoms of a fledgling

European individualism, though he was in general very positive and healthily curious. At the turn of the century Mohammad Abduh took notice, in his religious conciliatory *fatwas*, of the interests and needs of the individual within the framework of Islam. The Mufti of Egypt, who was fond of compromises, advocated

> the reform of the way of writing the Arabic language . . . there is still another matter of which I have been an advocate. People in general are blind to it and are far from understanding it, although it is the pillar of their social life, and weakness and humiliation would not have come upon them had they not neglected it. This is, the distinction between the obedience which the people owe the government and the just dealing which the government owes the people. I was one of those who called the Egyptian nation to know their rights vis-à-vis their ruler, although this nation has never had an idea of it for more than twenty centuries. We summoned it to believe that the ruler, even if it owes him obedience, is still human, liable to err and to be overcome by passion.[2]

The importance of what Abduh said can be seen in the context of the traditional Sunni Islam, according to which submission to a despot is a lesser evil than revolting against him, which is considered a plot (*fitnah*).

Unfortunately, what Albert Hourani called 'the liberal age' in the Arab world was doomed. Banning and censoring of books soon became the custom, and radical anti-western movements started to acquire fresh impact. The anti-colonial struggle served the rise of anti-western values as an ideological extension of its political activism.

The ideas of Adam Smith and Jeremy Bentham and their followers could not stimulate any real interest in the Arab world owing to the differences between the Muslim and the European historical experiences at that time. Smith's doctrine of laissez-faire, based upon a profound belief in the natural harmony of individual wills, and Bentham's utilitarianism, with the basic rule of 'each to count for one and none for more than one', went unnoticed. On the economic side, Smith's 'natural liberty', which portrayed the exchange of goods and services in free and competitive markets as the ideal system of mutual advantage, did not attract any attention either.

Thus the tendency towards depersonalization was never checked. For modern depersonalization was a consequence of the collectivist trends that ended up always having the upper hand in contemporary Arab politics and culture.

Over-politicization was preached by the non-liberal ideologies, which were very well received in the Middle East. Nationalism, statism and statist socialism all influenced, to certain degrees, the Arab elites who resented colonial France and Britain. The Shah of Iran, the Turkish military and the Arab 'modernist' experiences backfired. The Khomeini revolution and radical Islam in general agitated sentiment against 'the west', and in particular the United States of America.

All in all, the nation, the social class and political Islam served, each in its own way, to obliterate the individual as an independent entity and to insist that a person sacrifice his/her existence to a collective cause or belonging. In this regard women were asked for a double sacrifice: not only as individuals but also as women.

Alan Mintz observed, in comparing Judaism to Christianity, that 'although the individual is responsible for his actions [in Judaism], the meaning of his life is absorbed in collective structures and in collective myths. With the partial exceptions of mystical testimonies in the Kabbalistic tradition, Judaism, unlike Christianity, does not know the deeply personal experience of conversion, nor the nuanced inner drama of individual salvation.'[3] This applies historically and theoretically to Islam as well, where converting to it was always portrayed as an added value to Islamic civilization as a complete whole. Martyrdom, especially in the Shi'ite tradition, tied individualism to death. It actually made the martyr the only person who deserved to be recognized as an individual.

The Arab–Israeli conflict helped, on both sides, to perpetuate this tendency, for 'all of us' Arabs were expected to immerse ourselves in this epic war against 'all of them'. In this concentration on the struggle, which is often called 'the battle of destiny', no space was left for other tasks. The monumentality of history dwarfed the promotion of individualism or of democracy in the broad sense of the word.

What Isaiah Berlin called 'negative liberty', i.e. the protection of individuals from the abusive deployment of state powers, did not gather momentum in the political culture of the Middle East.

The military regimes, which, in the 1950s and especially in the 1960s, engulfed Egypt, Syria, Iraq, Yemen and Algeria, crushed what was left of a nascent Arab individual. It became the mission of every single Arab to fight individualism, to promote heavy industrialization, to establish socialism and to build Arab unity. The 'people' was proclaimed as the vehicle of the new dawn and also its target, and the state became the new patriarch.

Over-politicization meant that the evolution of civil societies, created by free individuals, who initiate associations and institutions and develop ideas and thoughts, became a remote possibility. On the other hand, the occasional demand for democracy meant that all the emphasis was laid on the rule of the majority and not on providing guarantees for minorities and individuals.

Poverty and underdevelopment contributed to this trend. Lack of investment in the non-oil countries and generous spending on defence throughout the area helped to create a certain analogy between individualism and unaffordable bourgeois luxuries. All in all, concern for national or religious sensitivities far exceeded any concern for democracy and civil society. Politics could go untested, and despotism felt immune to social and cultural changes. Immobility carried the day.

In a country like Lebanon, which escaped the military dictatorship option, individualism did not succeed in challenging the old social formations. The civil war that broke out in 1975 proved that religious sects have unmatched power, even after half a century of a parliamentarian regime. One of the results of this prolonged war was that the individual became more atomized, and the need for sectarian solidarity and protection increased in an unprecedented way.

When it comes to culture and means of expression, we come up against the negative effects of language or, to be more precise, non-reformed language. The magic of the Arabic word and its almost prophetic quality had to do with the special relationship between the language and the Qur'an. Its centrality is derived from the centrality of the sacred.

As is well known, Arabs write and read one language while speaking another. The vernaculars are the 'languages' of everyday life in the twenty-five or so Arab countries, but they are still considered unsuitable for writing, and representative of popular and 'low' culture. Some endeavours to turn the vernaculars in Egypt and Lebanon into written languages were met by fierce opposition. Their proponents, who belonged mainly to religious minorities, were classed as political heretics and cultural agents of colonialism.

When it comes to writing, our language looks not only alien and artificial but also epic and pre-modern. Its grandiose character does not help it to depict what is ordinary, practical or spontaneous, nor to develop a discourse concerning women, children, theatre, nature or personal feelings. It is, in this sense, the language of a group, not of an individual, a language inherited from the age of aristocracy and not a democratic one, a language that is suitable for describing great events and great turning points in history.

This, among other things, is still reflected in the means of communication and public speech, where the high epic style still imposes its hegemony. Announcers on Arab TV stations do not merely speak classical Arabic. They also give a sense of urgency and destiny to some of the least important details they announce. They look so serious, stiff and impersonal that any personal gesture or joke sounds rude, if not completely out of place. Their sense of time looks very backward in this post-industrial era of information.

In Arabic newspapers you rarely find the word 'I'. The news is, for the most part, written in the passive: 'It has been said . . . It has been done . . .'. Interviews are rarely accompanied by a description of the person interviewed.

Autobiography in the Arab world is still unestablished as an independent literary genre, although autobiographical sketches have had a long history in classical Arabic literature, to the point that Rosenthal considered Ghazali's *al-Munqidh min al-Dalal*, among 'the most personal autobiographies in Islam'.[4] Similar evaluations were attached to Usama Bin Munqidh, the great commentator on the Crusades.

Nevertheless, these records, which were written mainly by men, rarely exceeded what one might expect in a sophisticated curriculum vitae. Later on, some autobiographical elements found their way into the works of al-Tahtawi, Ahmad Faris al Shidyaq and Ya'qub Sanu', among others. In the late nineteenth century, the Lebanese Jurji Zaydan started following western patterns of autobiographical writing. After his 'biography of my life', many Arab writers tried this genre, among them the Egyptians Salama Musa, Tawfiq al-Hakim, Ahmad Amin and Lewis Awad, the Lebanese Mikhail Naima, the Palestinian-Iraqi Jabra Ibrahim Jabra, and the Palestinians Fadwa Tuqan and Hisham Charabi. Writers of biographical works who belonged to religious minorities were over-represented compared with the numbers of people in their sects and religions. But, as Stephan Guth has observed, Arab writers in general 'gave preference to novelistic rather than autobiographical approaches'.[5]

Taha Hussein's *al-Ayyam* (The Days) is still considered the classic Arabic autobiography. It narrated, in three volumes, the early years in the life of a blind Egyptian youngster, who was Hussein himself, but the 'I' was replaced by either 'he' or 'our friend'.

The autobiographies written by Arabs are, for the most part, still political and social in the broad sense. But when it comes to questions concerning religion and sex, the tendency to be indirect is still dominant. Many writers still apologize for dealing with personal matters, or invent excuses for so doing.

The practice of bringing up children in the Arab world is still very far from the modern theory, which holds that the interests of normal adults are best served by allowing them maximum freedom and responsibility for choosing their objectives and the means for obtaining them, and acting accordingly. Except among a few westernized urban families, the prevalent conservative education in the Arab world does not embody any opposition to authority or to means of control over the individual, especially when it is exercised by the state or by the wise elders within the family. Lately things have started to change, but they are changing very slowly. The art of the novel contributed to the change in this direction.

The Egyptian Najib Mahfouz, the most important Arab novelist, modernized not only the themes of Arabic literature but linguistic usage as well. Similarly, some non-political television programmes tried to bridge the gap between what is thought and what is said. Through the new means of communication, especially television, politicians in some semi-democratic regimes are starting to address their constituencies in direct and comprehensible language.

This new wave can be sensed in some movies and art works. The Egyptian Yousif Shahin and the Tunisian Nuri Buzayd, among others, epitomized this trend in the cinema. The Moroccan novelist Mohamed Choukri, in his *For Bread Alone*,[6] revealed, with admirable bluntness, his passage from street prostitution to the world of letters. The Lebanese Hasan Daoud wrote many novels that revolved around city life and the impact of wars on individuals. In the poems of the Lebanese Abbas Beydoun personal agonies are one of his central themes. The new women's writing, initiated by the powerful stand of Leila Baalbaki in the 1960s, introduced a fresh personal introspection in Arab fiction.

But in order to create different mainstream forms and expressions, a new individual politics and a new consciousness of the self as an independent entity within a group, there is still a very long way to go.

One can only hope that the few individual attempts we have witnessed will not be silenced nor their proponents intimidated in the future.

Notes

1. Bernard Lewis, *The Political Language of Islam*, Chicago, 1988, p. 63.
2. Quoted by Albert Hourani, *Arabic Thought in the Liberal Age 1798–1939*, Oxford, 1970, p. 141.
3. Quoted by Yaron Ezrahi, *Rubber Bullets: Power and Conscience in Modern Israel*, Farrar, Straus and Giroux, 1997, pp. 95–6.
4. See Ed de Moor, 'Autobiography, Theory and Practice: The Case of al-Ayyam', in R. Ostle, E. de Moor and S. Wild (eds), *Writing the Self: Autobiographical Writing in Modern Arabic Literature*, London, Saqi Books, 1998, pp. 128–38.
5. Stephan Guth, 'Why Novels, Not Autobiographies?', in ibid., pp. 145–6.
6. Mohamed Choukri, *For Bread Alone*, London, Saqi Books, 1993.

CHAPTER FIVE

The Crisis of the Individual in Egypt

Husayn Ahmad Amin

Since the dawn of their long history, and to this day, Egyptians have never in my estimation known an epoch free of autocracy or an age that made space for multiplicity, that permitted individuals to express themselves freely. In ancient Egypt, the state's absorption not only in waging war but also in irrigation projects, construction and serving the gods (all of which might be regarded as akin to military service) required that subjects see themselves as duty-bound blindly to obey the supreme authorities. Indeed, even Amenhotep IV (Akhnaton) – that supreme rebel in the spheres of religion and art – was unable, even as pharaoh, to escape the consequences of his rebelliousness and his individualism. The priests of Amon and their partisans in the army and the nobility entrapped him. Once they had got rid of him, matters returned to normal, for they revived the worship of the ancient gods that he had tried to replace.

For in the age of Akhnaton Egypt had witnessed a struggle between, on the one hand, forces calling for regeneration and innovation, for an openness to the world and a willingness to derive benefit from the fruits of neighbouring civilizations, and, on the other hand, the forces of conservatism, represented by the priests and their devotees, who saw any inventiveness or newness as posing a danger to their interests and influence.

In other civilizations and their arts they saw nothing that surpassed or even equalled the achievements of their ancient Egyptian forebears. They explained any reverse in political authority or any military defeat as a sign of the gods' anger against the Egyptian people, for having deserted the way of the ancestors and adopted foreign customs.

However, the truth is that the era's conservative spirit concealed a profound anxiety and a palpable erosion in self-confidence. It had been within the capability of the Egyptians of the past – in the ages of the Old and Middle Kingdoms, when geographical barriers protected them both from relations with those outside and from foreign incursions – to exist in a state of self-sufficiency founded on the conviction that they were far more advanced than all other societies. But when the Hyksos overran their country that firm belief was shaken. It was further uprooted (even after they had managed to expel the Hyksos) by the eventual outcome of their military forays into Asian territories and the expansion of their commercial exchanges with these regions, and by the constant flow of Egyptians outward from the borders of their state – soldiers, bureaucrats, merchants – as well as the profusion of foreigners coming to Egypt either to settle or to join the ranks of the Egyptian army. For all of this movement in and out of the country meant that Egyptians could not help but observe other, diverse civilizations; it meant that Egyptians now confronted visible signs that some aspects of other civilizations were not far behind the civilization of the pharaohs.

Akhnaton's master-stroke was his insight that the old worship then prevalent in Egypt had no place in the context of these new circumstances and the changing conditions of the world that he saw around him. If that religion were to retain its hold, Akhnaton recognized, it would consign Egypt to an inevitable petrification. Thus, he embarked boldly on a policy of closing the old temples and effacing the name of the supreme god, Amun. His innovation was to focus worship on the disc of the sun, whose favours flowed beyond Egypt's boundaries to embrace all of humanity. Wherever they voyaged in this wide world, Egyptians would find that orb, and others could find it too when they came to Egypt, all merely by glancing skywards. This revolutionary global view was a rational response to the new reality. After all, those Egyptians who had remained closed in on themselves for long aeons were astonished and bewildered, once they emerged from their burrows and began to open themselves to the world, to find the sun shining and sending light and warmth into every place to which they ventured outside Egypt, just as it did in their own land. They came to realize that, if all people participated in the worship of this benevolent global god who showered his grace on all human beings, ties of mutual understanding, fraternity and peace would necessarily be created between them, to the benefit of all. They saw that this made a stark contrast with those local gods who inherently divided and fragmented, rather than unified, those who worshipped them.

Akhnaton, then, was the first of the unifiers, first of the monotheists and first to seize on one of the implications of the modern concept of globalism. He was also the first in history to preach an all-embracing view of the cosmos. However, his followers were a tiny minority in a swelling sea of hostility. In support of him were those soldiers, merchants and administrators who had crisscrossed the far reaches of the empire, had observed the circumstances in which other people lived, had become acquainted with others' civilizations and religions and had experienced the variety of life and beliefs outside Egypt's borders. But he was opposed by the men of religion who abhorred foreign influences, by notable families whose interests and privileges were bound up in the worship of Amun and by the masses of common people who were submissively complicit with the deceit practised by the men of religion and the hegemony of the nobles. It was the strength of these reactionaries that led to the failure of this attempt to alter Egypt's path in order to adapt to the rising international ambitions in the territories of what is now called the Middle East. And the victory of this reactionism had long-term effects on Egyptian civilization and its arts and on the psyche of the Egyptian individual. For a start, the art of Tel el-Amarna, with its realism, vitality and individualism and its varied and liberated styles, was immediately abandoned, while the arts of sculpture and architecture declined noticeably in the age of the Ramessids, such that the focus now was on bulk rather than on beauty and human emotion. Likewise, Egyptians' tendency once again to face inwards and backwards to the past and the glories of 'the sound and pious ancestors' (al-salaf al-salih) took on momentous proportions. Once again, Egyptians turned back on to the path of the Old Kingdom in its traditions, beliefs and arts, even if tempered by the fact that there had by now seeped into the religion certain superstitions that could instil hope in the spirits of the downtrodden, sadly worn Egyptian people. Everlasting life in the gardens of bounty now became the right of all, something that was to be within their grasp rather than being the exclusive province of those whom the pharaoh blessed with his approval. Over time, it came to be sufficient to place in the burial casket, along with the corpse, a few talismans and magic amulets to guarantee protection from the dangers of the underworld.

Religion was always one of the principal bases for the politics of suppression and the erasure of the individual in Egypt. Perhaps there were motives other than religious ones behind the effort to get rid of Akhnaton;

but what happened to Hypatia in Alexandria at the start of the fifth century AD, under Christianity, may be the clearest example in the history of ancient Egypt of the way in which oppressive practices stemmed solely from religion. Hypatia (370–415 AD) was the first woman in history to stand out in the field of mathematics. A scholar of astronomy and geography, she led the neo-Platonist school in the Mediterranean region. With her eloquence, outstanding beauty, rare modesty and unique mental abilities, she was able to attract countless adherents to her philosophical circle. They regarded her as the epitome of knowledge and the scientific spirit. And since, among the earliest Christians, knowledge and the scientific spirit were the two writs that certified one's ties to paganism, Hypatia became the focal point for the conflict between Christians and non-Christians in Egypt. It was her presence above all that triggered the outbreak of strikes and violent clashes in Alexandria; in 415 AD, acting on the provocative counsel of the Alexandrian Patriarch, the rabble was able to kidnap and kill her, cutting her body into pieces. With her death, most of her followers fled Egypt. This event was a harbinger of change: it presaged Alexandria's slow fall into obscurity, after centuries during which that city had maintained its status as the centre from which the rays of knowledge and enlightenment spread.

Christianity was followed by Islam. 'And whosoever follows a religion other than Islam, it will not be accepted of him' (Q. 3. 85). Now the Muslims of Egypt experienced the same developments that had penetrated all of the other regions in the Abode of Islam, developments that had no intrinsic link with the religion of Islam but which became especially marked with the rise of the Abbasids and the closing of the door of *ijtihad* (the independent judgment of scholar-legists in questions of Islamic law). What prevailed from this time on was an attachment to the views of the sound and pious ancestors, a bond so strong that it precluded the right of the individual to think for himself about anything. It was as if, no matter what the subject was, the final word had already been said years before; there was no longer any course of action possible but to hear and obey, to follow and submit. Verification, whatever the issue at hand, became a matter solely of establishing the existence of a pertinent *hadith* (utterance or reported practice of the prophet Muhammad) or the opinion of an imam or jurist (*faqih*) on that issue; or, concomitantly, of denying the existence of a relevant *hadith* or scholarly opinion. It was unlikely to occur to anyone that one might present objective arguments either to support or refute the issue at hand. To put one's own mind to work on the problem was hardly seen as an option. Thus, among Muslims the concept of knowledge came to mean something already formulated, ready and waiting to be drawn from within the binding of a book – and the more ancient the book, the more correct the knowledge. This narrowing of the concept of knowledge was taking place at a time when, among Europeans, 'knowing' signified a process of utilizing what was already known to reveal what was as yet unknown. This sort of irrational stance provided us with a motive for obeying the opinions of the ancestors, whatever they might be, and solely on the basis that those ancestors had uttered them. This was the ruler's most forceful ally in strengthening his ability to exert autocratic power in our Islamic world.

At the beginning of the fourth century AH, a tendency emerged in the Islamic state to restrict the right to think to those who were already dead – to the senior jurists who had established the prevailing judgments on all matters. All others were forced to accept those judgments, 'for all major questions have already been settled, both in outline and in detail'.

And with the closing of the door of *ijtihad*, all that was now permitted to the Muslim individual was imitation: after all, no voice should be raised higher than the voices of the ancestors. It was widely said that it did not befit the believer to let himself be guided by the dictation of his mind; that the rational faculty was superfluous in the matter of eliciting the truth, which could be located within the ancestral utterances on faith.

At this point, coercion began to take its fullest form. Even the Mu'tazila – whom some regard as the adherents of free thought in the history of Islam – were not free of these taints. For, when the controversy over the nature of the Qur'an erupted, during the time when the Mu'tazila had political power, they resorted to torturing those of opposing views throughout the territories of the Islamic world, among them Egypt. They whipped and imprisoned those adversaries and divested them of their positions. As the political authority put an end to the individual's freedom to think and to choose for himself, so as to cleanse his beliefs of false conclusions and obsolete ideas, each person got into the habit of practising the same oppression and autocracy as he experienced at the hands of the political and religious authorities towards whomever was in a lower position. Leaders oppressed their followers, men oppressed women, fathers oppressed their children. When the subjects or the wife or the child asked of the ruler or the husband or the father, 'Why?', the response would be, 'Because that is my will'.

Westerners always found a special magic in the unknown, for they saw in it a challenge that invited them to adventure and experiment, to discover and invent, but in the Islamic world, the guiding principle among the majority was: what you know is safer than what you do not know. This was the case even in politics, where a prevailing compliance with a tyrannous ruler was evidence of a fear that this ruler would be succeeded by someone even worse. 'Yet it may happen that you will hate a thing which is better for you,' says the Qur'an (Q. 2.216).

The roots of this problem extend back to the concept of the *sunna* among the pre-Islamic peoples of the Arabian peninsula. In the Arabic language, *sunna* is the 'way' or 'road', the way of the ancestors who, in their travels through the desert, established that this was the one path that would lead them to the oases and wells without which they could not remain alive. As a result, it became a matter of danger – and a thing abhorred – for an individual to deviate even in the slightest degree from the path of the fathers and grandfathers. And so, wherever they were, including agriculture-based Egypt, Muslims inherited this habit of mind and the resulting aversion to innovation and novelty in every sphere. Whenever a *mujtahid* – a learned interpreter of the religious texts – offered an opinion, he would be asked, 'Is this something the Messenger of God said or is it an opinion that you conceived on your own?' If the answer was the latter, they rejected this view and dissociated themselves from him.

This inherited habit of mind paralysed the ability of the Muslims as a group to take risks or to innovate, and it obstructed the forward movement of inquiry and opinion and invention. It was blind imitation and rigidity that became widespread. Muslims justified that rigidity by pointing to the greatness of the Islamic state in its earliest centuries; they attributed that state's subsequent deterioration to circumstances beyond its capacity to exert control. In this, they were akin to someone who preserves the shop he has inherited in a state unchanged from the days of his father and grandfather. He does not take into account the transformations that have occurred in the interim – changes in styles of business and taste. Then he justifies his behaviour by referring to the flourishing business that the shop has once seen, in the days of his predecessors. He explains the current and inevitable stagnation of his business as a result of the flaws of the present age, or the corruption of people's consciences, or the ruinous state of anything but his own mode of thinking.

One factor alone allowed Egypt's agricultural society to preserve a limited measure of individuality and to maintain its ancient character amidst that sweeping sea of values coming from the desert and the Bedouins. I refer to the great zeal that Egyptians showed in the matter of reinterpreting the pagan aspects of their ancient religions to conform with Islamic beliefs and practices. They applied this reinterpretation to specific elements of those religions that they wanted to maintain and preserve. Historians of ancient Egypt and the Coptic era refer to the transformation of the ancient Egyptian gods into saints under Christianity, and into *awliya'* (friends of God and pious individuals) under Islam, noting that the phenomenon occurred without any change in the geographical sites of veneration associated with these figures or in sacred sites in general. Indeed, sometimes there was no discernible change in the accompanying rituals. As Ernst Renan famously said, 'Humanity from its beginnings always prayed at the same place.'

Gaston Maspero, for example, tells us about the *mulid* celebration for one of the *awliya'* in the city of Akhmim in southern Egypt. He says that its rituals follow very closely those that the ancient Egyptians practised in the very same city. Similarly, European travellers noticed the similarities between the behaviour of women visiting the tomb of Sayyid al-Badawi in the delta city of Tanta during the annual *mulid* celebration and their behaviour during their procession to Bubastis (Tell Basta in the Egyptian delta) as described by Herodotus. And so it goes also with certain infamous customs inherited from ancient Egyptian religions. There is a possibility, too, of a relationship between the pilgrimage of the Egyptians to the shrines of Tanta (among them the tomb of al-Sayyid al-Badawi) and the pilgrimage of their ancient forebears to Bubastis, or the Copts' pilgrimage in the past to the tomb of one of their saints there. It is known that the goddess of Bubastis, called 'Bast', was symbolized by the figure of a woman with the head of a cat, carrying on her left arm a small sack. Until not so long ago, the Egyptians retained the practice of accompanying the *mahmal* (camel litter) sent to Mecca each year at the time of the pilgrimage with a large number of cats in the care of a man appointed for this purpose and popularly called 'Father of the Cats'. (Observe, too, that many Egyptians still call cats 'Bissa', a loanword from the ancient Egyptian language.) To justify the continuation of this practice once Islam was adopted, the people attributed to the prophet Muhammad a love of cats, and claimed that he was partial to one particular cat, which gave birth to its litter in his lap!

Moreover, for a segment of the populace in Egypt's southern regions, to circumambulate the tomb of Shaykh al-Qenawi in Qena seven times is believed to be a legitimate alternative to performing the religious duty of making the pilgrimage to God's sacred house in Mecca. A number of religious scholars supported this view, recognizing the futility of mounting resistance to the population's notions and preferences. For if Islam's continued existence was considered the important thing, there had to be a measure of submission to and acceptance of the local pagan elements once they had been tinted in Islamic hues. If we then take into account the possibility that this Shaykh al-Qenawi was a legendary figure whose tomb was constructed on the remains of a temple to one of the ancient Egyptian gods, we arrive at a strange conclusion: the general populace in Egypt replaced one of the five pillars of Islam with a purely pagan ritual going back to the days of the pharaohs!

Thus, after Ibn al-'As had conquered Egypt for Islam, the Egyptian people succeeded in deceiving the conquerors and in bending to their own needs the religion that those conquerors had brought with them. The Arabs who had come from the Arabian Peninsula wanted the Egyptians to pay the *jizya*, or subject tax, if they chose to retain their previous beliefs, and they also slammed the doors of a number of important state positions shut in the faces of Egyptians who did not convert. To circumvent the special tax and attain the state positions to which they aspired, while preserving their beliefs, the Egyptians' strategy was to embrace the new faith while imbricating these beliefs and rituals in it. This ruse convinced the rulers; the religious scholars complied; and the subjects were content. The people obtained – or thought they were obtaining – the blessings of this world and also the recompense of the hereafter.

Thus, as we have suggested, it was easy for the Egyptians to preserve a measure of freedom to express themselves while preserving their distinct society, maintaining its difference from the other parts of the Islamic world. However, a momentous reverse transpired, beginning early in the sixteenth century, when the conflict between Shi'ite Iran and the Sunni Ottoman state emerged. It would become a major feature of Islamic history for the next three centuries. This was a clash so sharp that it made the conflict between those two states and Europe seem marginal by comparison. The consequence of this struggle between Sunnis and Shi'ites was that those who already held authority over the reins of state and over the religion, on both sides, became even more determined to hold fast to a rigidly conservative set of principles permitting no renovation or innovation, and disallowing any external factors or older religions from having any impact whatsoever. Their adherence to a traditional, rigid formulation of the Islamic *Shari'a* (legal code, based on Qur'an, *hadith* and scholarly interpretation) also intensified; here was a significant reason why the European renaissance had no echo, either strong or faint, in the Islamic world. The Sultans Salim and Sulayman the Lawgiver, in Istanbul, and Aurangzeb, in Delhi, saw danger signals in every new idea, every plurality of opinion, every call for reform, every aspiration to create things anew, every tendency to inquiry or review. Thus, the awakening in thought and the arts, literature and the sciences that Europe witnessed in that epoch had no parallel, not even the shadow of one, for no such awakening occurred in Iran or in the Ottoman state, including the territories it ruled, among them Egypt.

More disastrous still, the policy of repression practised by the Muslims' rulers and the men of religion towards every free intellectual initiative left terrible legacies from which the Egyptians (and others) still suffer to this day. For the reaction to those intellectual initiatives took the shape of an administrative measure by the central authority, not of an intellectual challenge coming from those who held opposing views. This violent repression paralysed every attempt to respond to changes in the world that surrounded the Islamic state or to face new challenges. The intellectuals found security either by remaining silent or by adhering to what the religious scholars dictated. This poverty of intellectual debate among those of differing views yielded a further harvest: the reactionary religious scholars, having become utterly confident that they had the full backing of the tyrannical rulers as well as the support of the political and military authorities, and being also sure that the intellectuals would lack the boldness to challenge them and debate their ideas, saw no urgent reason to arm themselves with added knowledge or information in order to guarantee their victory in any argument with their opponents. Thus they neglected study and eschewed further learning, with the result that their stock of knowledge grew meagre. In effect they vacated the outstanding intellectual legacy that had been theirs, finding it sufficient to rely on the government to safeguard the beliefs they stood for and to fight off attempts at innovation. And this is precisely what continues to go on in Egypt today: we see the official men of religion scurrying in alarm to the central authority each time there appears a book or an article that contests their thinking, entreating the government to ban such-and-such a book or to suppress the ideas of such-and-such a writer. Whenever even a single voice can be heard calling for an understanding of Islam that shapes it to the contours of contemporary world, a number of those who are labelled Islamic thinkers hasten to demand loudly that this voice be silenced, and express wonder at how the government could have permitted such a voice to rise in the heart of the Islamic world, the city of the thousand minarets!

Thus, the events that ushered in the sixteenth century constituted in themselves a forewarning that western Europe's civilization was emerging as superior to the rest, and that Islamic civilization was now on the wane in all the regions where it had held sway. Historians, both Middle Eastern and western, have ascribed the onset of Islamic civilization's demise to a set of causes, the most important of which was the impact of the European sea blockade on Muslims' commercial activity, and the latter's loss of the ample profits they had enjoyed as a result of being intermediaries between Europe and the Far East, particularly in the spice trade. However, the real reason for this decline – which might surprise some – was the fact that the Ottomans continued to enjoy military victories over their enemies in Europe and elsewhere for long periods after this European sea blockade had started, a string of triumphs that continued until the Ottoman armies were defeated at the gates of Vienna in 1683. If the Europeans' act of cutting off the Muslims' trade route to the Far East in the era of Sultan al-Ghuri had had the immediate effect that was intended, forcing part of Islamic society to realize that it was facing real external danger, and as a consequence spurring intellectuals to advance proposals for transforming internal conditions in a way that would ensure an adequate response to this danger – for adapting positively to new circumstances – then the condition of the Muslims would have been different. They would not have fallen into such a state of weakness. Instead, regrettably, the armies of the Ottomans (the new rulers over the greater part of the Islamic world) continued to win one victory after another, expanding the borders of the state east and west, north and south, for a period of nearly two centuries. Those Muslims who were the ignorant subjects of the Ottoman state imagined falsely that, with these victories, they had blocked dangers both external and internal. This gave them the peculiar, and fatal, feeling of assurance of the continued might and glory of the Islamic state and its superiority over the world of the infidel dogs. Such a belief yielded a spirit of extreme conservatism, a rejection of any and all innovation and a scornful attitude towards the civilization of the enemies, belittling the value of studying that civilization carefully in order to assimilate its beneficial aspects.

In this, not in the loss of the spice trade, lay the true affliction of Islam in the modern age; in this was concealed the secret of its failure. Another factor was also decisive. Ibn Khaldun indicated this in his *Prolegomena*, when he described the Arab as a person ready to remove a stone from a building in order to sit on it, even if that caused the whole edifice to topple! Commentators bothered by this description interpreted Ibn Khaldun's remark as referring to the Bedouins, not to Arabs in general; this circumvented the necessity of inquiring how this 'Bedouin' trait might have spread, for instance, to Egyptians, both in rural areas and in the towns, stamping their behaviour with a brand of extreme individualism, with an anxious and narrow self-interest, to the exclusion of respect for the general welfare and the sentiments of others. A familiar sight in Egypt today is the hand of a car owner emerging from the window to toss orange and banana skins on to the road; and when that person reaches his friend's home, the hand remains glued to the car horn until the friend peers out at him from the sixth floor, or the tenth, whatever the hour of day or night and regardless of the feelings of others, whether they be asleep, ill, studying or reading!

Personal interest has become both goal and slogan; neither homeland nor neighbour concerns us, and who cares if a crooked civil servant burns down an entire museum when the time for the annual inventory draws near, so that his thefts will remain undiscovered? Who cares if businessmen flee abroad with the embezzled savings of hundreds of thousands of people, even if their dishonesty shakes the economy of the state to the core? The moment a public park opens, it becomes subject to destruction by young people, yanking off and carrying away its blooms and tree branches. No collective endeavour succeeds. And the only sports in which we excel are individual ones where there is no call for cooperation among the members of a team.

In such a public atmosphere, devoid of sensitivity to other peoples' needs, lacking respect for the feelings of others, when it has become a common occurrence for every hand to reach into another's pocket to snatch whatever it holds, it is inevitable that we sense the barrenness of the milieu in which we live. It is no surprise that we feel there is no one who wishes us well, and that the law of the jungle rules our lives.

This brand of individualism is the natural harvest of the fact that another sort of individualism has been weakened to the point of erasure. This other kind of individualism is embodied in the individual's development of his self, his talents and intellectual leanings; his recognition and exercise of his right to differ from others; and his ability to play a part in the political, cultural, religious and family spheres. There is no doubt that the extreme passivity of the Egyptian personality is the inevitable result of the oppression that prevails in all of those spheres.

Ilyas al-Ayyubi, in his book *'Ahd Isma'il* (The Age of Ismail), mentions that in the first session of the Parliamentary Council that Khedive Isma'il ordered formed in 1866, Sharif Pasha, Minister of the Interior, delivered a speech to the representatives in which he said that European parliaments are always divided into two parties: one that supports the government and one that opposes it. This being the case, they ought to divide themselves likewise into two parties, one with the government and one against it. The men of the government party would sit to the right and those of the opposition would sit to the left, he said. Hearing this, the representatives all hurried to take their seats to the right, shouting, 'We are all the slaves of our Effendi [the Khedive], and so how could we be in opposition to his government?!' Likewise, Lady Duff Gordon recounted, in her correspondence, that one of the representatives said to her, 'We, the company of representatives, head to Cairo with our hearts in our shoes. The only response that any one of us can make to a superior with respect to any order issued to him, no matter how oppressive, is "Absolutely, whatever you say – I am at your service". So then, can you imagine us daring to oppose the will of our Effendi who owns our very necks, and can do what he likes with our lives, and can at any moment he wishes make the ground swallow us up and cut off- our existence?'

So the situation has remained, from that day to this, buttressed by Egyptians' tendency to flatter the men of government. (Recall the popular proverb, 'The man who marries my mother, I will call my uncle!'.) It was also buttressed by people's inclination to glorify the ruler at the expense of whatever issue was or is at hand, as illustrated by the common saying, in the days of the early twentieth-century nationalist leader and prime minister Sa'd Zaghlul, that 'Imperialism at the hand of Sa'd is better than freedom at the hand of 'Adli [Yakan]' (referring to his rival, the head of another political party). This subservience is equally evident in a saying prevalent in the time of Abd al-Nasir's presidency, that 'All of us are Gamal 'Abd al-Nasir'. In a song written by Salah Jahin in honour of Abd al-Nasir, there is a line that goes, 'Say what you wish, we are your men'. In the same vein, I heard with my own ears a director of the Diplomatic Institute attached to the Egyptian Foreign Ministry say to the students, 'Let us all praise God that we have no need to think, for He gave us an inspired leader – Abd al-Nasir – to think on our behalf.'

The ruler in Egypt, therefore, has little need to fake general election results (which he nevertheless does each time) or to caution that 'To the one who says "such and such" with his head, I say "thus and thus" with my sword'. Nor must he shout on every occasion, 'No voice shall be heard above that of the battle' (and for him the battles go on, one after another.) Even so, Anwar al-Sadat, during the span of his presidency, felt it necessary to add a new commitment, to 'the morals of the village' (a phrase that no one but himself understood) and to the traditions of the great family he headed (understood by everybody to allude to the necessity of complete submission by all members of the Egyptian family to absolute paternal authority). It was understood that any individual who attempted to express himself, to offer an opposing view, would be answered with the rebuke, 'For shame, lad!' (We should point out here that the word 'shame' was one of the most frequent words on Sadat's tongue in his orations and statements, and that during his rule he issued what he called the Law of Shame.)

Another anecdote is appropriate here. It is told of Ali Mubarak Pasha, the nineteenth-century reformer, leading educator and Minister of Education, that during his inspection of a rural school a peasant boy stood up and said loudly that he had an opinion contrary to something the Minister had said. When the headmaster scolded him, saying, 'Quiet, boy, for shame!', Ali Mubarak hastened to say, 'No, let him express what is on his mind, for as long as he has said "no" to the Minister, he will find it easy afterwards to say it to his father and to the village headman and to the

Ma'mur [commissioner, e.g. of the police]; and this is what we hope for and want to anticipate.' But Ali Mubarak's attempt to encourage dissent yielded no further fruit and was not repeated in the subsequent history of Egypt.

The family traditions, akin to tribal practices, that so delighted Sadat played a major role in allowing Egypt's rulers to suppress intellectual freedom in their society. The expanding power of the ruling apparatus, the state's complete domination of the media and its policy and its consequent monopoly over the distribution of senior positions and ability to freeze at will the income of those it disliked, all combined to produce a specific result, namely, that those who produced culture adopted a position of hypocrisy and appeasement towards those of power and influence. Such a stance shook their confidence in themselves first, and in their moral position and the cultural commodities they produced, and in the end led them to adopt a posture on life, values and culture that was saturated with scepticism and ironic mockery. Add to this the appearance of oil wealth in certain Arab countries, which nudged a large number of Egyptian writers and artists into announcing their loyalty to the authorities in those countries – most of which are reactionary in terms of intellectualism, politics and religion. Egypt's intellectuals and artists did so in order to benefit materially from publishing their works in those countries, but as a consequence they had to submit to stipulations, both announced and unannounced, on what they published, and in the end this destroyed all their creativity and intellectual independence.

A further negative factor is the relationship between the growth of a populist Islamism and the terrorism of extremist religious groups, on the one hand, and the positions taken by al-Azhar and official Islam on the other: the latter are in essence no less extreme than the former. The correspondence between the positions derives either from a fear of losing influence with the masses or of the possibility that the terrorists might perpetuate deeds such as their assassination of former Minister of Religious Endowments (*Awqaf*) Shaykh al-Dhahabi, whose outlook they rejected. Or perhaps the convergence in position is simply due to the pressure of Egypt's prevailing reactionary intellectual atmosphere. The government needs those 'official' religious institutions to support it against terrorism and the influence of the extremist groups, to grant the state 'legitimacy' in the measures it takes against those groups and to provide testimony of the excellence of its Islamic principles. This is because, with the passage of time, the government apparatus has become obliged increasingly to appease and satisfy those institutions and to offer them concessions. In these circumstances the state turns a blind eye when the religious establishment bans books or refuses to allow them into the country, when it forbids the screening of films or the performance of plays, when it closes down art exhibitions that display tendency towards freedom or independent thinking, when it issues judicial decisions against thinkers (such as the court ruling to separate Nasr Hamid Abu Zayd and his wife on the basis of opinions he voiced in certain books) or even when it commits repugnant acts such as the assassination of the intellectual Farag Foda.

The men of government and the media, or the Islamic thinkers who are labelled as 'enlightened' and therefore liberal, or the men of religion characterized as 'moderates' might react to this angrily, expressing disapproval of the assassination of Farag Foda and citing as proof the Qur'anic verse, 'There is no coercion in religion' (Q. 2. 256). They might describe that deed as contrary to the tolerant spirit of Islam, citing the verse, 'Call to the way of your Lord with wisdom and good exhortation, and dispute with them in a better manner' (Q. 16. 125). But those individuals from among the Islamic groups who do dispute with them are also able to take as witness a set of stories from the authorized versions of the Life of the Prophet, such as that by Ibn Ishaq, and the *Maghazi* of al-Waqidi, which relate how the Prophet delegated groups of his Companions to kill poets who had mocked him in their verses or who had incited the infidels of Quraysh against him in their poetry. al-Waqidi says:

> Ka'b b. al-Ashraf was a poet. He ridiculed the Prophet and his Companions, and incited the infidels of Quraysh against them in his poetry. So the Messenger of God said: Who will rid me of Ibn al-Ashraf? For he has harmed me. So Muhammad b. Maslama said: I will kill him. The Prophet said: Then do so. Ibn Maslama went with a small group of the Aws tribe until they came to Ibn al-Ashraf and struck him down with their swords. They carried his head to the Prophet, whom they found standing at the entrance to the mosque. He said: May your countenances prosper! They replied: And yours, O Messenger of God! They tossed down the head of Ka'b, and he praised God that Ka'b had been killed. And when the Messenger of God rose the next morning, he said: Whichever of the men of the Jews you lay your hands on him. The Jews were afraid, and not one of their senior men dared to show his face or speak. They feared that a plot would be hatched against them as it had been against Ibn al-Ashraf . . .

In such a climate, those Egyptian intellectuals who are atheists (and they are numerous) have lost their boldness about articulating their views on religion in public; if they do so in their writings and discussions, not a single reader or listener can comprehend what is hidden there, for they express themselves along the same lines as do the believers, putting themselves into the same discursive context, even though they maintain a contrary ultimate purpose. They make the same obeisance to the Messenger of God, they employ the same tactics of citing verses from the Qur'an and prophetic traditions and they offer the same expressions of zealous concern about protecting the interests of Islam and the Muslims. If, in their attacks on singers, the extremists depend on *hadith*s attributed to the prophet that forbid music and singing, and use the same or other *hadith*s to justify the destruction of musical instruments at performances, their adversaries respond merely that these are 'weak' *hadith*s (ones not transmitted by reliable sources) or fabricated *hadith*s (ones proven false). And then they counter by arguing the existence of sound *hadith*s that permit music and singing. This is the level of backwardness that we have reached! I might be able to understand the enmity that certain narrow-minded extremists have towards music and singing if it were on the basis of a *hadith* that they considered sound. But I do not understand how their 'enlightened' interlocutors can defend themselves by relying on a *hadith* or an anecdote from the prophet's life, rather than on articulations of rational thinking or logic. Can one imagine a German youth speaking of music in the following way?

I am infatuated by music because I have read that one day Martin Luther – God sanctify his soul – and his wife came upon some people in the village of Wittenberg who were playing music and singing. His wife began to sing with them, while Luther stood before her, nodding his head in time to the music (in another version, he began to tap his foot to the music)! And I know that music is one of the most important arts of humankind. According to the story transmitted by Edmund Ludlow (who heard it from Henry Leutreil, who took it from Owen Fleetham), in which one of Luther's companions asked him one day, 'What do you have to say, O Martin, concerning the Pope of Rome, who detests music?' And Luther replied, 'Do not talk of him, for he comprehends nothing.' (And this is a tradition generally agreed upon.)

So much for the Muslims. As for the Copts, there is no doubt that feelings of frustration and bitterness are present in their community, especially as the Islamists have broadened their reach; there is no doubt that Copts sense that attempts to cement sound relationships based on religious coexistence with Egyptian Muslims are threatened with failure. Six centuries of the history of Christian Egypt (longer than the entire history of the United States) – and the Egyptian Muslim knows barely a single detail of this history. Newspapers and magazines offer no podium for the expression of

Coptic thinking; in fact, they are practically restricted to a single publication, which is read only by Copts. At the same time Coptic writers are talking about the enormous dearth of portrayals of the circumstances of their religious community, its way of life and its intellectual compass, whether in novels, theatre or film. The Copts, in any case, bear much of the responsibility for the negative aspects of their position in Egyptian society, in that they have traditionally turned inwards and have shown passivity and caution, for which they are famed the world over. Many of the eminent ones – those with the most cultural capital experience, and skill – have elected to emigrate from their homeland without attempting positively and actively to confront what is happening there, without participating in the creation of some way out of their dilemma and without aiding the government to strengthen religious coexistence between the two groups, by making proposals to this end. For the most part, their stance does not go beyond reacting to whatever occurs, whether by emigrating abroad, complaining and grumbling among themselves, exercising a grudging patience or attempting revenge. But when it comes to planning in order to salvage national unity, they are mostly clueless. As for their rights to citizenship and full equality in a country where their due is equivalent to what Muslims are due, their intellectuals and leaders are satisfied with repeating, on public occasions, words that neither they nor anyone else believes: that everything is just fine; that things could not possibly be improved; and that Egypt's enemies – whether they be inside the country or outside – have failed in their efforts to fragment the nation!

Three ideological directions have remained salient. Two of them Abd al-Nasir embraced: socialism and Arab nationalism. His successor, Anwar al-Sadat, encouraged the third after Egypt's relations with all other Arab states ceased following the Camp David Accords. That third tendency was the resurrection of Egyptian nationalism at the expense of Arab nationalism. All of these courses failed to move the Egyptian people, yet they had fatal impacts on the personal and intellectual products of Egyptian thinkers in the opposition, as the authorities suppressed every attempt – and even every inclination – on their part to express views that diverged from those of officialdom.

Whether it was the Marxism that had appeared in Egypt at the start of the 1920s or the socialism that Abd al-Nasir adopted at the beginning of the 1960s, adherents to these ideologies remained permanently incapable of, or averse to, offering new, independent thinking rooted in Egyptian realities, even with the leaders's boasting talk of Arab or Egyptian socialism. For in spite of the fact that their outlooks originated in a fundamental concern with the issue of social justice within Egypt, with settling accounts with imperialism and ending exploitation, and with the relationship between the national revolution and socialist transformation, these marxists remained intellectually and organizationally dependent on the Soviet Union, bowing almost completely to its theoretical interpretations and tactical political positions. Their vacillations and the contradictions in their thought stemmed from the vacillations and contradictions in Soviet policy; they feared creative effort and neglected to draw inspiration from local reality, which critically reduced the appeal of their thinking among the masses, even of workers and peasants. In spite of their general restraint about entering into open battle against Arabic cultural heritage and Islam, they believed absolutely that those legacies were fundamentally unsuited to collective organization or political confederation. Here, we should add that the socialist regime of Abd al-Nasir had directed a mortal blow at civil society and its institutions or formations; and likewise at the individual's sense of responsibility for coming to terms with Egypt's social problems and trying to act to solve them. For individuals could observe that the state had taken on itself all of the responsibility for everything, and indeed that it had begun to gaze suspiciously upon any individual effort that was expended in those areas.

As to Arab nationalism, it had remained, through the era of King Faruq, a modest, humble concept that hardly expanded outside the writings of a limited number of thinkers or beyond the banquets at the royal palace for Arab leaders in which orators gave speeches and singers entertained. With the emergence of Abd al-Nasir and his ambitions, however, Arab nationalism assumed a new character, which contributed to the formation of fierce inter-Arab enmities and struggles for leadership of the Arab world (especially between Egypt, Iraq and the Kingdom of Saudi Arabia) and indeed to civil wars (Lebanon in 1956 and Yemen from 1962 to 1967). In Egypt, beginning in 1955, and for the first time in its history, broad-based, organized campaigns attempted to implant in the minds of the populace the concept of Arab nationalism and the notion of belonging to an entity defined as Arab. These campaigns utilized the national mass media, curricula at both school and university level and the writings of intellectuals who were either hypocrites or true believers, as well as the speeches of leaders and commanders and propaganda from the ruling 'Socialist Union', complete with its slogans and banner statements. At some point (and especially after the establishment of the United Arab Republic, which united Egypt and Syria in 1958), it began to appear that the idea of Arab nationalism was becoming reality, that it had begun to garner a large measure of success. Then came the war of 1967, which neutralized and then eclipsed Abd al-Nasir and led Egyptians to doubt themselves and their abilities. In broader terms, it also caused them to question the viability of the socialist regime and the wisdom of involvement in internal Arab affairs, especially since Abd al-Nasir's doomed interference in Yemen was thought to be one of the causes of Egypt's military defeat by Israel. The upshot was that in the last three years of Abd al-Nasir's rule – the man whom the Egyptians and the Arabs had imagined to be the new Saladin – he became no more than a Soviet satellite, his dependence a move of desperation to save him from his twin predicaments, economic and military collapse.

The fact is that the idea of Arab nationalism and Arab unity, which made an earnest appearance in Egypt much later than it had in many other Arab states, never did penetrate the people's psyches in any serious way. It really got no further than the minds of a minority of writers influenced by ideas of western provenance (rather than Islamic ones) and the imaginations of some urban Egyptians. It did not touch the overwhelming majority of peasants and workers, who never felt any compelling need for the concept. As for the intellectual class in the Coptic community, while some found the idea appealing out of a hope that it would make for an expanded secular political framework acceptable to them, most Copts remained fearful that the success of this idea would simply result in the formation of an organic bond between Arab nationalism and Islam.

Let us add to this several other considerations. First, the failed experiment of unification with Syria made Egyptians doubt the viability of unity and the possibility that it could be achieved in any practical sense. Second, many Egyptians continued to feel that their sense of belonging was not based on being Arab, but rather was nourished by their ancient history and the glories of their pharaonic forebears. Third, in general the Egyptian populace's link to an Arab and Islamic heritage was weak by comparison to that of other populations in the region – in, for example, Syria or Iraq. Fourth, Egyptians believed that the economic predicament that plagued them was the result of entering some extremely costly wars in which the rest of the Arabs had failed to participate as much as they should have. Moreover, they felt that Arab financial help to Egypt had been paltry, especially considering the sacrifices Egypt had offered for the sake of an Arab problem that concerned all (and this sentiment was nourished by the Egyptian press and other mass media during the era of Anwar al-Sadat). Finally, Egyptians' feelings of displeasure towards other Arabs also stemmed from their disgust at the behaviour of some wealthy individuals coming to Egypt (especially from the Gulf countries). They saw these wealthy Arabs as ostentatious and conceited, confident in their belief that their wallets gave them the power to demand whatever they wanted, to control all situations and to purchase everything, including the honour of Egyptian women. This antipathy arose also from a sense of humiliation experienced by Egyptian labourers in wealthy Arab countries, compelled by the economic crisis in their own country to seek income elsewhere and treated by their new employers as inferiors. The feelings were intensified by the fact that for a long time the balance of status between Egypt and its neighbours had been precisely the reverse.

All of this encouraged – for a time – the resurrection of the Egyptian nationalist sentiments that Sadat had embraced. However, the Islamists' expanding power was linked to claims of the superiority of factors other than the sense of national belonging and citizenship. These new criteria were embodied in the teachings of religion. The Islamists had mocked the notions of patriotic territorial nationalism and Arab nationalism, calling instead for fealty to religion and to the Abode of Islam. They rejected the idea that legitimate laws and constitutions could be fashioned by human hands, just as they dismissed the notion of specific, territorially delimited countries whose boundaries were drawn by human decision. They announced this openly and plainly when they claimed that there is no citizenship either greater or lesser in its extent than that of Dar al-Islam, and that there exists no right of the majority – even a majority of more than ninety-nine percent of the community – to change or abrogate a single text given to humankind by the divine Lawmaker. It makes no difference whether this majority considers such an alteration necessary to stay abreast of the demands of the age and to face its challenges. In their loyalty to this creed, some Egyptians have gladly abandoned their attachment to their homeland and given unconditional obedience to the non-Egyptian commander of an Islamic group, Osama bin Laden, in his endeavour to shatter Egypt's stability and economy by killing tourists and committing acts of terrorism against foreign investors.

Another tendency has contributed to weakening the sentiments of patriotic nationalism in Egypt. This is a growing sympathy with globalism, whose adherents see it as an inevitable and irreversible development, practically a phenomenon of nature that cannot be successfully resisted or blocked. Advocates of this line argue that today's world has shrunk to an unprecedented degree, bringing new circumstances that make change imperative. This requires, among other things, that states relinquish their local authority (or a great part of it) and that the world's peoples give up their old notions of citizenship and attachment to the homeland or the nation. This outlook has been accompanied – or preceded – by a great change in the values and moral compasses in Egypt, especially among the young. Gone is the idea of considering work that offers a measure of self-realization or fulfils service to the nation and their compatriots or even that suit their interests and mental capacities. Instead, they seek work that will bring in the highest possible income and allow the most consumption, such as in banking, in a foreign firm, in one of the numerous import-export concerns, or even abroad, preferably in an oil-producing country. This change has helped to undermine concepts of nation and citizenship, for the young people's slogan has become, 'There is no necessary relationship between you and a particular country; the best country is the one that sustains you'. Or they follow the maxim of 'Ali b. Abi Talib: 'Riches in exile are a homeland, and poverty in the homeland is exile'.

These factors lie at the roots of the crisis of the individual in Egypt, of the weakness of individual consciousness that prevents the development of a human being's capacity to be truly loyal to what is at his own core. However, the past few years have seen the emergence of some developments that may offer a measure of optimism. First, the system of patriarchal authority within the family is continuing to diminish and in the end must disappear completely. It is now acceptable for an individual family member to say 'no' to the head of the family, and it has become very difficult for that head of family to say to the member, 'Quiet, child – for shame!'

Likewise, the power in society of the most zealous Islamists is intrinsically and indissolubly bound up with the efficacy of their movement and with their ability to direct the course of events in their spheres of activity. It is possible that these movements will fall into oblivion or at least weaken as a result of having to face the modern state's exigencies and historical determinism.

In the atmosphere of globalization that we expect to prevail, the absence of transparency can only have negative effects such as the majority of Egyptians have already experienced in their everyday lives. The regime itself cannot remain unaffected by this. It will be forced to broaden the compass of privatization to include, in addition to economic activity, the spheres of education and the information media. It cannot prevent the ever-greater spread of private schools and universities, of radio and television stations, of newspapers and magazines owned by individuals. Human rights organizations, international, regional and local, have repeatedly shown their willingness to ambush the state in response to its continuing transgressions of human rights. Likewise, economic aid and loans that we receive from major foreign governments depend on the extent to which the Egyptian government respects human rights. These pressures will oblige the state to hesitate before embarking on any serious abuse of those rights.

Such developments, coupled with a growing consciousness on the part of many individuals, represent the positive face of Egyptian democracy's future. Let us also bear in mind the significance of what we saw happening in the final decade of the twentieth century: the destruction of many totalitarian regimes, right and left, across the globe. Thus we can predict a gradual but inevitable weakening of the role of centralized political authority in Egypt over the coming years, its waning interference in areas that will become increasingly the province of the business and finance sectors, and the restriction of its role to the preservation of public security, protection of financial interests and eradication of pockets of poverty that might lead to social unrest.

Such a conjuncture breathes life into hopes for an expanded sphere of freedom in which writers and artists can express themselves, intellectuals can offer their views freely and the list of taboos, which for long periods have prevented us from seeing the revival of, for example, a literature of confession, might shrink. Then indeed our society may adhere to John Stuart Mill's warning in his famous essay *On Liberty*:

> If all mankind minus one were of one opinion, and only one person were of the contrary opinion, mankind would be no more justified in silencing that one person, than he, if he had the power, would be justified in silencing mankind . . . the peculiar evil of silencing the expression of an opinion is that it is robbing the human race, posterity as well as the existing generation – those who dissent from the opinion, still more than those who hold it. If the opinion is right, they are deprived of the opportunity of exchanging error for truth; if wrong, they lose, what is almost as great a benefit, the clearer perception and livelier impression of truth produced by its collision with error . . . even if the received opinion be not only true, but the whole truth; unless it is suffered to be, and actually is, vigorously and earnestly contested, it will, by most of those who receive it, be held in the manner of a prejudice, with little comprehension or feeling of its rational grounds . . . the meaning of the doctrine itself will be in danger of being lost or enfeebled.

CHAPTER 6

Individualism in the Arab Maghreb

Saleh Bechir

The history of the individual has scarcely enjoyed any sustained attention or concern among us. The figure of the individual is either nonexistent – melting into the group – or heroic. In the latter case, perhaps by virtue of the heroic figure's gravity and as a crowning touch to that venerability – as a means to consolidate it – this individual 'sacrifices' all individuality, gives it up in a generous gesture for the sake of the very uniqueness that a hero can and must claim. For this uniqueness anchors the values of the group and is their bearer, offering the most conspicuous of images that give expression to the collective. Thus, the hero's individuality becomes the instrument of its own neutralization, its very denial, as it is cast in a mould of uniqueness that draws upon a mythologization already in place, upon qualities of transcendence that make it a node of consensus, whether institutionalized or mass-driven (in the sense of expressing a collective sense of the populace or the crowd).

It may be that the logic inherent in the language betrays something of this. The term 'hero' (*batal*) comes from a trilateral root, incorporated into a semantic field, the two together accounting for a range of significations: *al-batil* (false, unfair, apocryphal), *al-butlan*, (futility, falsity, invalidity), *al-ibtal* (abrogation, abolition), *al-batala* (idleness, unemployment, vacation) and the like. One can occupy the position of hero only by abrogating one's own individuality, through showering upon it an excessive uniqueness that makes the point. Moreover, one cannot do so without deploying some measure, large or small, of falsity (that is, of fabrication, arrogation or plagiarism). It is this that necessitates the mythological recounting of the figure's heroic qualities and accomplishments, of a biography intended for crowds and pitched to the intensity of their zeal.

This observation compels us to ask: in such a relationship between hero and audience, who is the sacrificial victim of whom? Is it the former, the hero, exercising power over the imagination of the audience as well as perhaps tyranny over its members' destinies? Or is it the latter, the audience, having charged their hero with tasks that are not in that figure's power by assuming the right to define and then demand the completion of those tasks? Perhaps one can hazard a guess as to which supposition is the more likely. For when all is taken into account, the hero is possibly no more than an anti-alter ego, occupying a position that is both polar opposite and reflection of the victim or sacrificial lamb. For to the extent that the latter figure is burdened with the sins, defects and infirmities of the group, the burden falls upon this figure alone, who receives the retribution or expulsion due to any or all, suffered in their name; who assumes the burden of doing silent penance for all.

The hero takes upon those heroic shoulders whatever the group has failed to provide, whether in the realm of momentous traits or in that of glorious deeds. The group then adopts those qualities, assimilates them in their generalized or abstract form, by embracing the figure of the hero as their own. Thus the two faces of the mirror meet, twin metonymies, ultimate and inescapable expressions of all that remains constant and steadfast in the existence of the ordinary people, as measured against a human scale that weighs the modest heroisms and petty depravities that help to shape their lives and give them strength to bear those lives.

Perhaps this phenomenon is simply a feature of universal human existence. Yet what appears 'universal' may instead be an anthropologically shaped humanity – defined first and foremost through rituals and rites, which may constitute practically all that sets the group apart as a collective entity. This anthropological model might not correspond to a modern and democratic humanity in which the criteria of the law have occupied a central position in the life of the group, such that the society has by and large adopted this mode (letting it define significant signposts of its collective existence) as its primary means to delimit identity and to parcel out responsibilities. Such dispositions have become individualized, and have been stripped of anything that smacks of traditional ritual practice; or at the least, energetic attempts in that direction have accomplished much. If effective, this is one of the keys to its transition to, and maintenance of, a stable modernity.

One of the most noteworthy points in this regard is that we faced the modernity of which we speak – which has been imposing many and various claims and associations of ideas upon us for more than two centuries now – in the role of learner, as a collective recipient of instructions, who remained convinced, by and large, that this was indeed the most suitable niche for us to occupy. As a consequence, this modernity was always interrogating us – roughly and with some hostility – on the identity or essence of our society, and what aspects of it could be considered foundational. What was at its core? But the questioning always swerved to focus on the issue of the individual person: what was the status of the individual? What was the nature of the individual's independence (within the individual's social formation, of course, whether as an ontological being, in the philosophical sense or as a legal entity)?

These reflections may amount to no more than a background that is already well known. No one will be surprised by the remark that, since the question of the individual in our society is akin to other issues that also touch on the institution of a modernity properly rooted in terms of its moral qualities, intellectual vigour and founding principles, the importance of trying to understand it fully was neglected in favour of seeing it as purely or nearly procedural. In other words, we wanted and hoped to take the procedures, regimes and material implements of modernity, to introduce them into our society, and then to disregard the rest of it – in other words, its spirit. We considered that to be a supererogatory gift of which we had no need.

The truth is that our approach to modernity may have altered the way we received or appropriated it. For so far we have responded to it either by mocking it, casting slurs on the west and its culture and seeing modernity as simply the sign and token of both, or by weeping over its failure to appear among us and our inability to bring it to fruition. The latter attitude causes bitterness towards our own societies for failing to open their doors, to welcome modernity in and to assimilate it. For the experience of more than two centuries of mutual communication and commerce with the world of modernity – in a region that lies directly across the waters from the ancient wellsprings of that modernity and has a thousand formal and informal ties with it – has yielded only the resistance that we now can observe. This poses the following question: what if a culture's assertion that it could and would withdraw, secluding itself from modernity, confident in the ability to restrict modernity's reach and to be on guard against it, were a presumption worth taking seriously? Supposing its significance and potency had been obscured by our readiness (whether consciously or innocently) to adopt certain laws of determinism? Moreover, would not that disregard of modernity's values (or rather, of those values that supposedly accompany the modernization process) and the 'success' our societies scored in this act of neglect, become a historic event whose very history would demand inscription? Would this not be especially so given the abundance of pertinent material on hand for such a writing of history, not to mention the temporal extent, the range of experiments and the accumulation of experience varying across specific countries and regions?

These questions demand articulation, although it is not claimed here that one can probe, much less, answer them fully. Indeed, within the confines of our subject, we will content ourselves with raising some questions, making some suggestions and gleaning some points that arise from contemplating the Maghreb and its experience with modernization, especially concerning the issue of the individual.

One must hastily recognize that to define the Maghreb as a unit may appear arbitrary, especially in the domain that concerns us here. For nothing can be more varied than the paths that these countries have followed (I refer particularly to Morocco, Algeria, and Tunisia). This is despite their substantially similar histories of enduring hardships, born of similar colonial situations; the differences have been ones of extent. Their liberation movements, too, have taken nearly congruent courses, whether in timing (with some variation) or in aspects of their programmes and practices.

We can elaborate the points of divergence in the paths they have taken as follows. Until the end of the nineteenth century and the beginning of the twentieth, Morocco (which never did submit to Ottoman rule) offered the most proximate example of a traditional imperial entity; even western sources did not disclaim this attribute, calling Morocco 'the Sharifiyya Empire'. This label was perhaps at its most precise in describing the political regime as well as the social/popular organization of elements in that country, and its custodian, the office of Sultan. This office was the outcome of a power balance – but one that was often fragile and always susceptible to petition or modification (even through means that fostered discord) – between, on the one hand, traditional towns that were the refuges of craftsmen and a traditional 'bourgeoisie', as well as the authority of the *fuqaha'*, and, on the other hand, one category of tribes that inhabited the plains and farmed and were most often submissive to the 'central' authority, and another set of tribes based in the mountain ranges and desert regions who were frequently in a state akin to total independence, bearing a merely symbolic fealty to the Sultan. Such a state of independence might be so advanced that it would overwhelm the authority of its own spiritual source of legitimacy, even if this was an authority couched in the framework of Islam, as represented in the Sufi brotherhoods. This is extremely significant, occurring within an order in which religion occupied the privileged position in which it could impart or withhold legitimacy.

Naturally, this brief descriptive characterization cannot encapsulate reality's broad and profound complications. The divisions I have presented are not as stark as it might appear; certain characteristics evident in one situation are distributed to lesser or varying degrees across the others. Nevertheless, what concerns us here is that such an order could extend to embrace the individual as individual only in that human guise that has already been mentioned, the figure of the 'hero' or of the 'sacrificial lamb'. Indeed, the most important thing to stop and consider, in Morocco's experience, is that Morocco absorbed modernity by preserving and then mobilizing its own pre-existing features and traditional elements. Thus, any innovation or reform on the intellectual and political plane took on the bearing and direction of a *salafi* reform; that is, it unfolded within the domain of retrieval or reclamation, through a search for ways to accommodate the age by means of that recovery, rather than through committing the transgression of introducing the new. Therefore, if we were to situate this Moroccan experience within a sphere defined by 'the movement of renaissance and religious reform' (*harakat al-nahda wa'l-islah*), which the region has witnessed ever since the time of Jamal al-Din al-Afghani, we would say that the country took from that movement its religious reformist (*islahi*) half – exemplified, for instance, by Muhammad Abduh – and discarded its secular, renaissance (*nahdawi*) half, symbolized in the persons of Farah Antun, Salama Musa and others. Here is where we find the distinct quality of Morocco's relationship to modernity, which certainly now obtains for that country and which exhibits a certain efficacy even if it is in a situation of crisis. The distinct and specific nature of this modernity has often been belittled or undervalued, amidst all of the proximate attempts that have privileged certain models of modernization.[1]

Algeria's case has been quite different. The country did not truly exist in the political sense, or at least it constituted a political vacuum in that no central authority existed and neither did any intermediate institutions. The authority of the 'Turkish' Beys and Deys was only salient in the large cities where they had their seats of power, while the other regions of the country – in other words, most of it – constituted the province of the tribal. Whether with or without the tacit support of the Sufi brotherhoods, this was practically the sole available channel for organizing social elements.

When, in 1830, the Dey of Algiers put his signature to the document that declared his submission to the French invaders, his signature was binding and effective only on the capital and its immediate environs. In the rest of the country, the forces of the imperialist power had to subdue the territory practically inch by inch, an arduous task that took decades and perhaps was not truly complete even at the moment of independence in 1962. It is not surprising that such a situation left no space for the emergence of the individual. The state of political 'savagery' (we are not passing judgment here on this descriptive terminology) left space only for the shelter of the tribe or other units of popular belonging, to the point of complete identification with them.

It was perhaps only the Tunisian experience of modernization that conjectured the individual and took the individual's significance into account, from early on. This process may have been in train even before the era of colonialism (which began there in 1881). Even if the notion did not develop to its full extent, it did find exceedingly strong expression at more than one stage of that country's history across the past two centuries. It might not be an exaggeration to say that Tunisia presented the clearest example of the potential for democratic progress: many of its preconditions were in place, but in the final analysis they were subject to a devastating collapse.

For, beginning in the precolonial period, we can trace certain sociological transformations, ones that to our knowledge have not yet enjoyed any comprehensive or profound scholarly attention. From an early moment that it is difficult to pinpoint, these transformations had led to the breakup of the tribal structure in some regions of the country, especially in the Sahel, that coastal area along the Mediterranean at the country's midpoint. In that region, a French officer charged by the colonial authorities, in the early days of their presence, with carrying out an extensive geographical and demographic survey, observed that the inhabitants were organized, for the most part and in some fundamental sense, within village groupings based economically on working the land and socially on the restricted family unit, to the extent that many had dropped from their names the reference to the tribes that might have been their ancestral clans or residential affiliations. This phenomenon is possibly supported by another occurrence, emerging in the first half of the nineteenth century, in the time of field marshal Ahmad Pasha Bey. He had led the Tunisian attempt at a modernizing reformist programme, one that resembled Muhammad Ali's designs, which were already under way in Egypt. Yet Ahmad Bey's programme was the bolder one in some aspects, including, for example, an edict in 1846 to abolish slavery. Among the most striking episodes of that endeavour was Ahmad Bey's serious attempt to form a regular army, the first of its kind in the country's history. What might be especially noteworthy in that experience is that the majority of those drawn into this army were from the Sahel region, either because the authorities had applauded and encouraged this – perhaps because they saw that soldiers with such a background could not be pulled away from their fealty to the state by other loyalties – or because generally the sons of that region were best prepared by their sociological profiles, alluded to above, to become part of an institution characterized by such a measure of at least theoretical 'abstraction' and neutrality in its relations with institutions of the traditional popular social organization. Or perhaps this predominance of soldiers from the Sahel should be attributed to the close interweaving between those two factors. If the historical experience of that regular army is ultimately measured by failure, still, the fact that it was formed at all is of the utmost significance.

In any case, it might not be coincidence that the greater and predominant proportion of those who later assumed leadership of the nationalist movement in its modernizing half came from that region – in particular Habib Bourguiba, who in 1934 led the breakaway group from the Old Free Destour Party, under the power of the urban notables, and founded the NeoDestour Party, which remains in power to this day under the name 'the Democratic Destour Grouping' (al-Tajammu' al-Dusturi al-Dimuqrati). Bourguiba was the first leader not to emerge in that capacity from the traditional sites of influence and notability. He was the first to give speeches to the populace in colloquial Arabic, first to address the Tunisians as 'countrymen and countrywomen' (*ayyuha al-muwatinin, ayyatuha al-muwatinat*). Moreover, he was unprecedented in taking the popular political initiative: going out to the people, circulating among them in their villages and amidst their own groupings, rather than waiting for their delegations to come to him. Throughout, he acted as someone who engaged with them as individuals who belonged to a people – at that time, a new concept indeed – not as tribes or collectives grouped on the basis of occupation or spirituality or the like among traditional alignments and folk identities, as had been the case previously. Indeed, that period, between the two world wars, was replete with such happenings – for instance, the organization of active vanguard labour groups and other associations in all sorts of spheres.

These were occurrences and occasions that plucked the individual out of a traditional state of nonexistence and set that person on untrodden paths. Indeed, this period witnessed the production of a text unique among the masterpieces of contemporary Arabic literature. I refer to the achievement of Mahmud al-Mas'adi, late in the 1930s (but which remained unpublished until 1972), *Haddatha Abu Hurayra qala*.[2] This is an extraordinarily beautiful literary text, elegant in both form and content; with respect to this emergent sense of individuality perhaps it should enjoy the status of philosophical manifesto as well as foundational anthem. The author presents his character, Abu Hurayra, in a marginal note with the following words: 'In one account Abu Hurayra is three: first comes the Prophet Muhammad's Companion – may God be pleased with him – while the second of them is the grammarian, and the third is this fellow.' Thereby the author bestows upon the persona a historicity that is borrowed or arrogated yet in one sense is firmly in place. The personality of this Abu Hurayra is that of the individual, of a persona who strives to put to the test his own existence, by seeking to find and extract his essence as an elixir purified of flaws and the filth of the fatal usual, the repugnant monotonous and the vulgarity of those fettered and ossified structures. And for the sake of that he risks disengagement from all bonds to roam as a vagabond; he rebels, he runs the danger of interrogation and he can never be at rest. And yet with all of that he is unrepentant; he does not desist from penetrating the ultimate: an uneasy heresy, a death that returns him to the purified state of nature, to its fathomless depths. This is a fundamental text of discursive Arab modernism, yet it has not received due recognition or renown. It is worthy of rediscovery.

Indeed, perhaps one can say that the elucidation of the individual and his production – even if in an embryonic fashion – were among the accomplishments of the national movements, specifically those of Tunisia and Algeria. However, once independence and liberation escaped the noose of imperialism, that newborn was quickly buried alive, as the new, modern nationalist states undertook to suppress it once again by inserting it forcefully and coercively into rock-solid consensuses that were to brook no discussion or resistance – consensuses of a different, and recent, mint.

In both countries it was clear that the tasks associated with fighting the foreign occupier were beyond the capacity of the traditional structures – with their organizations and men, their rhetoric and their dynamics, their forces and the mode of mobilizing them. They were incapable of engendering from this struggle a societal renaissance that would be effective and beneficial, and would not be ambushed at every turn by defeat. All of the tribal uprisings (whether or not they were directed by Sufi orders) that the long history of the occupation of Algeria witnessed with regularity, as truly heroic as some of them were, ended without attaining their goals because they were aborted by such means (among many other causes). Such was also the case, although in a different way and under different circumstances, for the many forms of resistance in Tunisia as it was put to the test.

In both cases it was imperative that individuals emerge who had shed the structures of these organizations and the traditional modes of belonging, or who were stripped of these by the jolts and transformations that the imperial-colonial period generated in these societies; and it was just as necessary that these individuals join alternative structures, varied and new, political parties and the like. Only then would those efforts at liberation efforts bear fruit, eventually attaining the goals for which they had been created in the first place.

This process is clearly illustrated in the Algerian revolution. At its beginnings in November 1954, this revolution was detonated by individuals whose initiative caught unawares not only the imperial authorities but indeed the Algerian people in its multifarious groupings and existing institutions, whether religious, political, occupational or otherwise. The deed was thus akin to a coup mounted by a small group of individuals who managed the entire show. There hardly existed among them anyone who could claim to representative status or who issued from any sort of 'authority,' either morally defined or concretely existing in historical time, from any formation or from one social elevation or other.[3] Indeed, among the most striking ironies of the Algerian revolution – which was later to usurp the markings of popular and universal representationality – was that it did not at all emerge from the heart of Algerian society in the sociological sense, but rather from its 'empty spaces' and remote edges. It was, in its beginnings and before it was able to absorb other groups, an act by those who were on the margins of the urban polity, those who, with their poverty, had been ejected from the rural regions to the suburbs of misery and the popular quarters; the modern sectors had not assimilated them. Then other individuals of like characteristics joined them. These same factors of want and deprivation impelled them towards the French army, which they joined in droves, after which they fled it to plunge into the war of liberation. From these elements came generals who rule Algeria today, or ran it until very recently.

In Tunisia events took a parallel course, although they took on a foundational or institutionalized cast and a cultural and civic patina that we do not find in its neighbour.[4] The nationalist movement was led by graduates of modern educational institutions, among them Bourguiba, who studied law at the Sorbonne, graduating in 1924. It had already come to depend in the first degree on sectors of the new organizational structures, party and syndical. It thus represented a transcendence or bypassing of the traditional structures of society, which it thereby vanquished, along with their tendency towards fragmentation and their inclination to stifle the existence of the individual, among innumerable other premodern associations.

In those two experiences, the Algerian and the Tunisian, what stands out is that to the extent that the experiment of national liberation birthed the figure of the individual, shaped the rise of that individual and employed him during the era of the nationalist liberation movement, it was also quick to bury him alive, as already mentioned, and to disclaim his very existence in public space – and this at the hands of the state born of independence. This state worked actively, and still does, to dissolve the small, local consensuses of premodern formations, along with the seeds of breakup and fragmentation that they might encompass and which the state dreads. The states accomplished this by interpolating the individual within a consensus of a different sort, one that is comprehensive, exclusive and broad. The state regards this consensus as the one championed by and expressed in a privileged and conclusive fashion by the nation's nationalist history – especially if it can claim this to have been a 'revolutionary' nationalism. That is because, although the liberation struggle succeeded in transcending traditional structures, yet it apparently did not deliver the coup de grâce to those structures. The nationalist movements eclipsed or bypassed those structures in a merely formal or procedural sense. Once they had become states, they saw no alternative but to attempt to monopolize the public sphere. This is the role delegated to Algeria's military institution and, in Tunisia, to the party of the ruler once the state administration had joined it.

Only the Moroccan experience presents a distinct, even unique, path in this course of events. For Morocco retained its traditional structure and was able to revive it in the framework of the nationalist movement, around the institution of the throne. This institution assumed a central role throughout, such that the part played by the modern or quasi-modern nationalist parties was one of completion or fulfilment, not one of replacement or expulsion. This in turn created a sort of balance of forces that has remained more or less in effect ever since. Thus Morocco is the only one of these countries that remained consistently characterized by a true plurality of parties, which has not even momentarily faded from its public sphere, even in the face of oppression at times. This is a crucial point; for the presence of this political plurality has been a constant if unimposing reminder to the central authority of its own relativity, a reminder that even the sovereign's religious cast and bestowal of the title *amir al-mu'minin* (Commander of the Believers)[5] could not erase. It is also beyond doubt that here was the early, active nucleus of a political transformation, heralding the country's institution of a democratic framework, as has in fact happened over the past few years.

This Moroccan experience might be the more promising one for the emergence of the individual as an effective social agent and independent entity. This is not because the traditional structure of that country makes space for the individual and the role that individual might play to a greater extent than other countries do, nor is it because its parties – inherited from the era of national liberation, unrealistic about their roles in forming greater unities – make the individual paramount. Rather, it is because the pluralistic structure currently existing in Morocco did open the door to the beginnings of a civil society that was energetic, varied and full of life. The discrete organizations emerging in this civil society began to make their voices heard in many spheres, and were able to impose certain demands in the halls of government and in the political parties. These organizations are currently playing the most effective role in combating corruption and they can take the credit for opening some closed files, for forcing the issue of human rights transgressions and demanding a response that goes beyond the expression 'May God forgive what is past'. Moreover, these entities have ceaselessly pressed for revisiting legislation that affects the status of women.

This essay has offered some preliminary conclusions, which certainly do not give the subject the full attention it merits. But what may be said in summation is that in our era – and in contrast to the classical period of European modernity – we cannot necessarily anticipate that the individual as political actor will emerge in and from the political sphere itself, from its articulations and its organizations. Indeed we cannot assume that the individual will emanate from the space of civil society and its groupings, based as they are on interests and concerns of discrete slices of society, rather than on those of the society as a whole, which would arise from the location of citizenship, its demands and the relative nature of those requirements, and not from a position of demanding power or authority itself. In this, the Moroccan experience of modernity might turn out to be more productive of good fortune than will be the experiences of its two neighbours: the experience of coercive autocracy in Tunisia – despite the definite progress evident in some of its legislative activities, especially in the arena of personal status law – and the Algerian experience of military domination, which does not appear to harbour any definite perspective but rather moves randomly across the political map.

Translated by Marilyn Booth

Notes

1. The reader will find a comprehensive approach to the components and possibilities of the Moroccan nationalist movement in Abdallah Laroui, *Les Origines sociales et culturelles du nationalisme marocain, 1830–1912*, Paris, François Maspero, 1977.
2. Mahmud al-Mas'adi, *Haddatha Abu Hurayra qala*, Tunis, Dar al-Junub lil-Nashr, 1979.
3. On the eruption of the national liberation front and the different stages of the Algerian war, see the works of Mohammed Harbi, especially his book *Aux origines du FLN: Le populisme révolutionnaire en Algérie*, Paris, Christian Bourgois, 1975.
4. On this see a comprehensive historical review that covers the period from the occupation of the country until the brink of independence by Shaykh Muhammad al-Fadil ibn (ben) Ashur, *al-Haraka al-adabiyya wa'l-fikriyya fi Tunis*, Tunis, al-Dar al-Tunisiyya lil-Nashr, 1972.
5. This title derives particular resonance from its semantic history as the title given to the Prophet Muhammad's successors as leaders of the Muslim community long before the modern history of state formation in the region.

CHAPTER SEVEN

Individualism and Politics in Sudan

Khaled Mustafa

When I arrived in Washington DC, a relative said, 'I'll take you to a place that will turn your head around. You can't have anything like it across the Atlantic in "old Europe".' We went to Tyson's Corner shopping mall complex and I was duly impressed. A few weeks later, the *Washington Post* (Monday, November 8th 1999) published a photograph of Tyson's Corner as it was in 1956 – a small shack stop at the junction of routes 7 and 123.

That year happens to have been the year of Sudan's independence. The contrast between the slide into disorder and dilapidation in our capital, Khartoum, and the amazing transformation of Tyson's Corner in the US capital since 1956 put me in mind of a short poem in Arabic by the late poet Salah Ahmed Ibrahim, who articulated the Sudanese conundrum thus:

Behold our condition
Despite the mighty Nile
And all the land fertile
Behold our condition.

Development of a sort did take place after 1956; but it was erratic and the series of coups were capped with theocratic control on June 30th 1989, which turned its back on modernity and began looking for answers in the theological tracts of the distant past.

What went wrong? As a contribution to the search for an answer to this question, this paper attempts to consider the role (or lack of it) of individualism, a phenomenon that drew the attention of several political scientists and analysts who tried to understand the American spirit. Is individualism the missing link that (among other things) explains the difference between the rising and falling graph lines of development in Tyson's Corner and Khartoum since 1956?

The concept

According to F. A. Hayek, individualism in its modern phase can be traced back to J. Locke, Adam Smith and Edmund Burke, and thence to Alexis de Tocqueville. Its basic starting point is the belief that 'there is no other way towards the understanding of social phenomena but through our understanding of individual actions'. The system of private property is the best inducement for individuals to act in their own best interest and by so doing benefit not only themselves but also society as a whole. That is why individual initiative should not be shackled by an overpowering state with its coercive or exclusive power.[1]

Modern individualism grew at the expense of civic and biblical traditions, which enshrined unequal rights and obligations (husband–wife, master–servant). Middle-class values became inseparable from individualism.[2] The economic expansion that began in 1800 produced the 'quest for material betterment' and utilitarian individuals strived to 'develop their own inherent tendencies in relative independence from civic and religious forms of life'.[3] The middle class 'embodied in its own continuous progress and advancement the very meaning of the American project'.[4]

The virtues of individualism have been summarized by Alan S. Waterman as self-realization of talents and abilities, personal responsibility and eschewing dependence, creativity, rationality and the capacity for dispassionate analysis, as well as respect for the integrity of all persons as being of comparable worth to oneself. Pluralism, tolerance for difference and respect of free expression are preconditions.[5]

The crucible of individualism is civil society. Although complete harmony in a society is not feasible, liberal democracy 'opens the political field to the demands of all sectors of society' and attributes legitimacy 'to the demands of those classes and groups who previously had no continuous open way to give voice to their demands'.[6] This civil interaction reduces conflicts of interest.

The rule of law makes it possible to regulate conflict between private success and achievement on the one hand and collective interests on the other. The balance between individualism and collectivism was best illustrated by the much-publicized US government case against Microsoft, the Internet giant. The company became so successful and dominated the market to a degree that, according to the judge's ruling, created a virtual monopoly,[7] which had a negative effect on consumer choice and interests.

The Arab–Islamic conflict

Arab culture and Islamic religion are the two predominant factors in the values and beliefs of most areas of northern Sudan. Any consideration of individualism in northern Sudan has to begin with a brief note on the basic Arab-Islamic parameters.

The ethnic group mentality does not recognize the concept of the individual. Since the ethnic group is one organic body, a person does not settle a score with another who offended him/her. The individual can take his/her wrath out on any member of that person's tribe or group. This mentality was displayed in a very clear-cut way during the Iraqi invasion of Kuwait on August 2nd 1990. The irate Kuwaitis kept a record of the reaction of different countries to their plight. When Kuwait was liberated in 1991 they penalized all citizens of those countries that had supported Iraq. They could not see the difference between some of those individuals (dissidents who opposed their governments and condemned the invasion of Kuwait) and their governments. It never occurred to them that such an action actually rewarded the countries that supported the invasion because it targeted their opponents and vocal critics.

In Islam the concept of collectivity is enshrined in both the Qur'an and the Prophet's tradition and in jurisprudence. According to the Qur'an all Muslims are brothers and sisters, regardless of their race, colour or social status.[8] The doctrine of 'consensus' in *Shari'a* law is based on the Prophet's statement that the Islamic *umma* cannot reach a consensus on something that is wrong. The poet Abul 'Ala' al-Ma'arri sums up this attitude in his lines:

If I was singled out for paradise
I would not want to be the only
One to enjoy it

May the rains not fall on
My field, if they are not going
To fall equally on the whole land.

In Sudanese culture and society, the concept of collectivism is overwhelming. Examples that illustrate this include the practice of *Nafeer* in hunting, construction of houses or harvesting. All able members of a community take part voluntarily, on the understanding that the beneficiary will – on a future occasion – repay them in kind by participation in a *Nafeer* for them. In the extended family there are no secrets and no privacy. The idea of a room for every person is out of the question. The bringing up of children is a collective responsibility. If children misbehave outside the home it is the duty of any adult around to instruct them. Major events in life are collective: the birth of a baby, marriage as well as death in the family are matters for the whole community, which also contributes financially to cover the expenses. There are no funeral directors; the rituals and practical aspects are shouldered by able members of the community. There are no hotels or motels in the countryside. Villagers build a good hut for travellers. At mealtimes they take their own food and go to the hut in order to share it with the travellers (if there are any).

Some common proverbs reflect this. One such proverb goes, 'You cannot clap with a single hand', another says, 'Two hands together can throw [something] a long way . . .'.

Marriage, away from the urban centres, is not between two individuals who have fallen in love. It is arranged by the two families. The bride and bridegroom do not even attend the ceremony in which the contract is signed. In extreme cases, a father can 'divorce' his son's wife and ask her to return to her family's home without her husband's knowledge or agreement. Men in their sixties get married to younger women (often selected by their first or second wives) and do not worry about the future of the children. The family as an institution would automatically take over all responsibilities if the father died.

It is not my intention to give the impression of a black and white social picture. There are different shades, which allow for a degree of individualism. The proverb, 'If your son becomes an adult, treat him as a brother', implies a degree of acceptance of 'separate personality' for the offspring, albeit within the family setting. Social relations usually linked with the countryside can sometimes be found in the urban centres and vice versa. It is nevertheless true that the predominant feature is the one outlined above, in which the collective ethos is paramount.

The roots of collectivism

The lack of individualism and the overwhelming collectivist mentality have some of their most important origins in the distinctive way in which Islamic religion was embraced. The main advocates were the Sufi missionaries who infiltrated the country (before it acquired its present geographical borders) over the period of eight and a half centuries until the last Christian Nubian Sultanate was replaced by the first Muslim Arabic-speaking Funj Sultanate at the beginning of the sixteenth century.[9] This manner of embracing Islam contrasts sharply with the way in which it was embraced in the heartlands of Islam (Egypt, Iraq, Syria and North Africa) in the wake of the armed conquest and occupation followed by extensive settlement of troops. Islam spread 'under the control' of the Caliphs in Mecca. By comparison, the Sufi missionaries in Africa did not have arms or armies, were few in number and had to 'give and take', making several concessions in their efforts to attract new believers. It is worth remembering that the Sufis themselves were not strictly 'orthodox' Muslims. Their worshipping innovations are unacceptable to most strict clerics.[10]

As a direct outcome of the Sufi background of these missionaries, Islam in the area that became the Sudan Republic acquired a distinctive characteristic, namely, 'saint-worship'. In the initiation process the disciple becomes completely subservient: 'Initiation was purely an act of blind submission to the shaikh.' Through an elaborate system of organization, the Sufi orders (*turuq*) 'demand absolute allegiance'.[11] The vital instruction to the aspirant (*murid*) is: 'Be with your shaikh like the corpse in the hands of the washer: he turns it over as he wishes and it is obedient.'[12] The influence of the Sufi orders is very strong because they were the most common expression of Sudanese religious life. Trimingham underlines the extent of their influence: 'In contrast with other countries where it is only certain groups or strata of the population who belong to a *tariqa*, all Muslims in the Sudan have attachment to some one or other.'[13] Time has diluted their hold a little since the publication of Trimingham's book in 1949; but on the whole they are very effective. Since, in them, the concept of individual will or initiative is unheard of, we can assume that they have played a role in the lack of individualism – and the characteristics that are fused to it – in Sudan.

A corollary to this is the fatalism inherent in Sufi practices (based on Islamic belief). If everything you do is preordained and determined before your day of birth, there is no room or inducement for you to 'make it', to change your fortunes, fate or position in society. Upward mobility never becomes even an aim.

The middle class

Since individualism is linked to the middle class, a discussion among the middle class in Sudan is relevant to the theme of this paper. Little has been written about the Sudanese middle class. F. B. Mahmoud quotes S. Amin, who traced the origins of the class to the pre-mercantilist period in the Sultanates (sixteenth century) when long-distance trade existed with Egypt and the east. After that time the Sudan was integrated into the capitalist market during the Turko-Egyptian colonial period (1820–85) when Sudanese nomads participated in trade by acting as middlemen for Turkish, Syrian and European merchants.[14]

Following the re-conquest of the Sudan in 1898, the middle class did grow; but the very nature of colonial rule (joint British–Egyptian) kept it in a subservient position. Colonialism perpetuated a legacy that continued long after it left the country. In 1976, the ILO noted that 'the Sudan, more than most developing countries, is an administrative state. In addition to the customary, regulatory and public service functions of government, the state operates or controls the greater part of modern-sector production.'[15]

Despite these limitations the middle-class intellectuals articulated the call for self-determination and formed the first political parties in the 1940s. The memorandum they submitted in 1942 (inspired by the Atlantic Charter of 1941, which was signed by F. Roosevelt and W. Churchill) contained typically middle-class goals, which include: self-determination; a say in the budget; separation of the judiciary and the executive; abolition of restrictions that hinder the flow of trade to the south; the passing of legislation defining Sudanese nationality; allowing the Sudanese to exploit the commercial, agricultural and industrial resources of the country; and the demand that colonial companies reserve a number of top jobs for the Sudanese.[16]

To their credit – and in contrast to the pro-Nazi sentiments of the Arab countries – the Sudanese intellectuals also supported the democracies against the Nazi–Fascist alliance. G. Warburg does not do the Sudanese justice when he states: 'It is interesting to note that throughout the war the Sudan, unlike Egypt, Iraq and other Middle Eastern countries, was practically free of Nazi propaganda.'[17] The leaders of the national movement actually cooperated with the colonial authorities in mobilization for the war effort.

The most dynamic leader of the middle class among intellectuals, a mathematics teacher at the Gordan Memorial College, formed the first Sudanese political party in 1943 and soon after that wrote his book *Attariq Ila al-Barlaman* (Road to Parliament). In that book Ismael al-Azhari (who in 1954 became the first elected transitional prime minister of the Sudan) showed that he understood the importance of the institutions of civil society. He defined the 'association' or 'society' as 'individuals who have one objective or principle in common and who devise a certain system or set of rules to which they adhere in order to achieve their goals'. Further, he expressed his conviction that the knowledge of rules for associations has to be instilled in the young generation as a way of preparing them for future respect of the parliamentary system.[18]

Indeed it was through the non-governmental schools, literary associations, sports clubs, cultural clubs, women's unions, workers and peasant unions that the country achieved independence – not through armed struggle.

In the aftermath of the 1953 elections, Ismael al-Azhari (who won the elections on the platform of 'Unity with Egypt') performed a U-turn, which has soured relations with Egypt to this day. In so doing, he put the interests of the local middle class first. Having rid itself of British domination, it had no desire to share the country with anybody else. It should be noted that this U-turn took place after the Free Officers' coup in Egypt that abolished parliament and went all out for nationalization and a one-party repressive regime (the antithesis of what al-Azhari advocated in his Road to Parliament.[19]

To their credit the two main middle-class parties in Sudan have established democracies, which were rated very highly by independent observers. The US academic P. Bechtold wrote: 'In terms of political culture the Sudanese have ranked among the most democratic in the Arab World and Africa . . . Multiparty elections in Sudan have always been open and fair in comparison with other Arab and African states.' In a footnote he adds: 'This perhaps startling conclusion results from this author's almost 20 years of study of Sudan and from professional visits and field research in 20 countries of the Middle East and North Africa.'[20]

Their blind spot was, of course, their attitude towards the south and their inability to realize that development of all areas of the country was bound to strengthen democracy as well as the business interests of the merchant and industrial class. The feeble and lacklustre performance of the elected government 1986–9 (including its lack of will-power to defend itself against the NIF terrorism that preceded the coup on June 30th 1989) poses the question addressed several years earlier by M. Ahmed Mahjoub after the 1969 coup: 'Where did we fail?'

It can be argued that the seeds of failure were sown in the formative years of the 1940s. The top British civil servant D. Newbold rejected the middle-class intellectuals' memorandum of 1942 in which they claimed to speak on behalf of the Sudanese people. As a direct reaction to his reply that they did not represent the public at large, they forged an alliance with Khatmiyya and later the Ansar sects. The two main parties in the Sudan are a result of that period.[21]

A conflict was inevitable between the Sufi mentors (expecting complete and unquestioning allegiance and obedience) and the individualism of the intellectuals, the merchants and the so-called 'modern forces' which grew up in the urban centres as a result of migration, inter-ethnic marriages and new forces of social solidarity (trade unions, civil society associations). At the beginning of the alliance between these two unlikely bed-fellows the leaders of the two Sufi sects, Sayyid Ali al-Mirghani and Sayyrid Abdur Rahman al-Mahdi, kept discreetly out of the political limelight and satisfied themselves with influence off-stage in the wings. Had their offspring followed the same strategy, tension would have been greatly reduced. What happened in fact was that the next generation of sect/Sufi leaders burst on to centre stage and assumed actual leadership of the *umma* and then of the Unionist parties.

This development had far-reaching consequences. First, these Sufi leaders were not well equipped (by the very token of the religious badge they inherited) to deal in practical politics. Second, their religious roles do not allow them to engage in double-speak, manoeuvres, half-truths and other 'tricks of the trade' of professional politicians. Their status bars them from sharp or harsh replies, even to opponents who go out of their way to insult them. Third, when a Muslim religious leader becomes leader of a political party, a message is sent to non-Muslims that the party is no longer broadly national. The 'catchment area' of the party is limited to Muslims and regions where non-Muslims are the majority are alienated.

As a result they were no match for the machinations of the extreme religious right (the NIF) and the communists. In addition, they gave the parties the wrong image, scaring away students and the educated young who were more and more attracted towards fringe extremist parties because of their understandable desire for modern change. They have limited and minimal interest in the democratic organization of a modern political party (meetings, elections, subscriptions) because their real power base, the Sufi sect, suits them best, with its unquestioning obedience and allegiance.

Mainly because of this fault-line the two parties split and reunited more than once. In 1956, the People's Democratic Party was formed as a 'sect only' party, which split from the National Unionist Party. In 1967, the old party was reunited under its present name, DUP (Democratic Unionist Party). In 1966 the Umma Party was split by the election of the modernizer Sadiq al-Mahdi (who became Prime Minister at the age of 30). The party was reunited because Sadiq's rival and uncle was killed by Numayri in 1970.

Immediately after independence in 1956 the Umma Party gradually changed from a rural-based party to a party with influence in the cities too and shared the middle-class ground with the NUP-DUP.

A case study

One of the attempts to redefine (or even put an end to) the sectarian middle-class alliance took place in the year 1985–6. As one of those involved in it, I can give a brief insider's report.

When the DUP was underground during Numayri's one-man rule (1969–85), one of its leading intellectuals (former diplomat Ali abu Sinn) visited me at the university and said, 'You are a moderate. We need your cooperation.' I said, 'Have you read what I write about political parties?' He replied, 'Yes. Those active in the opposition now are not the sectarians and Sufis. Come and listen.' I then met Sheikh Haj Mudawi Mohamed Ahmed, leader of the faction, a committed democrat and well-known merchant and businessman, and continued to work with the DUP.

When Numayri was overthrown, we were ambitious enough to reestablish the old NUP (before alliance with the Khatmiyya sect). We held a congress in 1986 and I was elected member of the Political Bureau. Businessmen and intellectuals flocked to the new party. We had a newspaper and a building in Omdurman as headquarters. When the elections were held, we did not win a single seat and got 17,000 votes all over the country. Later on I resigned over a technicality. The chairman of the party was asked by Sadiq al-Mahdi to draft 'alternative *Shari'a* laws'. The request was made to him in his capacity as a lawyer; not as party leader. He obliged. Our 'line' in the Political Bureau was 'complete abolition' of the *Shari'a* Laws (September Laws 1983).

When the extreme religious right (the NIF) staged a coup on June 30th 1989, the leaders of the two leading sects (orders) were at the helm of the establishment. Sadiq al-Mahdi was Prime Minister and Ahmed al-Mirghani was Head of the Presidential Council. Coup preparations were common knowledge. The name of the man who eventually took power, Omar H. Beshir, was even published in a London magazine. Top army generals knew about the danger. I interviewed the former third man in the army and he confirmed this information.[22] The Sufi background of the leadership explains at least partially why no decisive action was taken to protect the democratic system.

It is difficult to imagine a situation in which the next democratic rule can see a better performance without solving the intractable problem that has shackled individualism and initiative in the parties of the middle class. It is equally difficult to see a peaceful solution to the conflict in the south without the exclusion (or isolation) of the religious factor from the heart of the constitutional and inter-party debate. Hasan at Turabi, before he himself was ousted and imprisoned, suggested a reconciliation meeting between government and opposition to be hosted by the Saudis in the Holy City of Mecca,[23] knowing full well that the suggestion means de facto exclusion of SPLA leader John Garang who, as a Christian, cannot enter Mecca.

Conclusion

The obstacles to social as well as political progress in Sudan are not difficult to identify. Measures to ensure the release of the huge force of change can also be earmarked.

Fertile conditions for the flowering of individualism, the growth of the middle class and institutions of civil society can be accelerated after the end of the present theocratic one-party rule. Economic development (with outside, mainly western, encouragement and help) can increase the rate of disintegration of ethnic loyalties and divisions. People will move, intermarry or mix with others. Tolerance and pluralism can be guaranteed with a constitution that is either secular or impartial as far as religion is concerned. Education and literacy can undermine Sufi-based allegiances with a direct effect on the political landscape. Ethnic and Sufi loyalties will not and cannot disappear overnight; but they will shift from the dominant centre-stage location. When the middle-class parties organize themselves, the religions and communist parties will be confined to the fringe.

Restructuring the economy and ridding it of the overblown state sector inherited from the colonial era will encourage entrepreneurs and investors. This has to take place in an atmosphere of rule of law, transparency and anti-corruption mechanisms. (Not to the benefit of an in-group around the secretive, theocratic single party and corrupt circle as is the case now).

This is the only block-free road from dilapidation to Sudanese Tyson's Corner-like transformation.

Notes

1. F. A. Hayek, *Individualism: True or False*, Dublin, Hodges, Figgis and Co. Ltd, 1946, pp. 6–16.
2. R. N. Bellah et al., *Individualism and Commitment in American Life*, Los Angeles, University of California Press, 1985, p. 143.
3. ibid., pp. 47–51.
4. loc. cit.
5. Alan S. Waterman, *The Psychology of Individualism*, New York, Praeger, 1984, p. 4.
6. Edward Shils, *The Virtues of Civility*, Indianapolis, Liberty Fund, 1997, p. 76.
7. Rajiv Chandrasekaram, 'Judge Says Microsoft Wields Monopoly Power', in *The Washington Post*, Saturday, 6 November 1999.
8. 'The believers are naught else than brothers.' The Private Aps. Sura, no. 49, The Holy Qur'an, translated by M.M. Pickthall, Beirut International Publishing Agency, 1978, p. 339.
9. P. M. Holt and M. W. Daly, *The History of the Sudan*, London, Weidenfeld and Nicolson, 1979, p. 28.
10. J. Spencer Trimingham, *Islam in the Sudan*, New York, Barnes and Noble, 1965, p. 207.
11. ibid., p. 203.
12. ibid., p. 206.
13. ibid., p. 205.
14. F. B. Mahmoud, *The Sudanese Bourgeoisie*, London, Zed Books and KUP, 1984, p. 2.
15. Quoted in P. Woodward, *Sudan 1898–1989, The Unstable State*, Lynne Rienner Publishers, Boulder, 1990, p. 173.
16. M. Abdel Rahim, *Imperialism and Nationalism in the Sudan*, Khartoum, KUP, and London, Ithaca Press, 1986, pp. 117–8.
17. G. Warburg, *Islam, Nationalism and Communism in a Traditional Society*, London, Frank Cass, 1978, p. 244.
18. Ismael al-Azhari, *Attariq Ila al-Barlaman*, Beirut, 1965, pp. 6–7.
19. P. Bechtold, 'More Turbulence in Sudan. A New Politics This Time?' in Ed John, *Sudan: State and Society in Crisis*, vol. 11, Washington DC, Middle East Institute and Indiana University Press, 1991, pp. 6–7.
20. M. Abdel Rahim, op. cit., p.132.
21. Lieutenant General Mohamed Zein, Deputy Chief of Staff for Administration, interviewed in Washington DC, 15 October 1999.
22. News article by M. M., 'Sudan: Bashir-Turabi Showdown Deemed Imminent', *Mideast Mirror*, 17 November 1999.
23. A. El Bashir, 'al-Ma'raka al-Khasira', *al-Khartoum* newspaper (Cairo), 19–30 August 1999.

CHAPTER EIGHT

The Kurds and the Obstacles to Individualism

Sami Shourush

The Kurds are perhaps an ideal example for a study of the social and cultural shaping of the peoples of the Middle East. First, they are one of the most ancient peoples of the region, since their origins at the foot of the Zagros Mountains go back to the second millennium BC.[1] Secondly, the Kurds are situated in an important area of the Middle East within whose borders three of the largest and most important people groups of the Middle East meet, namely the Arabs, the Iranians and the Turks. As well as the shared cultural, economic and social traits that have linked the Kurds to these peoples at different times, the Kurds have also been witnesses, victims or participants in the relations between these groups of peoples throughout history, inevitably affected by their conflicts and their wars.

Nevertheless, the social and cultural fabric of the Kurds as a group and as individuals has some specific features springing from their geography and history. One clear feature is somewhat paradoxical. On the one hand, they desire to be free and to escape from the bonds of the state and its repression of the individual with his social and ideological identity. On the other hand, they are deeply attached to collective identities, whether religious, nationalistic, ideological or social, which have no less a tendency to eradicate the individuality of a man and his freedom from the state.

It may be possible to reconcile this paradoxical nature of the nationalist tendencies circulating amongst the Kurds in the following way. The Kurds are resentful of nations who have not maintained a place for them in their legal and constitutional framework. However, at the same time they long for a nation-state that will restore them to a more equitable position in relation to the other large nation-states in the Middle East. It is also true to say that, up until recent times, the Kurds have lived a primitive nomadic mountain life, and their lands have been dominated, occupied and divided throughout history. This has meant that they have been unable to find a way to protect themselves other than by sheltering in their rugged mountains and by taking strength from their group structures such as the tribe and the clan; more recently parties and ideologies have given them some protection.

However, despite all this, the Kurds remain a society whose developments and changes it is difficult to follow in the contexts of history and current events. This is due to their isolation, their dispersal over a wide area and the harsh historical circumstances that they continue to endure. We must also draw attention to the lack of Kurdish records and the marked poverty of references and sources on which the researcher can rely.

This brief study will attempt to throw some light on the most important causes and factors, historical and contemporary, that have hindered the development of a clearly defined individualist tendency amongst the Kurds. We begin by focusing on the Kurds on the basis that they are one society. However, when we deal with the period following the First World War and the resulting division of the Kurdish regions between a number of Middle Eastern countries, the focus narrows to the Kurds of Iraq. The reason for this is that the Kurds of Iran have mixed more with the Iranian state than other Kurds did with the states amongst whom they had been scattered. The Kurds of Syria were such a small minority that they were unable to establish a cultural, social and economic experiment distinguishable from Syrian society. As for the Kurds of Turkey, they lived in the shadow of great repression that did not allow any independent Kurdish activity. This was the opposite of what happened to the Kurds in Iraq. There, despite being exposed to numerous forms of repression, persecution and denial of identity, the Kurds remained capable of practising distinct cultural, social and economic activity. This short excursion into different periods of Iraqi history will help to crystallize an identity that we can then contemplate and study.

The Kurds and their clan system

The Kurds are famous for the strength of their family relationships and for their clan allegiance. This may be what moved the Russian orientalist Vladimir Minorski to conclude at the beginning of the twentieth century that the Kurdish man cannot live outside the framework of his clan.[2]

However, this system has taken different forms throughout history: local princedoms, religious sheikhdoms and armed rebellions mixed with religious tendencies. Nevertheless, allegiance to the clan remained, in most circumstances, the most distinct characteristic of the Kurdish way of life up until the 1940s. This was generally true, with little variation, throughout the different parts of Kurdistan distributed between Turkey, Iran, Iraq and Syria.

The clan system of the Kurds was not just a social order. Rather, it was the wider framework for humanitarian activities of various types. On one level, the clan system provided individuals with a framework for their economic activity, whether within the confines of the village or a number of villages. On another level, the clan provided military and political protection against enemies from the outside or against other clans. In other situations, the clan provided a religious reference point, especially when the clan head (usually called an *agha*) adopted a Sufi order and transformed himself into a religious sheikh. A clan would often combine all these roles, which would help bond individuals together and strengthen allegiance to the clan.

The Kurdish historian Muhammad Rusul Hawar[3] talks about a clan leader of the 1920s and 1930s, Sheikh Mahmud al-Hafid. He says that his fathers were Barzanji sheikhs and were founders of the Qadiriya Sufi order. They were prominent feudal landlords, owning tens of villages, and hundreds of peasants worked on their lands in the mountain valleys lying to the east of Sulaymaniya (currently in Iraqi Kurdistan). The same description would apply to the Naqshabandi sheikhs, of the family of Sheikh Siraj al-Din al-Naqshabandi in the region of Bayara near the Iranian border.

Geographically, the country of the Kurds, or what is called Kurdistan, lies in an important strategic quadrangle in the Middle East. Dr Abdul-Rahman Qasimlu has delineated the sides of this quadrangle by saying that the lands of the Kurds stretch from the north, from the Mountains of Ararat, and run directly to the southern part of the Zagros Mountains and Bashtakouh in Iran. From there a straight line can be drawn to the north-west in the direction of Mosul, then straight towards the port of Iskandaruna, and from there to Ardrum and eastwards to Ararat.[4] As

Qasimlu has drawn them, the lands of the Kurds are distinguished by the ruggedness of their mountains and deep valleys, the bitterness of their winters and the multitude of natural obstacles. Given these difficult geographical factors, it was not easy for the Kurds, who were scattered in the folds of their valleys and mountain chains, to communicate amongst themselves in the absence of a nation-state to organize and facilitate this communication. Nor was it easy to resist harsh nature or to organize economic and religious life. Hence there grew up the need for a local authority within the confines of the valley, the foot of a mountain or a group of neighbouring villages to take the place of the state. The establishment of scattered clans, with difficult communication between them, led to what Vladimir Minorski calls the lack of group bonding between the Kurds.[5] However, at the same time, it led to a warm clan allegiance that is still fiercely strong in the forbidding mountain regions of Kurdistan.

On the other hand, the difficult terrain of Kurdistan provided natural boundaries for the many rival empires of the east: the Achmaenids, the Medes, the Armenians, the Sassanids, the Greeks, the Muslims, the Ottomans and the Qajaris. Thus the Kurdish region was transformed historically into an arena for constant bloody clashes, wars and struggles between rival armies. In this sense, history too played a role in isolating the Kurds into small groups around springs in the valleys and the mountains. The natural result was that they developed a fierce allegiance to the clans, which they founded as a reaction to their isolation. The same explanation can be given for the emergence of the religious sects in Kurdistan, such as the Kaka'is, the Shabak and the Izidis. Like the clans, these sects were each concentrated in a particular geographical region and they established between themselves a ranking similar to that which developed amongst the clans.

However, what is remarkable in the Kurdish clan system, as has been said above, is that while geography and history encouraged the Kurds to remain loyal to the bonds of the clan and to maintain their allegiance to this collectivity, that same geography and history also drove them to maintain with equal vigour their individualist clan specificities and not to desire to be melted into larger loyalties.

A good example of this is the Daz'i clan, which is spread over the plains lying on the southern edge of the city of Arbil. Although this clan venerates group allegiance to Kurdish nationalism, it forbids its members to intermarry with the other Kurdish clans for fear of melting into the Kurdish collectivity. Another example is the Shi'ite Kaka'i (Ahl al-Haqq – people of truth) religious sect, which encountered much persecution at the hands of the Sunni Islamic states as well as fellow Kurds who were Sunnis. This sect demands, on the one hand, respect for distinctions between individuals and a guarantee of freedoms for all to enjoy their individuality and specificity; on the other hand it stresses veneration of excessive group allegiance to the sect and a stubborn zeal in maintaining its mysteries and its doctrines, rejecting every spirit of individualism amongst its followers.

Thus one can notice clear contradictions in the Kurdish clan system. The harsh nature of Kurdistan, the ruggedness of its terrain and the difficulty of its climate, in addition to the many bloody wars and struggles that these lands have witnessed throughout history, have imposed on the Kurds a deepened allegiance to the clan or the tribe. However, at the same time it has caused them to maintain with fierce determination individual specificities.

The blending of clan and religion

In the nineteenth century, clan allegiance amongst the Kurds blended with religious allegiances, particularly after the spread of the Qadiriya and Naqshabandi Sufi orders.[6] After the spread of these orders, the first at the end of the seventeenth century and the second in the middle of the eighteenth century, the Kurds began to become linked to religious sheikhs, which led clan leaders to contact the religious sheikhs, adopt their order and transform themselves into sheikhs who led Sufi orders. In this way, they gathered into their hands religious influence as well as economic and social influence over the clan.

The blending of clan and religion happened for the first time at the end of the fifteenth century when the Ottomans supported the religious sheikh Mulla Idriss al-Batlisi. However, the Batlisi experiment did not prepare the way for the exercise of absolute power over the clan by a religious leader. In this experiment the religious power remained balanced against the power of the head of the clan. This balance was altered only in the nineteenth century after the spread of the Sufi orders amongst the Kurds, especially the Naqshabandis. Many researchers agree that the Naqshabandis, who were started in Kurdistan by Khalid al-Naqshabandi, spread widely among the peasants, villagers and Kurdish clan members because of the social content of their message, which was based upon equality. However, this dissemination soon ceased to be confined to peasants and began to be adopted by clan leaders,[7] who probably realized that the Sufi religious sheikh would take away their power, influence and social base, unless they converted themselves into religious clan leaders.

Those clans whose leaders did not adopt Sufi orders soon suffered internal splits. B. Rush speaks about the great split that occurred in the nineteenth century between the religious sheikhs in Barzan, who followed the Naqshabandi order, and their original clan, the Zaybariya.

Thus was generated the combination of religious and clan leadership in the hands of the clan chiefs. Soon after, they also gathered national leadership into their hands. This was especially the case after the development of the first primitive forms of a Kurdish national movement in the middle of the nineteenth century by Sheikh Ubaydallah al-Nahri, the head of the Nafidha clan and guide to the Naqshabandis over a wide region on the outskirts of the city of Hakari, which is currently in Turkish Kurdistan.

However, the phenomenon of religious clan leaders was not the only example of the blending of clan and religion amongst the Kurds. This phenomenon is also seen in the lives of religious sects, which number about twenty in Kurdistan. These sects, like the Izidiya, the Kaka'iya and the Shabak, are distinguished by their purely religious development and their ceremonies, which are linked to a religious history that is deeply rooted in the past of ancient Iran and ancient Kurdistan. Nevertheless, they resemble the model of the clan in their system of ranking and the way they provide a framework for life. In fact, some of them, like the al-Haqqa sect on the outskirts of Karkuk, have changed through time into clans that are self-sufficient in terms of their economic, social and cultural life, as well as in their religious and worldly allegiance. It is likely that the dual allegiance to religion and clan is the reason why members of the clans are more solid and unquestioning in their allegiance to their clan and their sect than individuals belonging to non-religious clans. The Barzanis represent another example; they too see in their clan not only a framework for their economic life, but also a context in which to delight in their religion and their Sufi practices.

The beginnings of nationalist allegiance

The territory of the Kurds has been subject to two processes of division. The first took place after the agreement that was reached between the Iranian Safavids and the Ottoman Sultan Murad in 1639 following an intermittent war that had been going on since 1514. The second took place after the First World War and the collapse of the Ottoman Empire.

In the first division, the Kurds were split between the Iranian and Ottoman empires. In the second, they were divided between four countries in the Middle East that grew out of the destruction of the two empires, Turkey, Iran, Iraq and Syria. These countries, both the old and the new, played a dual role in relation to the Kurdish clan system. When they were weak or involved in wars and national struggles, they would try to improve relations with these clans by granting their leaders influence and wide political, military and economic powers.

However, when their struggles and wars came to an end and they felt strong enough to stand on their own feet, they would turn their back on the Kurdish clans and would try to strip them of the economic power and the social influence that they enjoyed, as well as of the rifles and other weapons that they had amassed.[8]

The following may serve as an example. At the beginning of the sixteenth century, storm clouds of dispute gathered between the Ottoman and Safavid empires, giving warning of a bitter war between the two sides. This being so, the Ottoman Sultan Salim Yawuz came to an agreement with the Kurdish religious leader, Malla Idriss al-Batlisi, that the latter should gather the support of the Kurdish clans around the Ottoman Sultanate based upon their shared membership of the Sunni sect, which linked the two parties in opposition to the Shi'ite Safavid state. In return for this support, Sultan Salim Yawuz issued a firman in November 1515, which acknowledged the independence of Kurdish princedoms and which permitted the establishment of sixteen independent Kurdish princedoms in the north-east of the Empire.[9]

When the Safavid state weakened and suffered defeat in the Jaldiran War in 1514, the position of the Ottomans changed. They turned their backs on the princedoms and the Kurdish clans and launched wide-ranging military campaigns against them, wiping them out in less than five years and subjugating the clans to the authority of the central state. The Iranians, for their part, began their campaign against the Kurds in 1608, when the Shah Abbas al-Safawi repressed the al-Baradousitiya clan.[10]

There are other examples of Ottoman attempts to weaken the role of the Kurdish clans and to merge them with the state. In 1826 the Ottoman Sultan Mahmud II began to widen the central administration in Kurdistan as part of his policy of reforming the Ottoman Empire. The central feature of this policy was to strip the Kurdish clans of their weapons. Similarly, in 1892 the Ottomans founded special schools, called clan schools, in Istanbul and Baghdad to disseminate the Turkish spirit in the hearts of the members of the Arab and Kurdish clans, and to bring them nearer to Turkey.[11]

Another case in point is the fierce campaign waged by the founder of modern Turkey, Mustapha Kamal Atatürk, against the Kurdish clans from 1925 under the pretext of establishing a modern united secular state. During the period of the Turkish war of independence against Greece and Britain in 1919 and 1920, Atatürk had made an alliance with the Kurdish clans. However, after things had returned to normal and the modern state had established its authority, Atatürk turned to crush the Kurdish clans and religious sheikhdoms. The most important thing he did in this connection was to sanction the decision of a Turkish military court to execute Sheikh al-Naqshabandi Sa'id Biran and a number of Kurdish Alawite clan leaders in the region of Darsim (currently called Tunjli).

The conflict between the desire of the central state to bind the Kurds in a framework of allegiances to the Turkish state and the desire of the clans to preserve their individuality rather than dissolving into the melting pot of the central state contributed to the growth of a nationalist movement, with a rudimentary structure and content that lay in the lap of the clan. In fact, the beginnings of the nationalist movement go back to the middle of the seventeenth century, which witnessed bitter struggles between the state and the heads of the clans. An example of these nationalist stirrings is the long *qasida*, *Mim wa Zin*, by the Kurdish poet Ahmadi Khani. It contains a clear nationalist complaint at the injustice of the Turks and the Iranians and the Kurds' lack of a king of their own who would rule them with justice.[12] Subsequently, this movement developed and its leadership fell to religious sheikhs who at the same time were chiefs of their tribes.

Thus at the end of the nineteenth century and the beginning of the twentieth century, the Kurdish man was no longer committed to a single allegiance. Instead, he had become besieged by three interpenetrating allegiances: his allegiance to the tribe, his allegiance to a religion, a sect or a Sufi order and his allegiance to Kurdish nationalism, which was also embodied in the clan and its leader.

This threefold allegiance severely curtailed the opportunity for the Kurdish man to preserve his individuality. He was also hemmed in by group allegiances; it was not long before he was being led to commit bloody atrocities. The three most glaring examples were the massacre of the Armenians in 1915; the killing of Mar Shim'un at the beginning of the 1920s; and the persecution of the Assyrian Christians after the First World War.

Poetry and the individualist tendency

In the years following the end of the First World War, the parts of Kurdistan became subject to two chief influences. One was the spread of thoughts of national liberation, which Europe had distilled after the

Industrial Revolution in the eighteenth century. The majority of those affected by these thoughts were young Kurdish people who had lived in Istanbul in the early part of the twentieth century and during the years of the war, including Mustafa Yamliki, Muhammad Amin Zaki and Tawfiq Wahbi, or Kurdish poets who had become acquainted with Turkish culture and its poetic experience, which had been influenced by the European literary movement, such as Tawfiq Bira Mirad.

The other main influence was the appearance of modern states in the eastern area of the Middle East (Turkey, Iran, Iraq and Syria) and the scattering of the Kurds among them as a result of international agreements. These states adopted non-Kurdish nationalisms, but their attempts externally to consolidate cultural, political and economic relations with the west, and internally to extend their authority, their administration and their influence to the Kurdish regions, by spreading schools, roads, hospitals, presses and means of education, influenced Kurdish ways of life deeply.

In fact, these states and the internal social and economic policies that they followed impacted on the way the Kurdish social and cultural fabric evolved. Nor must we forget that modern schools, means of communication, and means of modernization and developing civil life reached the Kurdish heartland for the first time through these states. The clans refused to accept the extension of the authority and the administration of these states into the districts under their influence. However, the states did not experience any great difficulty in establishing their presence and their administration in the large towns and kasbas and in spreading the beginnings of modern education among the Kurds. In fact, only a few years passed before there began to appear among the Kurds, in the framework provided by these states, a stratum of urbanized intellectuals with distinctive cultural characteristics of their own.

Of course, this stratum could not compete with the clan leaders who remained in effective control, particularly after the First World War, which had destroyed the authority of the Ottoman state and then raised up weak states who were absorbed in their internal construction. The clearest expression of the continuing role of the clans was the numerous revolts led by clan leaders or religious leaders. These include the movement of Isma'il Agha Shakkak in eastern Kurdistan (in the west of Iran); the movement of Sheikh al-Naqshabandi Abdul-Salam al-Barzani and Sheikh al-Qadiri Mahmud al-Hafid in southern Kurdistan (in the north of Iraq); and the movement of Sheikh Sa'id Bayran and then the movement of Sayyid Rida in northern Kurdistan (in the south-east of Turkey).

Nevertheless, Kurdish intellectuals tried to construct their independent selves by casting off the clan system. These attempts were embodied in two tendencies. The first was political and social and manifested itself in the establishment of numerous cultural institutions and associations and political clubs especially for Kurds in the cities of Turkey and in Beirut. The second was literary and poetic and manifested itself in the growth of a poetic movement led by the poets Tawfiq Bir Mirad, Nuri al-Sheikh Salih and Abdullah Kuran, which set out on the path of poetical renewal and returned to dealing with man as an individual. The most important examples of this work in the years following the World War were the long *qasida* written by the poet Mulla Hamdun, which expressed the sufferings of the individual under the shadow of war, and the subjective poems full of the spirit of the individual being crushed by war, collective allegiances and large-scale changes, written by Nuri al-Sheikh Salih.

The war led to the release of a widespread outburst of nationalist feeling amongst the non-Turkish ethnic groups residing in the Ottoman Empire. Although the clans played a major role in leading this outburst, the intellectuals, through the associations and institutions that they had established or the cultural or literary products that they had produced, were able to fall into line with great speed. There is no clearer indication of this than the cooperation that was instituted by the literary and cultural elite in the city of Sulaymaniyya with the revolution of the clan and religious sheikh, Mahmud al-Hafid. Among this elite were two who were assassinated in suspicious circumstances during the rule of Sheikh Mahmud: the first was Jamal 'Arfan, and the second was the man of letters and short-story writer Jamil Sa'ib, who became famous for his short story *Fi Hulmi* (In my dream), which has a clear individualist strand. Jamal 'Arfan was accused of spreading propaganda in favour of democracy and atheism, and was assassinated during the rule of Sheikh Mahmud al-Hafid by landowners who were followers of the Sheikh.[13]

During the period of the *hakamdariyya* of Sheikh Mahmud (1922–3), Sulaymaniyya witnessed an influential civil movement. This was the Kurdistan Association, which was founded by Mustafa Yamliki, the Minister of Education in the government of Sulaymaniyya at that time. al-Talibani has pointed out in his book that this association was tireless in criticizing the attempts of Sheikh Mahmud to facilitate the domination of the clan aristocracy. At the same time it called for the enactment of a constitution and for the renewal of the administration.[14]

Thus, some poets and intellectuals began to focus their attention on the necessity of respecting the individual, with deliverance from the bondage of group ties that crush creativity, imagination and value. However, they were very quickly confronted with violent opposition from the other side, who were most of the time invisible. In addition to the killings of 'Arfan and Sa'ib in obscure circumstances, the poets Mulla Hamdun and Nuri al-Sheikh Salih unexpectedly stopped writing poetry and absented themselves from public activities. Abdullah Kuran (1940–62), who continued to write *qasidas* that shed great light on the life of the individual, selfhood, problems and dreams, became the object of personal defamation and insults. Not the least of these was being accused of sexual assault and embezzling public funds, which eventually led him to prison. Kuran, who did not surrender easily, subsequently adopted the communist ideology and joined the Iraqi Communist Party in his desire to protect himself from the hostile social environment.

In the period between the two world wars, a large nationalist movement was prevalent amongst the Kurds, led by a quasi-coalition between the leaders of the clans and the Kurdish intellectuals. This movement was so widespread that it paved the way, for the first time, for the growth of nationalist party organizations amongst the Kurds. The Khawibun-al-Istiqlal movement, which was founded by Kurdish intellectuals in Beirut in 1927, and the Haywa-al-Aml movement, founded by clan leaders and Kurdish intellectuals in Baghdad in 1939, were the first fruits of this new behaviour.

The Second World War jolted the Kurdish social, cultural and political edifice. However, it could not reduce the influence of nationalist ideology and the role of the clans in Kurdish life. On the contrary, it prepared the way for the spread of another collectivist ideology, represented by the Iraqi Communist Party, which had been founded before the Second World War. It also prepared the ground for the establishment of a Kurdish national party, the Kurdistan Democratic Party, which was founded in August 1947.

The nationalist and communist streams polarized the Kurdish intellectual class with amazing speed. It is interesting that intellectuals in Sulaymaniyya, which is known in Kurdish history as one of the Kurdish regions that resounds most loudly with nationalist appeals, joined forces with the tribal nationalist stream, which had begun to be led by the Kurdistan Democratic Party. Prominent amongst the intellectuals of Sulaymaniyya were Ibrahim Ahmad, Nuri Shawis, Nuri Ahmad Taha and Mustafa Khushnaw.

The intellectuals of Arbil, which remained distanced from nationalist appeals as a result of its complex ethnic situation, joined the communist stream. Those involved included Nafic Younis, Hamid Othman, Aziz Muhammad, Jamal al-Haydari and Salih al-Haydari.

Within the wide spectrum of these nationalist and communist streams, there appeared poets and intellectuals who decided not to be drawn along by either of these collective streams. They preferred to focus on themselves and their concerns, emphasizing the importance of protecting the individual from melting in the collectivities of parties and appeals. The poet Yunis Daldar (1918–48) was one of these. However, strange to say, this poet died early in obscure circumstances. It is said that he was poisoned.[15]

In reality, the Democratic Party was a nationalist party with a strong emphasis on deepening the nationalist bond between Kurds, in spite of their divisions of clan and religion. It was able easily to extend its influence into the Kurdish regions. What helped it in this was that from the beginning it had convinced the clan leaders that it did not entertain a desire to compete with them for their role in society.

The Communist Party entered into fierce struggles with the Aghas, the feudalists, the clan leaders and the religious sheikhs. As a result of this struggle, the communists were able to establish themselves in the cities, the large kasbas and the villages situated near the cities, especially among intellectuals, literary figures and artists. Remote country regions remained subject to the influence of the clan leaders, whom successive Iraqi governments began to support militarily and to provide with arms following the appearance of the Kurdish armed nationalist movement in 1961. After it began, the Kurdish armed movement changed into the military wing of the nationalist ideology and began to crush personal individuality. In this respect the movement did not differ from the Iraqi state, which, from the time of its establishment in 1920, fell into the grip of a Sunni Arab nationalist stratum.

In all this, collective allegiances remained dominant amongst the Kurds, in spite of conflicting forces that pulled them in different directions. The state was trying, through its schools, culture, policies, administrative structures and military power, to subject them to allegiance to the Iraqi state. Then there was their social structure, composed of clans and sects. Third, there was the religious allegiance and the influence of the sheikhs and religious leaders. Fourth, after the Second World War, parties appeared, as did totalitarian nationalist and communist ideologies.

These ideologies were the strongest forces calling for group interests to prevail over individual interests and feelings, nationalism in the case of the Democratic Party and class in the case of the Communist Party. The literature of both parties is full of calls for the individual to sacrifice himself in the interests of 'nationalism' and 'the homeland' and 'higher class interests'. What helped the two parties in this was that the Iraqi state had begun, especially after the army invaded political life in Iraq in the coup of 14 July 1958, to impose allegiance to it by force on the Kurds.

The Ruwankeh *experiment*

At the beginning of 1970, a number of Kurdish poets and literary figures living in Baghdad launched a new literary and poetical movement to which they gave the name *Ruwankeh* (the Watch Tower). The founders of *Ruwankeh*, including the short-story writer Hussein Arif and the poet Shirku Beyks, said that the goal of their movement was to renew the artistic, aesthetic and linguistic edifice of Kurdish literary and poetic activity.[16] However, the reality that their literature expressed made it clear that *Ruwankeh* wanted to jolt the Kurdish intellectual and cultural status quo and to reconsider humanitarian issues that had been crushed by ideological factors and political and social allegiances.

As is well known to those, including myself, who have followed the establishment and background of this movement, the call to respect the individual, and not to sacrifice him and the value attached to him on the altar of the collectivities proclaimed by ideologies, was one of the chief concerns of this movement and its founders. This was perhaps natural, as the founders of *Ruwankeh* had recently emerged from difficult party and ideological experiences. Hussein Arif had recently left the Iraqi Communist Party (the Central Leadership) and Shirku had also recently left Kazik, the extremist Kurdish nationalist organization. The chief problem that Hussein and Beyks suffered from in their political life was that the parties did not respect their individual characteristics and their literary activity. Instead they continually tried to turn them into tools of the party who would simply repeat the party line.[17]

One year before the appearance of *Ruwankeh*, the city of Karkuk, well known for its ethnic and sectarian diversity, witnessed a Kurdish artistic experiment calling for renewal and urging man to return to himself. Among them was one of the brightest Kurdish short story writers, Latif Hamid, and a number of young poets like Latif Hilmat and Salam Muhammad. This movement coincided with a wider Iraqi poetic movement led by Iraqi poets from the city of Karkuk such as Anwar al-Ghassani, Fadil al-Azzawi and Salah Fa'iq.

The Kurdish Karkuk movement faced difficulties stirred up by the Iraqi authorities on the one hand and Kurdish religious and clan leaders on the other. One of the clearest examples of these difficulties is the death of Latif Hamid in suspicious circumstances less than one year after the launch of the movement. Similarly, others, including Latif Hilmat and Salam Muhammad, were forced to abandon their city and live rough in Baghdad.

Ruwankeh was more mature than the Karkuk movement in its propositions and its emphasis on the importance of the individual. Perhaps we can trace the reason for this to the cultural and political easing of the Kurdish situation following the signing of the agreement of March 11th 1970 between Milla Mustafa al-Barzani and the Iraqi government. This agreement laid down the right of the Kurds to enjoy their cultural rights and to use their language in the various stages of education as well as allowing them to publish newspapers and magazines in the Kurdish language. *Ruwankeh* published a literary magazine in Baghdad, of which only three issues were printed, and clubs started large cultural activities. However, their main focus was on offering models of literary work, poetry, short stories and drama, as well as contributing articles to the Kurdish newspaper *Haoukari-al-Tadamun*, urging respect for the individual, his creativity and his initiatives.

However, *Ruwankeh*, like the few other individualist tendencies in modern Kurdish history, was promptly met with a stream of sharp criticisms and threats to kill its founders, which came not from the Iraqi government but from inside Kurdish society itself. Foremost among those issuing these criticisms and threats were the religious leaders, the Kurdish Democratic Party and the Iraqi Communist Party.

The most important event that can be pinpointed was the *fatwa* of the religious leaders of Sulaymaniyya in June 1971, authorizing the spilling of the blood of the founders of *Ruwankeh* because they had called for the liberation of women and the dissolution of morals, had damaged the spirit of the collectivity and national and religious unity and had promoted the spread of Zoroastrianism, Christianity and western values amongst the Kurds. The communists additionally levelled accusations of their own, which condemned *Ruwankeh* for being bourgeois, calling for the spread of liberal western values and trying to quench the fire of class consciousness in the working man.

As for the Kurdish nationalists, of both left and right, they criticized the movement for its attempt to weaken the will of young Kurdish people and their spiritual preparedness to sacrifice themselves for the sake of Kurdistan. Kurdish nationalism was being threatened with destruction.

The *fatwa*s of the religious leaders forced a number of these innovative poets and men of literature to leave Sulaymaniyya and Arbil and to lose themselves in the crowds of Baghdad. At the same time, Baghdad proceeded to close the *Hawkari* newspaper for two weeks and to change its editor-in-chief, as this newspaper had become a cultural mouthpiece for *Ruwankeh*.

All these circumstances forced the founders of *Ruwankeh* to call an end to their movement, close down their magazine and avoid participating in public cultural events. This was another reverse for the advocates of individualism under pressure from the power of ideologies and collective allegiances among the Kurds.

Conclusion

It could be argued that the fact that the Kurds do not enjoy a state of their own has helped free them from allegiance to a state that is considered in the east to be one of the most repressive instruments for crushing individuality and imposing collective allegiances. This does not mean, however, that there are not numerous barriers to individuality in Kurdish society, including clan, religious, nationalist and communist allegiances, not to mention attempts to impose national allegiance by the states of the Middle East throughout which the Kurds are scattered.

These institutions have succeeded in spreading their influence not just because of cultural and social backwardness and the high rate of illiteracy amongst the Kurds, but also as a result of other factors, including the geographical and historical factors that govern the life of the Kurds. In addition, there are the bloody wars and struggles, which have raged over their territory, both external wars and civil wars between Kurdish clans and parties.

These factors together have prevented the growth and development of individualist tendencies in Kurdish society. In fact, these tendencies have often been met with forcible repression when any trace of them surfaces. Individualism remains in Kurdish society a point of condemnation. It is accused of damaging the unity of the clan, of religion and of nationalism for the Kurds. There is no clearer sign of the hatred entertained by totalitarians towards individualist tendencies than the attitudes of the leader of the Kurdish Workers' Party, Abdullah Ujallan, who used to boast of creating a collective imagination so that this might become the individual imagination of every Kurdish man. This general picture and these details are not confined just to the Kurds. They reflect the generalized state of the ordinary people of the Middle East, of whom the Kurds are just a part.

Translated by Basil Hatim

Notes

1. Vladimir Minorski: *al-Akrad: Mulahazat wa Intiba'at* (The Kurds: observations and reflections), translated, annotated and introduced by Dr Ma'ruf Khazindar, Baghdad Press, 1968, p. 23.
2. ibid., p. 64.
3. Muhammed Rasoul Hawar, *al-Shaykh Mahmud al-Hafid*, vol. 2 (in Kurdish), p. 127.
4. Dr Abdul Rahman Qasimlu, *al-Jawanib al-Iqtisadiyya lil Mas'ala al-Kurdiyya* (The economic sides of the Kurdish question), Prague (edition in Czech), 1962.
5. Minorski, op. cit., p. 31.
6. Ayoub Bey Rush, *Barzan wa Harakat al-Waii al-Qawmi al-Kurdi 1826–1914* (Barzan and the movement of the Kurdish national consciousness), publisher unknown, 1980, p. 13.
7. ibid., p. 14.
8. Jalal al-Talibani, *Kurdistan wa al-Haraka al-Qawmiyya al-Kurdiyya* (Kurdistan and the Kurdish national movement), 2nd edition, Beirut, 1971, p. 69.
9. Gerard Chaliand (ed.), *People Without a Country: The Kurds and Kurdistan*, London, Zed Press, 1980, p. 22.
10. ibid., p. 117.
11. Minorski, op. cit., p. 29.
12. Hazar Mukriani, Ahmed Khani, *Mim wa Zayn* (Mim and Zayn), Paris, Kurdish Institute, 1989, p. 11.
13. Jalal al-Talibani, op. cit., p. 107.
14. loc. cit.
15. Abdul-Khaliq 'Ala' al-Din, *Yunus Delwar: al-Sha'ir al-Thawri* (Yunus Delwar: The revolutionary poet), Baghdad, Dar al-Afaq al-Arabiyya, 1985, p. 29.
16. *Ruwankeh* magazine, 1st issue (in Kurdish), Baghdad, al-Hawadith Press, 1971.
17. Personal correspondence with Hussain Arif.

CHAPTER NINE

Individualism, Communalism and the Quest for Democracy

Iliya Harik

As a communalist of long standing, the view that I offer in the following pages on the quest for individualism is likely to be one of dissent. The varieties of communalism under consideration here pertain to traditional social formations such as an ethnic group, a religious sect, a kinship group, a town or village community, where the sense of solidarity is based on preconceived identity and relatively intimate proximity rather than on a formal organization or explicit ideology. Commitment in the former comes to the individual as an inheritance, whereas in the latter it is made by a voluntary decision. Members of a community are held together by bonds that are in place when individuals are born. The context is one in which the individual and the group remain identifiable, yet inextricably linked entities. Communalism seen from this perspective is not an exclusive nor an intrusive category, but one among other coexisting bonds of secondary nature in a pluralist order consistent with a democratic arrangement.

It should thus be readily understood that the concept of communalism under discussion here does not have anything to do with collectivization or with the idea that the community stands before or above the individual. This collection of essays on individualism in the Middle East is inspired, I suspect, by the historical process in advanced industrial societies towards attaining the almost complete autonomy of the individual from impositions by kin or other primordial groups, though not from voluntary organizations. It is thus part of the modernists' aspirations to see Middle Eastern societies break away from traditional social forms and catch up with what is supposed to be the ideal. This forward-looking outlook, which yearns for creativity and freedom, considers the realization of these values to be a product of increased individual autonomy.

It is not to be denied that the historical struggle against oppressive regimes from traditional monarchs to fascist ones in the west has brought about constitutional guarantees for the integrity and autonomy of the individual. This achievement was meant to protect the individual against political regimes, not against community constraints. The disintegration of the latter has been the product of modernizing forces, such as industrialization, education and mass communications, among other factors. In the Middle East, the quest for individual autonomy is associated not only with political freedom but also with the notion that communalism is out of date, divisive and oppressive. It therefore must be 'abolished', a term prominently displayed in the catalogue of slogans by some prominent political parties in the region. The professed view laments the continued presence of coherent communities and what is called their crushing effect on the individual. In particular, modernists with a nationalist outlook fear the exclusivity sometimes exhibited by ethnic groups, which could threaten national unity and cause debilitating domestic strife. There has been plenty of evidence for such self-centred attitudes and destructive tendencies in communal societies, especially religious and ethnic, in Middle Eastern and other countries, to make such fears credible.

In contrast to individualists, though, my apprehensions relate to the problem of disintegration of communities under the impact of industrialization and mass communications. Social and geographical mobility, universal education, extension of transport systems and the mass media are unstoppable forces acting on societies the world over. Social mobilization is the way of the present and of the future, without any doubt, but it has undermined traditional social formations, among other things, a process that is now in full swing in most Middle Eastern countries.

Although individual rights are constitutionally guaranteed in many countries undergoing social mobilization, hardly any communal rights are recognized in countries of the Middle East, other than in Lebanon. The existence or institution of constitutional guarantees of group rights, secondary as well as primary, would instil more confidence in us that no violence or coercion of any kind would be inflicted on such constituent members of society.

My other concern is that the universalist ideals sought by advocates of individualism have given rise to attitudes of exclusion on the part of ideologically orientated, secular-leaning political parties, as well as of revivalist religious groups active all over the Middle East. Centrifugal and exclusivist tendencies often observed among communal groups are actually manifested to a greater degree among modern ideological groups such as political parties.

The issue here, though, is not to make a stand for or against such social formations, but whether the persistent sense of community, which has not yet given way, is ethically wrong or against human progress, as envisioned by advocates of modernization. Does communalism stand in contradiction to modernity and individual creativity, and should its demise therefore be hastened? To this writer the answer is clearly 'no'. Individualism is a more healthy phenomenon when it occurs in the context of communalism and less so when it expresses atomized societies, which is the target envisioned by westernized modernists.

The arguments against communalism that carry some weight relate first to its oppressive effect on the individual and its exclusiveness. With the exception of the undeserved status of women in some communities, I see no community-crushed individuals in the Arab countries that I have known. Rather, I see regime-crushed individuals and politically oppressed communities, including under secular regimes. Secularism, it should be remembered, is a correlate of the modernists' ideology of individualism. What I see in the Middle East are individuals and communities groaning under the political weight of overbearing states.

The markedly modernizing phase of the 1950s and after has been particularly characterized by the unbridled growth of patron states, which justify their heavy and cruel hands by reference to such ideas as progress, secularism, patriotism, social justice and nationalism. Insofar as the plight of women is concerned, those states have been colluded with civil society in maintaining unfair and oppressive conditions.

Not only political systems but also modernizing forces have left deleterious effects on society. Wherever one looks in the Middle East, the landscape is marked by rural-to-urban migration with its attendant dislocations affecting members of previously intact communities such as families, tribes, villages and small towns. Formal education is strongly in evidence and its effect has been to take individuals away from independent, family-oriented small businesses in farming, trade or crafts and turn them into salaried individuals working for impersonal corporations, if indeed they are fortunate enough to find work at all. The cash economy has accentuated the individual's instinct for capital accumulation, leading him/her to bond first and foremost with property rather than with people. The communal sense of equality, which had prevailed within clans in Arab countries such as Iraq and Syria, was undermined by the introduction of private land property laws, starting in the middle of the nineteenth century.

The capitalist spirit, where everyone is out for his or her own enrichment, is not limited to big business, but is pervasive wherever cash is the dominant mode of exchange. In the patron state, whether communist or single-party system, one can see a throwback, in which there is considerable reduction in the use of cash and instead reliance on exchange in kind, such as subsidies and the like. The power of the mass media, which primarily addresses the individual, has made community-based social knowledge and decision-making irrelevant, to the detriment of whole classes of people.

In effect, we witness the individual floating in a mass of humanity in a city disconnected from his/her social and emotional bonds. Left deprived of an intimate social and economic support base, the individual becomes easy prey to insidious influences. The anguish associated with this state of transition and the need for new forms of support is turning Arab societies into mass societies, which respond to the call of the manipulator of the mass media and of political demagogues. This anti-social development, which affected European countries first, has not been averted in the Middle East, except perhaps by the fact that urban growth has been associated with a new phenomenon known as ruralization of the city, causing the persistence of some forms of old ties.

Most vulnerable to modernizing forces have been communities based on family ties, neighbourhoods and guilds. Sectarian and ethnic communities have endured, indeed one may say have revived, under the impact of modernizing forces, and perhaps for this reason are a major target of modernists.

As for the argument that communalism entails exclusion, it may be noted that traditional forms of organizations have had very clearly marked open and closed spaces with explicit rules for crossing the lines in and out. In that respect, they have functioned as a more practical basis for an open society. The communal identity of the individual has been preserved, as is also his or her association with the rest of society. Racism is another matter, and it has not functioned in the Middle East as a basis for segregation, in the way that it has in the west. The Ottoman Empire is an example of such a traditional pluralist model in the Middle East.

In contrast, a strong sense of exclusion is evident among modern-day organizations with a universal orientation, such as nationalists, communists and religious revivalists. Anybody who does not share in the movement's ideal is viewed with hostility as a 'son of darkness', misguided, an enemy, anti-social, selfish, reactionary, a subject of lower status – in short, is excluded. The concept of the individual is thus debased and the great value of the individualist concept of citizenship is lost. The exclusion clause, advanced as a charge against communalism, can be more truly attributed to modernist and individualistic forms of organizations. The divisiveness that is so often considered a plague concomitant with communalism, is just as characteristic, if not more so, of modern organizations such as political parties. In Iraq, for instance, far more turmoil and bloodshed have been caused by conflicts among rival political parties than by sectarian differences between Sunnis and Shi'ites.

A more complex case such as that of Lebanon will be commented upon later. New forms of social organization have naturally arisen, such as clubs, trade unions, school bonds, political parties and philanthropic and social organizations. The literature on civil society has properly acknowledged the social and political value of these new structures. However, advocates of the civil society ideology have excluded traditional structures from their purview as being, explicitly or implicitly, irrelevant to modern society. Civil society advocates run the risk of missing the value of the function of communalism as a buffer zone and mediator between the individual and an impersonal central power, as well as its value to pluralist democracy. Tariq al-Bishri, an Egyptian intellectual and jurist, is one of the very few modern Arab ideologues who has repeatedly tried to draw attention to this vital role of traditional social formations. There is no justification for excluding communal attachments from civil society.

Moreover, it should be added here that in many new states primordial sentiments are very much in evidence in modern organizations, presumed to be of voluntary nature. Dislocated individualism is emerging not as a voice of freedom and democratic order, but of a new dependency and a new form of authoritarianism, which we have already witnessed in the patron states in some Arab countries. The primacy of citizenship, which individualists advocate over communal attachments, is no sanitized social doctrine of democracy. Indeed, the secular ideal of citizenship is dominant in fascist and communist states, not only in democracies, which is to say that it is not necessarily linked to civil and human rights. A Turkoman in what was once the Soviet Union was equal in terms of citizenship with a Russian or a Ukrainian, but none of those citizens of different ethnic backgrounds enjoyed civil or political rights as they are articulated in the various declarations of the United Nations.

Let us remember then that citizenship as a secular concept and a pillar of individualism is not enough. One might dislike communalism for its divisiveness in politics, as is often the case in Lebanon, Syria, Iraq, Algeria, Morocco, Turkey and Iran, but not for its oppressive impact on the individual. Traditional and divisive communalism may be, but internally oppressive it is not. The power of a community, ethnic or religious, over its members is extremely tenuous and rarely enforceable. Communities are not formally organized, nor are they endowed with enforcement mechanisms. Aside from their application against women, which is itself a formidable injustice, social controls such as community sanctions, meddling, violence or ostracism are not much in evidence.

Moreover, many ideologically oriented political parties have a sectarian or ethnic base, as is the case in Lebanon, Turkey, Algeria and Morocco, but no sect or ethnic group is co-extensive with a political party. Within each sect and/or ethnic group one finds many different parties competing with each other for support among the same group members. Moreover, individuals move in and out of these traditional formations, act independently, join secular political parties and move into residential areas of other sects, without incurring group sanctions or recriminations. In many cases, individuals had religiously mixed marriages and some even changed their religion.

What is it then that advocates of modernity decry? Is it oppression, backwardness or the absence of democracy? If it is one of these, then they have not shown how communalism contributes to these undesirable conditions. There has been more freedom (social, economic and political) in sectarian and family-oriented Lebanon than there was in European states with higher levels of individualism such as Portugal, Spain and Italy during the first half of the last century.

It is difficult to understand the fascination of western-oriented Arabs with the idea of individualism, especially when they are aware of the degree of anomie in societies where individualism prevails. Perhaps the force behind it is the lure of the cultures of the advanced industrial countries of the North, whose universities served as the source of knowledge for Arab intellectuals.

Nor do westernized intellectuals seem to mind the fact that individually acquired knowledge, when transplanted to other societies, remains unintegrated and to a certain extent extraneous. western thought is acquired and its ideologies are adopted in the abstract, unlike communal knowledge, which is socially learned through shared experiences and deliberation in a local context and setting. That is why slogans launched by modernizing intellectuals are detached from and in contravention to peoples' practices. Such slogans are mostly irrelevant to the life situations of ordinary people.

Political parties and their ideologies have rarely addressed the concrete needs and problems of citizens in the Arab countries; rather, they have provided propositions regarding universal and national issues of a remote nature, such as national unity, class struggle, sovereignty, secularism etc. Is it surprising then that in countries such as Lebanon, where there are real and keen competitive elections, political parties receive one third or less of the national vote, while the remaining votes go to constituency-oriented, independent candidates?

But what is this individualism that we desire so much? Is it a positive quest for freedom and autonomy, or is it a negative drive whose aim is to destroy established and harmless social linkages? One is compelled to say that the answer is clearly the second, considering the weak commitment shown for individual liberties and for democratic practices in general. Secular ideologies, which have come to us during the first half of the twentieth century and were stridently advocated during the second half, are authoritarian and nationalistic. The individual did not fare well under secular regimes, politically or economically.

In contrast, individuals who belong to primordial groups scarcely feel the weight of oppressive communal controls. Members of such communal groups as have not yet disintegrated are autonomous and open to alternative options in various spheres of life. In many Arab countries a person today displays multiple loyalties coexisting side by side and moves in and out of some of them at hardly any social cost. If an Arab citizen now suffers from the lack of freedom, the source of his or her distress is likely to be an oppressive political regime, which may be secular, religious or plainly militarily opportunist. In comparison, social pressures exercised by a community over its members are pretty mild.

It would be in order to ask here why is it that most individuals in Arab states have communal affiliations while at the same time they enjoy individual autonomy. Indeed, why does the idea of individual autonomy come so naturally to them?

Undoubtedly, there are multiple factors, but the one that impresses me most is the fact that individual integrity is preserved in the communal setting, and in religions practised by the Arabs, such as Islam and Christianity, the individual is the centre of the edifice. At the same time, those religions endow their members with a sense of community, the *jama'ah* in Islam and the 'brotherhood in Christ' in Christianity. Although these religions bring to their members a sense of community in the faith, the essentials of the doctrine and practice are individualistic: each person is individually responsible for his or her sins and indiscretions. Moreover, salvation is an individual matter; the divine message is addressed to the individual, who is provided with the religious knowledge that makes individual choice possible.

We are repeatedly told that individualism is a western concept and practice, but in fact it is also essentially Islamic: faith, relation with God, salvation, responsibility for sin and understanding religion are all individual matters. There are no intermediaries. Economically, private property is almost sacrosanct; the individual is free and market-oriented. Yet, nowhere has this native sense of individualism been reduced to solipsism or to a lost sense of the social nature of man. In matters of justice, it is western culture that gives precedence to society over the individual; in Islam the issue is more complex. In the case of a crime, the state courts in western societies prosecute on behalf of the victim but also on behalf of society, for crime against an individual is ultimately seen as a crime against the civil order, the state. In Islam, punishment for a crime is intended primarily to set things right for the victim, be he or she an individual or a group. In classical Muslim societies, if a victim of a crime or the victim's family renounce their rights and forgive the culprit, the case is closed and the state washes its hands of the matter. Society in Islam has no corporate personality; it is the individual members that matter. This is even so in cases in which the death penalty is imposed. Once the judge has given his verdict, a victim's family or next of kin has the right, if he so wishes, to strike the blow that executes the culprit. What this means is that the state considers the crime as a matter between two individuals or kin groups, not against the state as in western culture.

Nowhere in Muslim societies have I encountered unfamiliarity with such ideas as freedom and equality, or strong and open opposition to them. In practice, though, Muslims are constrained when it comes to expressing their feelings or views because of fear of oppressive regimes. With respect to women, it is true that a great many Arab men still do not see that women are entitled to the same amount of freedom and equality. However, ideas of freedom and equality among men are part of the high culture of Islam, and this is why they now interpret *shura* as rights for participation and representation in one form or another. While their heritage discourages differences in what is basic and essential, it does not take the idea of *ijma'* (consensus) literally. As a matter of fact, no one seems definitely sure of the meaning of the term, nor does it seem ever to have been practised. In the everyday context it has come to mean mostly a measure of considerable agreement on a matter of law or religious interpretation and as such has increasingly become interchangeable with the term 'public opinion'.

Individualism in western culture

There is no doubt that individualism as a concept has since the Enlightenment occupied a central role in western culture and in democratic ideology. Moreover, the impetus for individualism in industrial and post-industrial societies is understandably tremendous. Great as its role is, one can hardly be sanguine about its salutary effects on the health of human society. This is a question for the sociologist and ethicist to discuss; our concern here will be with the philosophical foundations of individualism in western culture and its exaggerated relevance to democracy.

As a modern intellectual phenomenon, individualism can be traced back to the emergence of the concept of natural rights, advanced first by John Locke as a counter-argument to the pernicious and disputed practice of divine rights of kings. If individuals were endowed by their creator with inalienable rights, then no human being, king or bishop, could have any justification for using arbitrary power or oppression against them. The times were ripe for a rationalistic concept of legitimacy and it caught on rapidly with a wide segment of the population, reaching its greatest fruition across the Atlantic in colonial America, where it served as the cornerstone of American democracy. In a society made up of immigrants who had made new lives for themselves in practically virgin lands, individual freedom and personal achievement were greatly cherished values.

Practical and opportune, the concept of natural rights enjoyed remarkable success, but success does not necessarily make it epistemologically sound. John Locke, for instance, one of the most prominent founders of empiricism, claimed a rational and a religious basis for the concept of natural rights. Philosophically, this is quite idiosyncratic. The concept of God, which is the only force that makes sense of the idea of natural rights, is not itself a subject of empirical inquiry. Locke knew that much, yet he invoked divine power in support of his idea. One can say that the concept was, in effect, a strategic tool and an ideological contention adequate for the time, rather than the daughter of truth or rationalistic philosophy. Deviation from the empirical method in this case did not seem to trouble Locke, nor did the divine source that he claimed for those rights deter him from investing in the slave trade across the Atlantic.

Rationalist philosophers too could not establish the concept of natural rights on firm cognitive grounds any more than empiricists could. The concept is after all normative and therefore not subject to the criteria of truth and falsehood. Unless one accepts it as an act of faith, it has no force at all. No longer could one therefore attribute to the doctrine a binding force on rulers or citizens, unless all sides hold on to it as a shared doctrine of faith. Without being based on firm grounds such as the principle of natural rights, individualism ceases to be philosophically sound and leaves its advocates rudderless at sea.

Here is the rub. Decoupling the concept of the individual from the concept of natural rights leaves it dangling. For where does the individual stand if he or she is not shielded by inviolable rights from claims of subordination made in the names of other gods? A religious person, of course, could continue to claim the Christian God as the source of the concept, which is perfectly legitimate. The only drawback is that if others do not share his or her religious faith, then the claim remains an empty shell.

Would sharing by others give the concept of rights, natural or not, a social force? Undoubtedly it would, but it should also be admitted that the force is derived not from the presumed source of the concept but from the acceptance of others to live by it. The concept of rights is social, not natural; it acquires its cogency from its acknowledgment by others who live by the same rules. Let us then speak of socially constructed rights, not natural ones, and explore the implications arising from that position for the idea of individualism.

What are rights? A right is a claim made against others and must be acknowledged by others as a necessary condition for it to take hold. The acquiescing 'other' could be a family, a clan, a city, a state, any community or organization, which makes the claim good among its members. Quite often, a claim is acknowledged by one group in society but not by others, in which case a political solution backed by force, legitimate or not, sets in to give the matter a final form. A sizeable group of Americans today do not believe that a woman has the right to abortion. The American authorities, however, backed by constitutional judgments and majority rule, have decided otherwise. Abortion in America therefore is a right, a qualified right, but a right nevertheless. Ethical 'rights' remain something distinct, in that they may be held as a matter of faith based on the source from which they are believed to be derived, rather than on recognition by some human agency; in other words, with or without the recognition of others. Relying on an acceptable source for one's idea of 'right', whether it is God, tradition or predilection, is all it takes for the individual to claim an idea as an ethical 'right'. It could come from religion, reason, traditions or emotional reaction, among others.

There are, in effect, many contending views as to what constitutes rights in society, but only those acknowledged socially have the character of being authoritative. Validation of the diverse claims, of course, remains dependent on the legitimate social procedure established by society for that purpose.

The source itself, though, is not sufficient to settle the diverse groups' claims, and without social or political mechanisms for the resolution of conflict, they can go on arguing forever or fighting forever. To become an official right, a privilege will have to be shared and acknowledged by others willing and capable of enforcing their preference.

If this is the case, then rights are socially, not rationally or divinely, defined within a commonwealth. Under this perspective, the individual enjoys no inherent integrity or safe status, except by the privileges endowed on him or her by society. Where, then, does the claim of superiority and priority of the individual over the group come from? It remains to the individualists to answer that question.

As far as this essay is concerned, the philosophy of rights points to the importance of groups in the formation of a civil order. It also points to the mediating role played by intermediate groups linking the individual to the larger society. Among other things, such an intermediary role inhibits the tendency among political actors to concentrate power at the centre. In addition, it underlines the social absurdity of individualism.

To respond by saying that individualism is the right of the individual to choose, to become social, i.e. to become a member of a community or of an organization, is to beg the question. The right to choose is no right at all unless it is acknowledged first by rules already established by society.

It is important to note here that the argument that rights are socially defined does not give the group any superiority or priority over the individual, it simply asserts that the individual is not a separate and sovereign being, but subject to rules and social norms. The individual is autonomous only to the extent that he or she can make choices within the limited options permitted by the social order; and also by virtue of the right to participate in making the rules that govern a community.

In contrast to the social definition of freedom and autonomy of the individual, there is the sense of existentialist freedom, which we encounter in philosophical literature and in novels. It is thoroughly individualistic. According to this view, the will of the individual is supreme, but it should also be recognized that in that situation individual decisions are unrelated to social consequences. For, once consequences enter into the picture, the supreme will of the individual becomes socially constrained. Hence, while no force in the world can stop the individual from making his/her own decision, it remains a fact that the individual may pay an enormous social price for that decision. After all, one can decide to take one's own life. Rebellion and self-destruction are thus the only unquestionable sovereign rights of freedom one enjoys in life, and that, I am sure, is something that philosophers of individualism have not braced themselves for.

We come back at this point to the idea of citizenship as the political coordinate of individualism and its desideratum. Citizenship is the formal recognition by the state of its members. The state claims the loyalty of its members and citizenship is considered the modern egalitarian and legitimate bond in political life. It is a very secular idea. According to the principle of citizenship, 'the other', by whose acknowledgment claims become rights, is viewed as all the members of a formal commonwealth who constitute a civic order. The civic order, though, is the sum of all the groups who constitute society in its organized form, unless the state is an expression of the will of one person and therefore a dictatorship. A democratic state is based on the consent of and concordance among diverse groups and classes, whose claims, though derived from diverse sources, must be subject to some changes and compromise in order to become acceptable.

Otherwise, the body politic will break down into several units. The point is in effect that citizenship is not the only legitimate bond. Traditional as well as voluntary groups have membership and identities, which coexist with the state; they influence it and are influenced by it. A democratic state therefore enjoys no monopoly on loyalties, nor could it be democratic without subscribing to the condition of coexisting multiple identities subsumed under the ultimate rubric of citizenship. Citizenship that is based on secularism and patriotism alone acknowledges exclusive loyalty to the state-society and is therefore a dangerous, rather than a salubrious practice. As indicated earlier, many despotic regimes relied on the exclusive legitimacy of citizenship alone.

In conclusion, let us point out that communalism is not only part of the texture of the state, but also necessary for the survival of individualism. It plays a major role in maintaining the democratic order, especially in developing countries. Communalism leads to actual distribution of power in society and constitutes an obstacle to anyone who wishes to usurp power. In developing countries, where formal constraints such as constitutions do not necessarily serve the purpose of preventing concentration of power in few hands, socially based checks on the central government become essential. A pluralist social structure creates de facto division of powers and may prevent the incidence of dictatorship.

In Yemen, tribalism, anachronistic as it may seem to us, still has the effect of putting limits on the excessive power of a modern institution such as the military in domestic politics. The limits that communalism places on dictatorial tendencies have been one of the main stories of politics in Lebanon.

The civil war that shocked well-wishers for Lebanese democracy and devastated the country has been blamed fully on the communal system. It is very important for the future of democracy in divided societies everywhere to correct this erroneous impression. The various Lebanese communities were living by the rules of the game, in full exercise of their ability to keep political power balanced, at the time the war broke out.

The crisis came about as a result of a confluence of circumstances partly domestic and partly external. On the domestic side, the demographic imbalance had reached a marked point in the 1970s, thus underlining the growing powers of the Muslim community. The changes required to accommodate that development formally were blocked by external threats, primarily against the dominant Christian minority, upon whom rested the responsibility to cede power to the new majority. The Christian minority, rightly or wrongly, saw a political and military alliance between the domestic forces as a challenge to their political pre-eminence and to the external actors, particularly Syria and the Palestinians. The situation was such that the Lebanese tendencies became aligned along the contours of the Arab–Israeli conflict and overlapped with the strategies of the protagonists, and in consequence the small domestic Lebanese game turned into a protracted and vicious conflict. Some measure of tension would have accompanied the transition to a new majority regardless, but in no way would it have taken this violent and intractable turn, if it had not been for the conjunction with external exigencies. It may indeed be conjectured that, if the political structure had been dominated by political parties rather than communities, the outcome would not have been different.

This is not an argument for shifting the blame on others for one's own folly, as critics of the Lebanese system sometimes charge. It is an argument that stresses the significance of the moment in the convergence of external and internal conditions. There are times when external interference will not have much effect, and other times when it will be devastating, depending on the formula defining other variables, i.e. conditions under which interference takes place. To blame the war on communalism alone therefore is a gross mistake and a misreading of the facts. The conflict was much more complex.

The political history of independent Lebanon clearly shows that it was the strong centrifugal forces in society that prevented presidents from expanding their powers into monopolies as happened in the rest of the region. Thus, the strength of communalism in Lebanon and an underlying formal respect for its status preserved the constitutional system as the longest surviving constitutional order in the region. Advocates of secularism, in their ideological zeal, are now jeopardizing the principle of democratic representation in Lebanon by trying to devise electoral laws whose effect would be to violate the integrity of communities and, in fact, stimulate sectarian sentiments. It is hard to make self-styled modernizers understand that democracy means the faithful representation of the voters' actual wishes and interests, not a means of fulfilling the ideological predilections of intellectuals. Trying to impose a uniform secular and nationalist ideology on a divided society by means of legalistic tricks such as the post-Taif electoral law is hardly different from imposing such an ideology by force. To be credible, individualist ideology has to dissociate itself from such endeavours and define its stand vis-à-vis 'natural' groups in divided societies in a more pragmatic and tolerant fashion.

It is not communal or group identities that constitute a threat to national coherence but the culture of bigotry, whatever its kind, plus the tendency to exclude others. Exclusion results in violence and injustice, regardless of whether it is based on some communal principle or on formal organization, such as a political party. Modern history indeed shows that severe conflict and deep biases sometimes occur as a result of competition among political parties. Regardless of the type of society in which the individual operates, he is bound to have multiple loyalties of various degrees of intensity. There is no shame in that. The shame lies in viewing a person as a creature of one affiliation, thus reducing him to less than himself and denying the fact of his subscription to an overarching national identity.

Note

See my defence of communalism as a basis for democracy in my book *The Political Elites of Lebanon* (in Arabic, *Mann Yahkum Lubnan*), Beirut, 1972; also in 'The Ethnic Revolution and Political Integration in the Middle East', *International Journal of Middle Eastern Studies*, vol. 111, no. 3, 1972; reprinted in Sa'd Eddin Ibrahim and Nicholas Hopkins (eds), *Arab Society in Transition*, American University in Cairo, 1977; revised edition printed and translated into Arabic, London, Abwab, August 1996.

For the work of Arab writers based in the west who are staunchly against traditions of communalism, see Hisham Sharabi, *Neopatriarchy: A Theory of Distorted Change in Arab Society*, Oxford University Press, 1988; and Barham Ghaliun, *Islam et politique: la modernité trahie*, Paris, Editions la Découverte, 1997; also some of his articles such as 'Ishkaliyat al-Islam wa al-siyasah', in *Shuun al-Awsat*, Lebanon, no. 67, November 1997. This tendency, of course, constitutes the common culture of the literati in the Arab world.

For discussion of that concept, see my book *Economic Policy Reform in Egypt*, University Press of Florida, 1998.

Modern dissenting concepts may be found in the literature on consociationalism, and among philosopher critics of liberalism, e.g. M. Sandel, *Liberalism and the Limits of Justice*, Cambridge University Press, 1982.

PART TWO

Culture and Creative Expression

CHAPTER TEN

Individuality, Collectivity and the Arts: The Human Being as an Individual

Els van der Plas

The French philosopher and author Jean-Paul Sartre regarded humans as acting beings. According to him it is precisely at the moment of choosing to act that a person ultimately becomes conscious of his/her existence and life becomes meaningful. In his trilogy *Les Chemins de la liberté* (*L'Age de raison*, *Le sursis*, *La Mort dans l'âme*) the leading character's life gains true value only at the point at which he, after weeks of boredom in the trenches, comes face to face with the enemy and decides to fight. It is through this struggle of life and death that the leading character, Mathieu, experiences the true meaning of life. For Sartre this wasn't too late. On the contrary, the death struggle is characterized by an extreme feeling for life.

In his 1937 essay 'Die menschliche Persönlichkeit und die überpersönliche Werte' (Human Personality and Superpersonal Worth) the Russian philosopher Nicolai Berdyaev (1874–1948) makes a distinction between the individual and the human personality.[1] He sees the individual as a natural, biological given, while the personality is created by the choices a person makes. Emmanuel Kant too distinguishes between the individual, who is part of the natural order, and the personality, which, for him, falls under the notion of freedom. Making choices means freedom to Berdyaev too. In general, humans are inclined to adapt to the law of the majority; the largest common denominator. A strong personality is someone who dares to choose and who does not allow himself or herself to be led by social circumstances such as family. 'There exist only collective individuals, but no collective personalities,' wrote Berdyaev.[2]

His theories, furthermore, had a religious flavour. 'The archetype of the combination of one and many in a single personality was given to us in Christ, the God-Man, in God-made-Man.' The personality of Christ is finally a human one. Moreover, He is unique, the One. 'In the personality ... appears the universality of the divine and spiritual principle, albeit in a single and unique form.'[3] Berdyaev assumes that the notion of personality is not equal to egocentric action. On the contrary, the preservation of the personality after all relates to the preservation of the 'divine image in the human being, of the divine idea of the human being, of the dignity of the Son of God'.[4]

The ability to distinguish in part determines the personality. At the moment one is able to make a distinction between one's own 'I' and the 'I' of another, one is also able to place oneself in the other's position, which precludes egocentricity. Or, to put it more strongly, the personality needs the other precisely in order to be able to form itself. This may be another, a group of others, God or something holy or an idea.

Berdyaev experiences the personality as an interruption in the natural order. For him this proves the presence of something higher; something divine in the human being who creates and disseminates this personality, the ultimate personality, of course, being Christ.

Both Christianity and Islam believe in one deity, known as God or Allah. This one God is all human beings need and all they could wish for. For Muslims, 'There is nothing like him, for he is the all-hearing and all-seeing' (42:12). In Islam, as in the Judaeo-Christian tradition, the mind, the body and the soul are created in God's image.

The divine image in both these religious philosophies has had an enormous influence on the formation of the cultures. The arts reflect the ideas of the people and the culture. These religions still form the cradle of the arts in both the east and the west, albeit in a far more complex way than in the days when patrons were primarily religious.

In 1999 the Iranian artist Shirin Neshat (born 1957, Iran) won the prize for best international artist at the Venice Biennale for her video installation *Turbulent* (1998). *Turbulent* comprises two films, which are presented opposite one another. One of them shows the Iranian-Kurdish singer Shahran Nazereri performing a thirteenth-century poem by Jalal ed-Din Rumi. While he sings he stands with his back to the entirely male audience.

At the end of his performance he turns to receive the overwhelming applause. The other projection shows a woman who, while the man sings, stands with her back to the camera. When the male singer stops singing, the woman begins to expel strange sounds that caress one's ears. The camera moves around her and it gradually becomes apparent that she is standing before a large, empty auditorium. The public domain seems to belong to the man, not the woman.

In this work it becomes clear that the male experience (of the thirteenth century) is experienced collectively and, it would seem, unanimously. The woman, on the other hand, here represents the idiosyncratic individual. She does not sing a classical text, but utters apparently meaningless sounds and cries. 'She sings an impassioned, wordless song of supernatural sounds, breaths, wails, cries and moans, as if a thousand voices were pouring out of her. It's amazing – a primal scream. You think you hear birds, brooks and the secret sounds of the human heart.'[5]

Neshat has chosen to allow the woman to transgress the collective code; she presents her as strong and emotional. Unlike the man, she has no words, but a sound poem, while language and writing are considered the most important traditional foundations of the arts in the Islamic world. Neshat not only allows the woman to perform alone in public – which is forbidden in Iran – but also has her intone senseless sounds. The woman here acts as Berdyaev's much admired Personality, as an interruption in the accepted order. It is also the case that women in Islamic societies primarily control the domestic, familial domain, which paradoxically enough only seems to enhance their individuality. The art critic Octavio Zaya referred to this controversial individuality in his essay about Neshat's work: 'In addition, since a woman represents the domestic, personal domain, she carries with her an individuality which is disruptive for the social order. Therefore, when in public, a woman must be contained, silent and invisible. In other words she must be "veiled".'[6]

However much Neshat criticizes the traditional Islamic/Iranian social norms, she respects the people who make up these societies. The singer is sympathetically portrayed and, what is more, he sings beautifully. Neshat portrays very matter-of-factly the male position she is criticizing. She seems to say that the man too has been born into a society that dictates to him how he should live. Collectively accepted norms and values in the end determine the course of history, which consequently comes to seem almost inevitable. Individual action, admired by Neshat, does not automatically lead to social change. However, it can have a direct influence on the personal development of an individual.

The individual as artist

Western, modernist, art-historical thought is primarily characterized by admiration for the individual. This admiration goes so far that a good artist is described as a genius, someone who is, as it were, 'utterly individual', which in turn means someone who is idiosyncratic, non-conformist, inventive and before his or her time. The genius is described as the frontrunner of art, to use a sporting metaphor.

The *Oxford Dictionary* defines a genius as 'a person with a natural ability or tendency, with special mental endowment, with exalted intellectual power, with instinctive and extraordinary imaginative, creative or inventive capacity'. Thus a genius is someone who combines enormous imaginative power with an instinctive and inventive mind. It is interesting to note that instinct is characterized as an element of genius, but at the same time often regarded as something base, almost bestial. Yet in modern times instinct has been admired as an exotic quality, a pendant to the scientific and the rational. This is expressed in Pablo Picasso's and Georges Braque's admiration for the old painter J. J. Rousseau. They admired his unflinchingly naïve approach combined with a unerring feel for colour and form.

These ideals, together with the competitive nature of science and industry, became the basis of the most important quality criteria in western art, which could be formulated thus: Is the art work really the most individual expression (creativity) of the most individual emotion (instinct)? Humans were endowed with an almost divine gift, enabling them to accomplish superhuman feats. Human instinctive/original and creative capacities (creation) were therefore brought into a relationship with the divine. This definition of the artist comes very close to Berdyaev's definition of the Personality. Museums became the stamps of approval in the west – and still remain so.

It is a tenet of Islam that no human can approach Allah's powers and strengths. People, created as they were in God's image, were not allowed to be portrayed. This founding principle led to the development of a different visual tradition from that of the west. Through time this principle also inspired the individual to explore the 'limits of creativity'.

One of the most important and developed visual expressions in Islamic art is calligraphy. It is in this tradition that artists could excel and expand their boundaries. Without breaking with predetermined premises, artists tried to find a way to create innovative art works. As the artist Rima Farah (1955, Amman, Jordan) asks: 'Is there a point where a letter ceases to be a fragmentary symbol of language and becomes instead a visual feast?' Keeping close to tradition, and at the same time searching for innovative approaches, calligraphers and decorative artists came to occupy a position comparable to the European ideology of the creator (a divine concept). As is stated in *Forces of Change*: '. . .The fascination with abstraction has also a significance which extends beyond any depersonalization of the world. Geometric and abstract forms represent the best way to signify infinity through the conversion of form into pattern.'

The artist Saloua Raouda Choucair (1916, Lebanon) recalls how her professor at the American University in Beirut told her that 'Arabic art is a decorative art of a lower degree, far from being pure art, because the Arabs were not inspired by the nude'. His statement had the opposite of the desired effect and inspired her to explore the geometry and abstraction of Islamic art and to find a 'unity between the spirit of God and her spirit as an artist'.[7] When she arrived in Paris in 1948 she was overwhelmed to discover that the experimental Parisian painters understood what she was doing.

'The art work acquires its meaning through contact with others, it comes to life only in the eye of the viewer. Of course the art work comes from somewhere, but it above all goes somewhere,' says the artist Soheila Najand, who originates from Iran. She takes this to the extent that she prefers to make the art work with the viewer.

Najand lives and works in the Netherlands. Because of her socially committed attitude, the political and cultural centre De Balie in Amsterdam commissioned her to go to live in Rotterdam's notorious and ethnically diverse Spangen neighbourhood and to produce a public report on her findings. Najand traces the origins of her desire to penetrate such a community, and to become part of it, back to her life in Iran, where one lives by the grace of the social structures. She finds the west far more individualistic, which is not necessarily a positive feature. She finds individualist behaviour that slips into intolerant egocentricity extremely disturbing. But, she says, she also fled Iran precisely because she could not say what she wanted. In Tehran she could no longer represent what she considered important. In short, she was caught in a society that denied space for individual freedom. This freedom she enjoys in the Netherlands. 'In the end I feel at home here,' she once said, 'because here I can say what I want.' For the idiosyncratic Najand, individuality and freedom are highly complex notions, which are enmeshed within society in a very specific way and which have a very specific role. Najand appears to understand the complexity of the notion of freedom and to use it in her work. But she also has the wish to share this freedom of choice with others.

The freedom that Berdyaev and Sartre referred to had, of course, everything to do with a political system in which people are able to make choices. Berdyaev suggested that for him the ideal life meant complete freedom of choice.

Picasso and Braque, being independent artists, were always regarded as the exponents of this freedom. Both artists gave an account of the process of their joint project, which gave rise to Cubism, one of the most important modernist movements of the twentieth century. 'Picasso and I were engaged in what we felt was a search for the anonymous personality. We were prepared to efface our personalities in order to find originality.'[8] Braque was willing to give up his individuality in order to reach an original idea – at a time, interestingly, when it was still generally accepted that originality and individuality were closely linked. He goes on: 'I reckoned the personality of the painter ought not to intervene and therefore the pictures ought to be anonymous. It was I who decided we should not sign our canvases . . .'.[9] The approach of these two artists would appear to be almost religious. They served something higher (originality) and to that end they entered into a pact, a collective. We can draw a comparison here with medieval book illuminators, church painters and the artists who decorated mosques. They too did not sign their work; the only true creator was after all God/Allah. It may have been the collective nature of their work that accounted for Cubism's being more than just an incident, and instead becoming a historical movement with many followers. Picasso endorsed the search for supporters: 'We were trying to set up a new order and it had to express itself through different individuals.' But 'Individualism was already too strong and that resulted in a failure.'[10]

The tension between the individual and the collective here comes to the fore, just as it did later in the calligraphic work of Jackson Pollock: '"irreducible individuality" and endless, anonymous sameness confront one another nakedly.'[11]

By accepting originality and innovation as quality standards, western art has given itself a problem. If you take these attributes as the norm, then all artists will attempt to comply with it. This creates a uniformity comparable to that found among Chinese landscape painters or the calligraphers in the Islamic world. In some cultures imitation is part of the artist's training; only at the point when the artist has truly mastered the technical skills is he or she in a position to stand out. Some modernists also idealized repetition: 'A rose is a rose is a rose,' wrote Gertrude Stein. In her lecture 'Portraits and Repetition' she said: 'It is not repetition if it is that which you are actually doing because naturally each time the emphasis is different, just as the cinema has each time a slightly different thing to make it all be moving.

And each of us has to do that, otherwise there is no existing. As Galileo remarked, "it does move"."[12] Stein therefore suggests that repetition as such does not exist. The signature is always visible in the repetition.

This puts into perspective the clichéd western view that modern 'Islamic art' is uniform, unoriginal and always related to traditional calligraphy. First, this is far from true, and second, the same accusation can be levelled at western modernism, which, after the development of Cubism, has continued to use form and colour as starting points and in turn this has led to many abstract and minimalist art works by such artists as Malevich, Mondrian, Pollock and Donald Judd. It has always amazed me that this body of art works, all of which originate from the beginning of the twentieth century, are all interpreted as original and innovative in their own right. The opposite would seem to be true. However, in my view, this does not detract from their quality as art works, given that the quality-characteristic 'original' is not the one and only benchmark for judging art works. But it does place both western and eastern twentieth-century modern art in another perspective.

The artist as part of history

As has already been said, Berdyaev assumes that personality is determined by acting, in the sense of the undertaking of a personal act. At the moment a personal act repeats itself or is repeated (the revolutionary has many imitations), the threat arises of a mass following and the undermining of the personality. The tragedy of the personality is the conflict with the power of the many. The power of the many finally determines the course of history. History consists of moments of collective acting.

There is a tension between history and the personality. Berdyaev describes history as the lot of the personality. The personality works actively in that history, which in its turn stands, indifferently, opposite the personality. Humanity sees history as its tool. The personality is therefore its own opposition; the history that it partially creates turns against it. And history is more powerful than the personality. What is the artist's position in this world? Can she or he influence history or is it precisely the other way around?

We have seen in the case of Braque and Picasso that in their collective search for a new representation of reality they placed the goal above all else and regarded individuality as inadequate. Has this collective act had any effect, or was it the individual Picasso who finally gave shape to the modern art of the twentieth century? After all, he described the collective act as a 'failure'. Furthermore, of the two it is still Picasso who is regarded as the genius. Many art historians would take issue with Berdyaev and argue that Picasso wrote his own history. And although he had many imitators, he stands alone on tip of the iceberg of the twentieth century.

Berdyaev's ideas also seem to overlook the importance of minor changes in a society or for an individual. It is, after all, a significant result if small changes can be realized, such as raising people's awareness of other points of view or contributing to small, perhaps highly personal histories. In this way Neshat influences the stereotypical image of people in Islamic societies, both 'here' and 'there', while Najand, who is just as critical in the Netherlands as she is in Iran, generates a national debate about a multicultural neighbourhood in the Netherlands.

The role of the artist must not be overestimated, but neither must it be underestimated. Recently in Colombia a well-known comic, Jaime Garzon, was murdered for criticizing the government and the problems of his country. His death led to a protest demonstration by hundreds of thousands of people. In the west there is a saying, 'One swallow does not make summer', but the Chinese know that a single stone thrown into a river can cause a tidal wave.

Notes

1. 'De menselijke persoonlijkheid en de bovenpersoonlijke waarden' (Human Personality and Superpersonal Worth), *Nexus*, 1998, no. 21.
2. ibid.
3. ibid.
4. ibid.
5. Gery Saltz, in *Village Voice*, 1998.
6. Octavio Zaya, 'In between: Shirin Neshat', in *Genders and Nations, Artistic Perspectives*, exhibition catalogue, curator Salah Hasan, Ithaca, New York, Herbert Johnson Museum of Art, Cornell University, 1998.
7. All three quotations from Salwa Mikdadi Nashashibi et al., *Forces of Change, Artists of the Arab World*, Washington DC, The National Museum of Women in the Arts, 1994.
8. Georges Braque, 'Against Gertrude Stein', in *Transition*, July 1935, no. 23, Supplement 13–14, quoted by T. J. Clark, *Farewell to an Idea, Episodes from a History of Modernism*, Yale University Press, 1999.
9. ibid.
10. ibid.
11. ibid., p. 223.
12. Gertrude Stein, 'Portraits and Repetition', in *Lectures in America*, New York, Modern Library, 1935. Reprinted London, Virago Press, 1988.

CHAPTER ELEVEN

Arrested Individualism in Arab Culture

Muhammad Abi Samra

It is rare to come across writings or research that deal with the phenomenon of individualism in contemporary Arab culture and society. However, this is not the only phenomenon in our cultural and social lives about which this may be said. For writing, and in particular the keeping of records, like education, is one of the novel phenomena that have only recently begun to become widely and generally available in indigenous Arab societies in the countryside and the miserable city suburbs. Moreover, illiteracy, which is inseparable from poverty and ignorance and is related to traditional society based on clan membership and loyalty, is still high, perhaps on average more than 80 percent in Arab societies, according to some statistics. This is especially the case in cities that are far from coasts and urban centres. Sociological studies agree unanimously that illiteracy, unemployment, high birth rates and high population density are major factors in the spread of this new radical and violent Islam, which has happened in Arab and non-Arab societies in the wake of the triumph of Khomeini's revolution in Iran.

My purpose in mentioning these factors right at the beginning of my essay is not only to emphasize the close link between education, reading and writing, on the one hand, and the growth of individualism, on the other, but also to point out that the majority of the social and cultural phenomena that we are experiencing, as well as much of our modern and more distant history, are still outside the range of writing and the taking of records and have not yet become the subject of investigation, research and field studies. This is due to three factors, which may be concomitant and interlocking:

- The great historical rift in our Arab lives between the classical, traditional culture and its written and oral sources, and modern contemporary culture.
- The great rift as well between classical and written Arabic and the local languages and dialects that are spoken in Arab countries.
- The fact that the majority of the phenomena of our social, cultural and historical lives are outside the scope of historiography, written narrative and description, and investigative research and field studies. The Arab historical memory is still oral, and in the most part outside the scope of written records. Oral history and memory are disintegrating and falling into oblivion, generation after generation, owing to the scarcity or total lack of written records.

Neither clothes nor food; neither education nor the written and spoken language; neither folk traditions nor customs and culture; neither song nor music and dance; neither marriage nor sexual life; neither architecture and accommodation nor family life; neither emigration from the countryside to the cities nor emigration abroad; neither means of transport nor means of communication and exchange, nor patterns of production and consumption, etc. – none of these has benefited up until now from effective historiography and studies in contemporary Arab culture. Because of this great lack, all our history, society and culture remain stored in our silent oral heritage, which is threatened by loss and oblivion. This is what has made researchers consider that Arab societies are ahistorical, on the basis that history is concomitant with writing and the keeping of records.[1]

The beginnings of the literary renaissance

In the second half of the nineteenth century, in other words just before their emergence from the long Ottoman period at the end of the First World War, Arab Muslim societies, especially urban and coastal ones in Egypt, Lebanon and Palestine, experienced culture shock as they came face to face with western European culture and civilization. One result of this was that the first writings in Arabic appeared, including descriptions of scenes and impressions and comparisons between our local life and culture and the civilization, life and culture of the west. The pioneers in this field were the Egyptians, who undertook educational missions to Europe, the most famous being, perhaps, Rifa'a Rafi' al-Tahtawi's account of his journey to Paris. Our focus on studying such writings, which reveal the first signs of individualism in Arab culture, stems from the fact that the genre is a novelty. The writer creates a dialogue between his culture and the culture of the other society. Among other things, such a dialogue presupposes that one has ability, as it were, to take long-distance photographs, standing on the border between two worlds, two epochs, two civilizations and two cultures, comparing and stating preferences between them. The Egyptian elite was in the vanguard of this movement because Egypt had emerged from the Ottoman period before other Arab societies, thanks to the stimulus provided by Napoleon's military campaign against Egypt in the eighteenth century.

Egypt being in the vanguard of these developments, the Egyptian urban centres became the focus of immigration by eastern minorities, the majority of whom were Syrian Christians, whose biggest and most vigorous source was the Christian heartland of Mount Lebanon.[2] This immigration was particularly vigorous just before, during and after the First World War. The immigrants mixed with European communities of large size and diverse origins – Greek, Italian, French and British – in Cairo and Alexandria, which were the two largest cosmopolitan cities, as also in Istanbul. Cosmopolitanism is a fertile ground for the appearance of aspects of individualism in life and culture, since the ties of clan break down, racial and cultural mixing begin to take place and the characteristics of urban culture blossom. In this cosmopolitan climate newspapers in Egypt became lively and flourished. As well as Egyptians, Lebanese Christians were among the pioneers. It was in the climate of that intercultural mixture that Lawrence Durrell wrote *The Alexandria Quartet* and the Greek poet Kafafi his Egyptian poems. The so-called Era of the Arab Literary Renaissance dawned, inciting new cultural visions and genres of writing and allowing the appearance of images of individualism in looking at the world, the self and society. The new genres included drama and autobiography, which require of the writer a certain awareness of his individuality and distinctiveness.

One of the social factors that put Egypt in the vanguard was the development of an educated Egyptian middle class, some of whom helped to administer the state of Muhammad Ali Pasha. To be an administrator requires one to distance oneself from one's ethnic roots and from inherited traditional culture.

The emigration of Christian Lebanese from the mountains of Lebanon to North and South America was another factor in the Arab Literary Renaissance, from the latter part of the nineteenth century onwards. In America Lebanese *mahjar* literature appeared, whose stars included Jibran Khalil Jibran, Mikhail Naima, Iliya Abu Madi and others. Abandonment of the 'land' and the 'homeland', a romantic longing for it, the call for renaissance, political and social 'liberation' from the 'yoke' of Ottoman rule and revolt against local inherited, 'backward', social customs were some of the main literary themes in Lebanese *mahjar* literature.

Education and emigration

The broadening of the base of mission education and foreign emigration constituted the two pillars of the social and cultural renaissance in the society of Mount Lebanon in the period of the Mutasarrifiyya, beginning from the second half of the nineteenth century. Let us pause to examine one aspect of this renaissance, taking as a tangible example the career of the Bustani family. They were well known for their work in the fields of literature, lexicography and linguistic renewal, in business and the liberal professions and in high administrative and governmental posts between the latter part of the nineteenth century and the middle of the twentieth. The Bustani family were of ordinary peasant stock and came from Mount Lebanon and so typify the Christian families of that period, some of whose children entered either into the monastic system or into mission education. As they did so, their organic link with the land and with its cultivation, and subsequently with the countryside and village life, dissolved. However, although this dissolution led, on the one hand, to a diminishing of the family's ties with the rural way of life, on the other hand, it strengthened an inner bond constituted by family solidarity and mutual responsibility. The basis of this was that the sons of the family should pursue their education and reap its benefits. When the priest Abdullah al-Bustani (1780–1866) was consecrated as bishop responsible for the diocese of Tyre and Sidon and then later elevated to the archbishopric of Bayt al-Din, members of the family in the village of al-Dibbiyya, south of Mount Lebanon, were freed from the need to submit to the mores of rural life (the land and agriculture) and enabled instead to embark on careers in religion or education. According to the author of the Bustani family biography, Melhem Ibrahim al-Bustani, Bishop Abdullah was the first to concern himself with educating his own people, at a time when the number of schools in the country could be counted on one's fingers. They could not pay the school fees and related expenses, so he sent four of his paternal cousins in al-Dibbiyya to the well-known school of Ain Warqa, as well as sending a similar number of his in-laws to Dayr al-Qamar. Of the latter, two famous Butruses stood out, one in the religious sphere, who succeeded him as Archbishop Butrus al-Bustani, and the other in the worldly sphere, as the teacher Butrus al-Bustani.[3]

Thus the pursuit of knowledge spread far and wide and from generation to generation among the al-Bustani family throughout the Mutasarrifiyya period and beyond. Some excelled as linguists and compilers of dictionaries and encyclopedias, as translators and men of letters, others in the liberal professions and administrative, governmental and diplomatic posts in Lebanon and abroad. Large parts of the memoirs of Anis Furayha, which cover the period between the two world wars, in his two books *Isma'ya Rida* (Listen, Rida) and *Qabl 'an 'ansa* (Before I Forget), recall how he gradually cast off ties with the village environment of Ras al-Matin, moved from one mission school to another, arriving at the American University in Beirut and thence universities in America and then how he worked as a lecturer in the universities of some Arab countries and finally returned to the American University of Beirut.[4]

The biography of the Bustani family shows that involvement in education, administrative posts, the modern liberal professions and capitalist connections, and liberation from the earth and classical traditional society took place on the basis of family and denominational solidarity. This is the conclusion that Iliya Harik comes to in his book *Political Change in the Modern History of Mount Lebanon*.[5]

However, in the long term the education of which family solidarity was the basis and driving force caused the scholars of the Bustani family to soar high above the family safety net and far from the village of al-Dibbiya and from Lebanon. The translator of the *Iliad*, Sulayman Khattar al-Bustani (1856–1925), the son of Archbishop Abdullah al-Bustani and the pioneer of the family in the religious and educational sphere, helped to compile the famous *Da'irat al-Ma'arif*. He had mastered fifteen languages and amongst his achievements were the founding of a school in Basra, Iraq; managing the Ottoman and Khedival Omani Shipping Company; building an iron foundry; travelling between Iran and India and living in Istanbul for seven years before travelling to America as director of the Turkish Section in the Chicago Exhibition, and publishing a Turkish newspaper there. On the eve of the First World War, he was appointed Turkish ambassador extraordinary in Europe, and then he was given the Ministry of Commerce, Minerals, Forests and Agriculture in the Ottoman state. Afterwards he moved once more to the USA, where Jibran Khalil Jibran met him and wrote about him, his achievements and his experiences, in the *mahjar* magazine *al-Sa'ih* (The Traveller).[6]

Manfalutism and Jibranism

This biography of the Bustani family gives some indication of the eastward and westward movements of some of its leading scholars and how their careers were characterized by a shedding of their local framework, as well as by disjointedness and dispersion, which are all indications of individualism or of some sort of individualistic streak. However, the literary writings of the Lebanese *mahjar* convey other pictures of individualism in terms of literary expression, manner of address and ways of looking at existence, the soul and the self. Perhaps the writings of Jibran Khalil Jibran are the most pertinent example of these literary images. They are typically romantic in terms of the society they depict, in terms of the expressions, literary style and language he uses, and also in their ambiences, their systems of symbols and their intellectual content. More than others of its time, the literary style of Jibran displays an undisciplined leaning towards an injured romantic personalism that vaunts itself and its wounds. This leaning is similar to so-called Manfalutism, a term coined by the Egyptian writer Mustapha Lutfi al-Manfaluti, who lived from 1876 to 1924 and whose widespread popularity and pervasive influence preceded Jibranism by a short time.

Naji Najib has traced the reasons for the spread of Manfalutism and its very great influence on Arab readers. He considers[7] that Manfaluti stamped the didactic literary writing that was prevalent at the beginning of the renaissance era (in the latter part of the nineteenth century and the beginning of the twentieth century) with a subjective or personalist character, which enabled it to escape from the woodenness of the traditional lexicon and rhetorical criteria of Arabic and refreshed it with draughts of new waters. This created an intimate bond between the writer and words on one side, and between the writer and the reader on the other, reflecting the demand of the times.

Both Manfalutism and Jibranism embraced and fostered this demand. They made it the basis of their expressive texture, which responded to individuals' feelings of selfhood, their freedom and their independence, as well as their desires, which were constrained and repressed by traditional society. The shock of local Arab societies rubbing up against the influx of a western culture and a new model of modern life was a decisive factor in allowing these feelings to appear. Manfaluti himself expressed this cultural clash, the breaking up of the local, traditional, inherited structures of culture and society, in his book *al-Nazrat* (Perspectives): 'I saw names losing the things which they named, and the confusion these things felt in choosing between different names. I saw the boundary stones of definitions being shaken loose from their places.' The 'weakened ability of the world of the senses to penetrate reality' was one of the symptoms of this bewilderment. The middle and lower middle classes sublimated this feeling of weakness by means of projection and compensation. These were the classes that had grown up in the cities by virtue of the new schools and the expansion of the administration and the service sector. However, these classes were frustrated in their desire to be liberated from 'the bonds of traditional society', to be fully and completely enlightened and to appear on the stage of public life and influence events.

Naji Najib called this frustration 'the sadnesses of the petty citizen' who needs a feeling of his own selfhood and his own distinctiveness. Manfaluti writing in Egypt and Jibran writing in Lebanon held a mirror up to this feeling. Such literary writing lightened the hearts of a generation, indeed of successive generations, from Damascus to Fes, with the throbbing of the hearts of its characters – in the *al-Nazrat* and *al-'Abarat* of Manfaluti and in the *al-Ajniha al-Mutakassira* and *Marta al-Baniya* and *al-Nabi* of Jibran. In a later era, that of the 1930s and 1940s, the hearts of the Moroccan 'women of the harem' in Fes beat faster as they listened to the songs of Asmahan and her brother Farid al-Atrash over the air waves, so the Moroccan Fatima al-Marnisi relates in her book *'Ahlam Nisa' al-Harim* (Dreams of Women of the Harem).[8] In the third quarter of the twentieth century, the voice of the Lebanese singer Fayruz, which evoked the atmosphere of Jibran, embodied the longing of new generations who had originated in the country and recently moved to the city, for selfhood and individualism, which they could not realize other than through imagination, compensation and fantasy, in words and in ceremonies.

However, the sadness and hurt are almost totally confined to a 'psychological, internal and intimate activity' that has only a very weak link to the outside world but that induces a feeling of liberation and unfetteredness, linked with a frustrated, almost Sufi, rebellion and a generalized withdrawal from the world and its obscure accusations. The result of such withdrawal is a split between the inner and the outer, the private and the public, described by Naji Najib as 'happy sadness', 'blessed sadness', 'the romanticism of grief', 'the pastime of sadness', 'the eternal grief', 'the happiness of tears', 'beautiful poverty' and other similar appellations. al-Shihada (the testimony) or al-Fana' al-Sufi (Sufi self-annihilation) are in the first rank of these accumulated sadnesses that the literary texts of that era exposed and celebrates – literary texts with an essentially weak link with the practical realities of life.

The Arab reader, most of the time, was reading the literature of Manfaluti, and later on Jibran, searching for the experiences of others in order to compensate for his own personal lack of experience, to counteract the closedness of his world and in order to pacify his lewd hunger for the emotions and pleasures of life, which had been hidden, suppressed and repressed as a result of centuries of concealment and of the taboos that had frozen over them. It was as if the function of this literature was to stir up subjective and personalistic emotions unconnected with their reference point and source in living experience. In this situation emotions were sought in order to excite 'blessed sadness', grief and comfort and to feel individualization in a culture that killed all individualization. Thus a love of sadnesses and pains evolved, becoming in its intensity and constancy almost a form of worship, resembling exactly the love about which the Star of the east, Umm Kulthum, sings and the love that Hazim Saghie has in mind in his book *al-Hawa duna Ahlihi* (Love without Lovers). Saghie writes of a love 'always making light of the burdens of the earth and the weight of relationships and society, in order to remain a love without a relationship and without an other, aiming at sublimation and projection'.[9] The love of which the Star of the east sings praises Manfalutian, personalistic, romantic, Jibranian sadnesses. It is a passion for nobody and for millions at the same time.

In short, the personalist tendency, whose features appeared in the writing of the era of Arab literary renaissance and in song, does not issue from or express individualism itself, achieved or realized, nor does it express living tangible experiences. Rather this tendency is the cheated and frustrated expression of a bitter thirst for an individualism whose birth is being prevented, so it finds solace in a literary style and emotional recitation that express the difficulty of this birth.

The modern poetic movement

In his book *Awwal al-'Urubah* (Early Arabism),[10] Hazim Saghie considers that the literary and cultural renaissance, which was called political in the Great Arab Revolution, constituted a fertile soil for the birth of nationalist and ideological rallying cries in the countries of the Arab east between the two world wars. Among them were the Syrian National Socialist Party, the Arab Socialist Ba'th Party and later on the Arab Nationalist Movement. In Egypt the decisive role was played by the Nasserite military coup, then the Nasserite Republican Movement, which embraced many of the Arab countries. In turn, these nationalist movements and ideologies prepared the ground for the Modern Arab Poetry Movement in the early 1950s. What is noticeable is that the social and cultural cradle of this poetic movement was in the countries of the Arab east: Iraq, Syria, Lebanon, Palestine. By contrast, the writing of prose and of novels witnessed a renaissance in Egypt, some of the leading writers being Najib Mahfouz and Tawfiq al-Hakim.

In fact, modern Arabic poetry is an echo of nationalist cultures and gives expression to them much more than does prose. While poetry in many of its forms and genres has given itself over to the expression of the popular collective imagination, prose writers have tried to approach particular local circumstances and issues. Modern poetry is ablaze with the totalitarianism of calls to nationalisn and their transcendence of local backgrounds and cultures, social tendencies and differences. In departing from traditional, inherited forms of poetic speech and writing (metre, rhyme, romanticism and symbolism), it has made the embodiment of the spirit of the umma the cornerstone and ideal, addressing it and glorifying its revival. This has led many of the leaders of the Modern Arab Poetry Movement to create prophetic and noble images of culture and the umma, of the poet himself and of the nature and effectiveness of poetry itself. Perhaps the reason for this was the desire to fill the void and the dislocation between nationalist culture and nationalist poetry and the actual living history and events of the present time. Those literary figures who grew up in the heart of the nationalist currents made culture into a prophetic and magical fact. However, many modern Arab poets have used poetry as a ceremony to celebrate their success in escaping from the darkness of the womb of local communities and their traditional cultures, and to celebrate too their birth as modern poets and men of culture, who long for individualization as much as they long to dissolve in the spirit of the collectivity of the nation which soars above society, time and the present.

In this sense, nationalist and modern poetic culture expressed a clannish, delirious 'individualism', transcendent and inflated on the one hand, and defiled, hurt and broken-winged on the other.

The Modern Arab Poetry Movement and its leading figures, who were called the *ruwwad* (pioneers), dominate the view of Arab cultural life in the third quarter of the twentieth century (1950–75). One of the prominent aspects of this poetic movement expresses images of this composite of individualism. The titles of the collections of poems written by the *ruwwad* poets give an impression of this composite entity. *Wounded Thunder, The River of Ash* and *The Threshing Floors of Hunger* were composed by Khalil Hawi, a Lebanese poet who in his youth belonged to the Syrian Nationalist Socialist Party, then to the Arab Socialist Ba'th Party, and who wrote his doctoral thesis in literature about Jibran Khalil Jibran. He chose an incident witnessed by all, the Israeli military invasion of Lebanon in 1982, as the occasion to commit suicide in his accommodation in the American

University in Beirut, where he was studying Arabic literature. One of his most famous poems, 'The Bridge', dates from the early 1950s:

> They march light-footed across the bridge.
> My ribs are stretched out for them to form a sturdy bridge
> From the caves of the east, from the marshes of the east
> To the new east
> My ribs are stretched out for them to form a sturdy bridge.

The 'bridge', across which the vanguard of the nation is passing to its resurrection and renaissance, soon changes to a bridge of desolation, as the poet writes:

> They will pass but you will remain
> An idol left behind by the priests for the wind,
> With empty hands, crucified, alone.[11]

Two noteworthy collections of poems by Adonis (Ali Ahmad Sa'id), a Lebanese poet of Syrian origin, who belonged for a short time in his early youth to the Syrian National Socialist Party, were *A Singular with the Form of a Plural*, and *A Time for a House of Ash and Flowers* (which he presented to President Jamal Abd al-Nasir). Here are some lines from one of the poems in the second collection:

> Wiping out all wisdom
> This is my fire
> No holy verse remains
> My blood is the verse.[12]

'Register Me as an Arab' is, to date, the most celebrated poem by Mahmoud Darwish and, of all the works written by poets of the Palestinian Resistance, the one that sold in the greatest numbers.

> Register me as an Arab
> Number my identity card 50000
> I have eight children
> The ninth will arrive at the end of summer.[13]

The purpose of citing these extracts in this context is simply to indicate the general poetic mix, which had a powerful presence in, indeed was basic to, the Modern Arab Poetry Movement. The slogans of movement included:

'Poetry is a way of salvation'; 'Poetry is a way to change the world'; 'Changing the world with poetry'; 'The poetic revolution'; 'Rejection, destruction, resurrection, creation'; 'The explosion of language'; 'The revolutionization of language'. The group involved in the magazine *Shi'r* (Poetry) were among the first to coin these slogans to indicate the general impression that the Modern Poetry Movement wanted to give about itself and its role.

In its images and its content, the poetic writing of most of the leading lights of this movement was based on the following principles:

- To anchor poetic speech to a cultural ego, public and fictitious. It presents itself as a pole of the world, the context of the world, the conscience of the umma and the group, the pivot of the resurrection of its civilization. Usually this cultural, collective ego transcends history, recalling images, examples and symbols that may illuminate a bygone culture and that will serve as a guide for the present.
- To exclude living, individual and mere fragments of small experience from poetic discourse, which should not touch the present except to declare its decadence and the need to escape this decadence in a salvational and heroic manner, by merging the cultural or poetic ego with the fantasized history of the umma and its conscience.
- To merge the self and the nation into one, sometimes to glorify and praise that unified entity, at other time to belittle its powers, leading to a poetic discourse whose language is cut off from the living world and which eschews the material, the sensual and the personal. This is what makes poetic writing a jelly-like, chaotic phenomenon based upon binary oppositions: ego/world, present/absent, decadence/revival, strength/weakness, etc. Here poetic energy can be displayed only in the mix of lexical loading, tension and ferment that the poet injects into it.

It may be true to say that the individualistic features in such poetic works are revealed in a feverish 'fictitious individualism', which is the other side of an equally feverish fictitious collectivity. This is what brings poetry close to a heroism of fantasy and Sufi delirium and to language whose distant reference point is the heroism, bragging and vitality of ancient and classical Arabic poetry.

However, individualistic features are not present to the same extent in the writings of all the pioneers of the Modern Arab Poetry Movement. The poetry of Khalil Hawi, for example, contains bitter expressions of corruption, guilt and sin, transcending the self, the world and the city. At the same time, the guilty and deeply corrupt self never stops seeking and pursuing an impossible purity. In the poetry of Mahmoud Darwish, the features of individualism and the images mentioned above are reduced to make way for humanitarian, revolutionary motifs on the theme of the tragedy of the nationalist Palestinian people.

Individualism displays different faces in some modern Arabic poetry.

- Vagabond individualism, as manifested in the writings of the Iraqi poet Badr Shakir al-Sayyab, whose life, social career and personal experiences formed the source of his poetry. In the writings of the Syrian poet Muhammad al-Maghut also, there appear living and bleeding images of a material world, whose focus is brutality, fragmentation and decay. Vagabond individualism contrasts with fictitious individualism. It reflects the pains, the tragedy and the torments of the individual self as it undergoes the frightening experience of discarding the collectivity and tradition of the old world whose framework disintegrated, but is then unable to enter or even connect with the modern world. This struggle takes place in the context of a modern world that has not been consummated or realized in practice.
- Don Juan individualism, whose images appear in the poetry of Nizar Qabbani. This individualism draws its images from the unveiling of the woman in the modern Arab city. Using and developing such images in his poetry, Nizar Qabbani changes the woman, her body, her possessions and her clothes into a sensual geographical world, as if they were desirable, sparkling goods displayed in a supermarket.
- Purposeless or playful individualism, whose features and images appear in the poetical writings of both Unsi al-Hajj and Shawqi Abi Shaqra. This individualism is demonstrated in word plays, slippages in meaning, linguistic ambiguities and shifting textures. Thus they produce a prose *qasida* liberated from the traditional criteria of Arab eloquence and style. Perhaps the ultimate motive for this playfulness and liberation is a Lebanese desire to lighten the historicity of classical Arabic and its structures, rhythms and texture.

Mahfuz's novels: the anti-literature

Naji Najib mentions that the effects of the 1919 nationalist revolution in Egypt, under the leadership of Sa'd Zaghlul, on the Literary Narrative School were profound, and constituted a turning point in its development. One of these effects was to produce a demand for realism, truthfulness, real life issues and the expression of the experience of the self in literary writing.

This development echoed two political and social changes: the emergence of the Egyptian people as an influential and effective power on the stage of events and the entry of women into public life.[14]

It was in this atmosphere that narrative writing started in Egypt, although the tone of sadness and weeping that predominated in Manfalutian writings was not abandoned altogether.[15] Mahmud Taymur, Yahya Haqqi, Hussein Fawzi and Tahir Lashin were some of the leading lights of this initiative in narrative and novel writing. However, Najib Mahfuz emphasizes that the writing of narratives and novels took place on the margins of literary and cultural life, which was dominated in the Egypt of the 1930s and 1940s by Tawfiq al-Hakim, Abbas Mahmud al-Aqqad and Taha Hussein. Although these men wrote short stories and novels, such writings were peripheral to their main work and they did not own up to them. Taha Hussein used to write a novel in the summer, during his holidays: the 'real' Taha Hussein, the doyen of Arabic literature, was a 'thinker'. al-Aqqad wrote *Sara*, although he too had a reputation as a 'thinker' and indeed he claimed to despise the short story and the novel. In this respect, Tawfiq al-Hakim, who wrote *Awdat al-ruh* (The Return of the Spirit), was a similar case in point.[16]

The testimony of Najib Mahfuz shows three interrelated things:

1. Short story and novel writing had not yet become an independent literary genre, separate from the writing of essays and stories of emotion and fantasy.

    The leading writers in Egypt between the two world wars were embarrassed to admit that they were short story and novel writers, given that the theme of this sort of writing was the self, with all its grief and anguish. They believed that the images they used in such writings would deprive them, personally and socially, of the awe and the status that they were accorded as thinkers, opinion formers and public figures.

2. Short story and novel writing became an independent and distinct genre of writing, thanks to Najib Mahfuz and after he had settled a long internal struggle between his attraction to literature and his attraction to philosophy.[17]

    Najib Mahfuz's desire to devote himself to the short story and the novel, his realization of that desire, the priority he gave to this type of writing over other cultural and life concerns and his willingness to remain on the sidelines of public and cultural life – all presaged a new model of writer, unprecedented in Arab cultural life. His single-mindedness and all-absorbing concern with his pursuit kept him in his position as a minor official in the Egyptian ministry of Awqaf and prevented him from rising to any position of cultural, political or social influence or even from participating directly in public life. This was an essential concomitant of the requirement to be detached and objective in order to create coherent fictional narrative. Without these conditions and circumstances, Najib Mahfuz the novelist would not have become the unrivalled and most dedicated exponent of the genre in recent times.

3. What was new and unprecedented in the writing of Najib Mahfuz was that he did not take himself and his life the theme of his story and novel writing. Instead, his stories revolved around many different characters with different temperaments and passions. Their social, personal and professional lives were distinct from and independent of the writer of the novel and of the narrator as well. Najib Mahfuz's novels created a society, a range of places and types of humanity and their interrelationships of harmony and disharmony over time. Particularly successful was his famous trilogy, *al-Sukkariyya* (Sugar Street), *Qasr al-Shawq* (The Castle of Desire) and *Ben al-Qasrain* (Between the Two Palaces). Here he displayed clearly the detachment of distance, painting a vision of society and its changes, observing the novel's characters and charting the changes in their fortunes and their progress over a long period of time. Mahfuz's trilogy is a living social and historical documentary of the under-classes of Egyptian society before the Nasserite coup. In this trilogy, there is a mixture of recollection, imagination, conjecture and insight, which together constitute the pillars of novel writing. Najib Mahfuz may be the first Arab writer to compose an integrated fictional world and an integrated fictional time that are not those of the writer.

In the fictional writings of Najib Mahfuz, his own ego, feelings and reactions are not the source or the theme. The novelist, a literary figure who has mastered a literary style, has receded into the background and is completely hidden behind the fictional characters, who have lives, inner beings and destinies of their own. The texture of the writing of Najib Mahfuz is totally different from the texture of the writing that came to be venerated in the era of the Arab literary renaissance, which was constructed round a subjective literary style. Mahfuz's writing is structured and complex, drawing its nourishment and material from the history, society, places and different human types found in Egyptian society at a particular period of time. He was so successful that the characters of his trilogy, Ahmad Abdul-Jawad, his wife Amina, his sons Fahmi, Yasin and Kamal, and his daughters too have become real beings in the imaginations of readers and in the history of Arab novel writing. These characters strive for and achieve, to varying degrees, a presence, a power to represent certain types of life, relationships and social values that do not exist in other literary or artistic works.

The concealment of the author's ego, his rebellion against the style of literary writing that clings to the expression of open reactions and feelings, his focus on fictional characters with clear features: these factors indicate that the writer possesses a coherent individual ego that demonstrates the wounded and frustrated individualism expressed in the literature of Jibran and Manfaluti. Unlike those works, however, the pioneering works of Najib Mahfuz as an Arab indicate that he has broken away from bipolar individualism and has accepted that there may be complex and structured mediators between the ego and the self on the one side and the world on the other.

The novel after Mahfuz

In their style and the individualistic tendency contained within them, Mahfuz's novels created a new tradition in Arabic prose writing, especially in Egypt, where poetry had not blossomed as it had in the countries of the Middle East such as Lebanon, Iraq, Syria and Palestine. We have explained above some of the features of the individualist tendency in poetic expression. Observing the features of this tendency in prose writing, in the short story and novel, is more complicated, more structured and more varied. In this context it is possible to draw up a group of general initial observations.

1. In the short stories and novels produced in the Arab world, in spite of the variety of styles and the differences in situation, the writers have generally produced social types rather than believable fictional persons and worlds. Arab novelists usually disdain the notion of constructing fictional persons with precision and accuracy, preferring to present characters as general social types representing a faction, a class, a group or an issue, be it social or political. Thus the characters lose their uniqueness and individuality and change into masks through which the writer or society speaks. The masking of fictional characters happens

because of the domination of society and its deep-rooted and weighty values over individuals – individuals who exist in Arab society only because they have been cast out and forced to take to the streets as a vagabond.

2. In Egypt, Syria, Iraq and Palestine, the post-Mahfuz novel concentrated on the concerns of the political and social struggle and the imprisonments and exiles that followed. There are few Egyptian, Iraqi and Syrian novels written in the 1960s and 1970s in which struggle, prison, torture and exile are not present. The cultured people and writers of this era were so caught up in leftist and nationalist sectarian and ideological attachments that writing became a weapon of the struggle. Meanwhile, according to Kanan Makiya, an Iraqi writer living in the USA (*Samir al-Khalil*), the military authorities who had staged coups and who were ruling in these countries were engaged in destroying and choking the voices of these societies, and changing them into republics of fear.

    Indeed, Najib Mahfuz himself testifies that 'life around us appears harsh, so our personal lives in our local reality sometimes appear absurd'. That is because ' . . . we have been living through continual interior frustrations ever since we became conscious. Even when we simply want to breathe, we find somebody perched on our chests to smother us and ruin our lives . . . We began to become conscious just as the generation of the 1919 revolution was beginning to break up. [When] we were able to breathe after 1952, the situation very quickly suffered a relapse . . . and I fell into absurdity for some minutes after the defeat of June 1967.'[18]

3. Of the generation of novelists after Najib Mahfuz, the Egyptians Yousif Idriss, Sana' Allah Ibrahim, Abdul-Hakim Qasim and Edouard al-Kharat, and the Sudanese al-Tayyib Saleh, Abdul-Rahman Munif (of Saudi origin) and Ghalib Halasa stand out. Najib Mahfuz is exceptional and has become famous for not leaving his country throughout his life, apart from a quick visit to Yemen. However, both Ibrahim and Qasim spent intermittent years of their youth outside Egypt. Perhaps it was these breaks abroad that developed their individualist sensitivity and contributed to their cultural development. They certainly tried to penetrate to the depths of this in their novels as they contemplated the self and the social and cultural environment from which they issued. By contrast, al-Tayyib Saleh, in his *Season of Migration to the North*, the most famous of his novels, considers that the exodus of the intellectual from

this environment to Europe leads to an unending, never-satisfied sexual perdition that is never satisfied and whose end is never reached. As for Abdul-Rahman Munif, leaving and being cut off from Saudi society enabled him to write his fictional battle, *Mudun al-Malh* (Cities of Salt), about the development of and changes within that society as it became an oil-based Bedouin society. Ghalib Halasa, in his biography and his novels, is perhaps one of the Arab novelists most separated from his first homeland and his local environment, in his case Jordan. From one point of view, his novels are almost successive episodes of the progress of this ongoing separation, and of his temporary and uneasy sojourns in the cities in which he divided his time – Cairo, Baghdad, Beirut and Damascus – where he died the death common to uprooted foreigners. He seems to emphasize the fact that uprootedness, abandonment, separation and exodus are some of the essential constituents of the individualistic tendency in Arab culture and society.

4. Novels from pre-war Lebanon are few and do not fit into any framework. One of the clear features of these novels is the vilification of the city because it forces those who flock into it from the countryside to lose the original innocence that they enjoyed in the country. Tawfiq Yusif Awwad is not an exception to this, one of his novels being called *Tawahin Beirut* (The Mills of Beirut). Nor is Fuad Kanan, whose first novel is called *Qaraf* (Sick and Tired). Nor is Yusif Habshi al-Ashqar, who was described as afflicted with an existential stain – hence, perhaps, his novel *La Tanbut Judhur fi al-Sama'* (Roots Do Not Grow in Heaven). However, he went on to acknowledge that roots do go down deep into the soil and social life of the village, an environment that promotes tranquillity and deliverance from the unease of existence.

Arrested cities

Vilifying the city, treating it as a source of guilt and disintegration, fearing its influence on the innocence and purity and the native rural disposition of the soul are all clear signs of the weakness of the individualistic tendency that city life encourages. However, such images of the city occur in Arab poetry and novels, and their presence is not confined to Lebanese novels. The novels of Yahya al-Tahir Abdullah in Egypt are an example. In fact, the weakness of the individualistic tendency in Arab culture is but one aspect of the polarity present in Arab cities. At one extreme is the model of the city with a royal foundation, where society is based upon bonds of blood relationships; at the other is city-civil society model, where society tends to encourage its inhabitants and its immigrants to act as individuals in their demeanour, their decisions, their life style choices and their preferences in terms of pleasurable and profitable pursuits. Thus to varying extents individuals are cut off from agglutinating collectivities.[19] Waddah Sharara has called the city that fluctuates between these two extremes an arrested city. This means that the individualism in this city is in turn arrested. The mixing, abandonment, separation and weakening of organic solidarity do not proceed far in the arrested city before they are stripped of logic and legitimacy and violence becomes the only means and the only end.[20] Hence, when Beirut emerged from the civil wars that raged through it for fifteen years, it was more arrested, more backward than it had been during the third quarter of the twentieth century, when it embraced the Modern Arab Poetry Movement and its pioneers and became the stage on which they became acquainted, mixed with and addressed one another, albeit reluctantly and for a short time.

Translated by Basil Hatim

Notes

1. See: Hasan Qubeisi, *al-Matn wal-Hamish* (The Mainstream and the Margin), Casablanca-Beirut, 1997.
2. Masoud Daher, *al-Higra al-Lubnaniah ila Misr* (The Lebanese Emigration to Egypt), Beirut, 1986.
3. Melhem Ibrahim al-Bustani, *Tarikh wa Sirat Hayat al-Bustani fi al-Dibyih* (History and Biography of the Bustani Family in al-Dibyih), no publication data.
4. Anis Furayha, *Isma'ya Rida* (Listen, Rida), 4th edn, Beirut, 1979; and *Qabl 'an 'ansa* (Before I Forget), Beirut, 1979.
5. Iliya Harik, *al-Tahawwul al-Syasi fi Tarikh Lubnan al-Hadith* (Political Change in the Modern History of Lebanon), Beirut, 1982.
6. Melhem Ibrahim al-Bustani, op. cit.
7. Naji Najib, *Kitab al-Ahzan* (The Book of Sadnesses), Beirut, 1983.
8. Fatima Mernissi, *Ahlam Nisa' al-Harim* (Dreams of Women of the Harem), Casablanca-Beirut, 1997.
9. Hazim Saghie, *al-Hawa duna Ahlihi, Um Kulthum Surat wa Nas* (Love without Lovers: Um Kulthum, the Image and the Text), Beirut, 1991.
10. Hazim Saghie, *Awwal al-'Urubah* (Early Arabism), Beirut, 1993.
11. Khalil Hawi, *Nahr al-Ramad* (The River of Ash), Beirut, 1972.
12. Adonis, *Haza Hua Ismi* (This is My Name), Beirut, 1971.
13. *Diwan Mahmoud Darwish* (The book of Mahmoud Darwish), Beirut, 1971.
14. Naji Najib, *al-Nuzu' ila-al-'Alamiyah* (The Drive to Internationalism), Beirut, 1985.
15. ibid.
16. Gamal al-Ghitani (ed.), *Najib Mahfuz Yatazakkar* (Najib Mahfuz Remembers), Beirut, 1980.
17. ibid.
18. ibid.
19. Waddah Sharara, *al-Madina al-Mawqufah* (The Arrested City), Beirut, 1985.
20. ibid.

CHAPTER TWELVE

The Peripeteia of Commemoration

Emmanuel Sivan

Even my loves are measured by wars;
I am saying this happened after the Second
World War. I'll never say
before the peace of '45–'48 or during
the peace of '56–'67.

Yehuda Amichai[1]

A budding Israeli novelist, Amos Oz, in the introduction to a 1968 booklet commemorating his cousin, fallen in the Six Day War, describes a meeting of friends and relatives during the ritual week of mourning:

> Words: commonplace words and unforgettable words. Tearful words. And also unspoken words . . . and between the words – silences. It is impossible, ineffable. We cannot explain. There were things, moments, deeds; yet we're unable to name them. There once was a boy in Jerusalem, we loved him, we still love him, we cannot let go of him. How little we can say about him. We remember moments, laughs, conversations. Beloved smithereens of never-to-return days.

They talk in confusion. Cutting into each other's words, repeating themselves. Dazed by the dazzling sword of death . . . Here, now, what can we say. Now there will be a commemorative booklet.[2]

Oz takes us into an intimate, typically Israeli scene, a sort of vigil; a wake in which comrades-in-arms, friends and family gather and recollect, tell stories, sing songs of praise and lamentation, one after another. Together we conspire somehow to keep the beloved man around a little longer, fixing him vividly in language, before memory fades. Oz depicts an act of remembrance, part of a process of coping with death, interlaced with a rehearsal of memory traces. Unlike wakes in other cultures, the Israeli one is likely to end up as a written and edited product. The making of a memory artefact – the commemoration (Yizkor) book or booklet – is virtually inevitable, as though the mourners were programmed by their society to express their grief thus while also creating an artefact, several specimens of which are to be found in virtually any Jewish-Israeli home (ultra-Orthodox ones excepted).

The therapeutic potential of the activity is what primes it – as evidenced with particular poignancy in letters to the dead soldier (by mother, wife, etc), or excerpts from diaries of family and friends, which ponder the question of coping with grief. Yet almost as important is the remembrance aspect of this activity. It is best encapsulated in a terse poem by a farmer included in a book in memory of his son (and five of his comrades) killed in the Lebanon war (June 1982):

You also were felled.
It's spring, Memorial Day approaches,
almost two years since your death,
the passing time doesn't blunt the pain
your twenty years erased
as though they had never existed.
Only your name
drawn in the cement path, in our yard,
testifies you had been on the earth.[3]

One notes indeed a nagging fear running through all the generations who participate in the production of this folk historiography – namely, the fear that memory, personal, familial and particularly social, is fallible, that the fallen may very easily be forgotten, unless some rearguard battle against forgetfulness is fought. 'Why write about him? For whom? For what?' notes another bereaved father, one of the heads of the Israeli intelligence service, in his diary, soon after the 1948 war.

> I do not want this figure to sink like a stone in the Sea of Galilee, leaving a few ripples and that's all. He was my son and thus, thanks to kinship, I may have understood this unique human being better than others. I've learnt from experience that one cannot sketch out an authentic description of a great figure without an intimate affinity. This affinity suggests, nay even commands me, to try to do just that for my son.[4]

Both fathers echo the conviction that to forget is all too human. Indeed, did not William James suggest that forgetting may well be essential to the health and vitality of the mind? The upshot is that the perpetuation of memory requires 'memory work', or remembrance. And in this particular case, memory work is intertwined with grief work. Fear of oblivion propels these two fathers, among a multitude of other relatives and friends, towards an effort against the tide of oblivion; that effort is bereaved commemoration.

The singularity of the Israeli case, due perhaps to the fact of its being a small, democratic society, is that the bulk of effort is carried out through spontaneous activity of civil society rather than by the state. Parents, relatives, friends, army comrades – separately or together, usually in ad hoc groupings – but also sports clubs, youth movements, kibbutzim, schools and the like produce the booklets, which have been dedicated to about half the total number of fallen soldiers.

This form of commemoration through civil society is even more popular than monuments. The booklets still occupy pride of place in the library of most Israeli homes. It is thanks to these books that the children born after a war (or too young to have been aware of it) are exposed to the war experience and its human costs. Moreover, this folk literature constitutes a unique attempt to catch and preserve the individuality of the fallen, going beyond the mere mention of their names and the circumstances of their deaths. Each soldier – or group of soldiers (members of the same kibbutz, graduates of the same high school, members of the same platoon, etc.) – has many pages consecrated to him; his biography is composed by family, friends, teachers or comrades-in-arms, often illustrated with photos; parts of diaries or letters are published; other creative mementos, such as drawings, add their own singular touch.

Individuality was thus present in commemoration even in the early days of the state (and of the pre-1948 Jewish Yishuv of the state). But, make no mistake about it; this individuality is subjected to the hegemony of the collectivist ethos. If commemorating is part and parcel of an effort to rehabilitate the bereaved, it is a rehabilitation of a special kind, in that it intends to contribute to society at large while at the same time endowing the death in question with meaning. It does not seek to divert one's mind from the dear departed or to provide substitutes for him/her (in activities, new relationships, etc.). It rather endeavours, by objectifying the person's individuality, to transfer his or her memory to a wider social circle. It seeks to transmit to others, from an in-group into an out-group(s) what this person has represented for his or her intimates. A personal-familial memory may be integrated thereby into a collective memory through the mediation of 'agents of memory' such as family, groups of friends, etc.

It is no coincidence that most 'booklets of commemoration' appear on the first anniversary of the soldier's death. The Jewish traditional calendar of bereavement – followed even by most secularized Israelis – dovetails with the conventional insights of psychology. There is the practice of mourning in the week after death, the rest of the first month, then the following eleven months, corresponding roughly to the three stages of the grieving period during which there is a lessening of the rigour of ritual obligations and a growing integration of the bereaved into the normal life of the community. The first anniversary is the ideal point for the completion– or rather near-completion – of a rite of passage, as future anniversaries may enable the bereaved to deal with the lingering sense of loss. (Half of the booklets appear on the second to fifth anniversaries; and the majority of private monuments are erected during these years.)

In order to objectify the private memories of the bereaved and thus contribute to collective memory, a vast amount of social activity is called for: preparatory conversations, the establishment of an informal committee, fund-raising (rather limited in scale in the case of most booklets), the collection of documents, the soliciting of articles and the writing down of oral testimonials (sometimes at a special gathering). If one counts copy-editing, typing, production, and distribution (usually to a privately drawn-up list of addresses), each booklet involves the help of at least a dozen people, all associated in some way with the fallen soldier, shocked by his sudden, violent and untimely death, and trying, according to their varying degrees of intimacy with the departed, to cope with their sense of loss, but at the same time trying – through this very social activity of writing and publishing – to enlarge the social circle for which his death may have meaning. The dynamics of the support group and of group therapy are quite evident in these booklets, especially the reliance of parents on the help of comrades-in-arms (or friends) of their sons, and the collaboration between parents whose sons fell in the same battle.

Interviews conducted many years later with editors of commemorative books, as well as remarks interspersed in the booklets themselves, indicate that the idea of commemoration was usually broached during the first month after death (sometimes during the first week), that is, prior to the ritual visitation of the grave, which in the Jewish bereavement process marks the end of the first year. The decision to edit and to publish is taken either at that stage or during the months immediately after. Sometimes later steps are taken to have a multiple commemoration, but the book form was and is, more often than not, the only or the first option discussed. The idea is usually first discussed at the moment when the definiteness of the soldier's death lodges in the mind: the traumatic moment of viewing his body or – more typically – when the parent or friends stop writing in their diary, 'I still cannot believe he is dead'.

The guilt that comrades-in-arms often feel for having survived, out of sheer chance, is present in a different guise in the parents' generation. (Very few grandparents were involved in 1948, for they were not numerous in Yishuv families, which were founded for the most part by people who had immigrated young and without their own parents.) As one might perhaps expect in the highly ideologized society of the 1950s, parents – but also former teachers, who are frequent contributors to booklets – evince a deep sense of responsibility for the soldier's death, an event viewed in a way as the end-result of having brought their children up to serve the nation. In a broader context, death is seen as the upshot of their very immigration to Palestine. When parents recount their own life story in a booklet, they begin, as a rule, with their immigration; life in the Diaspora is, typically, disregarded. In what was then a strongly conformist society and in the context of a war deemed a 'good war', fought in self-defence and for the undisputed ideal of national independence, none of these issues gave rise to doubts as to the sense of this death, but they did provoke a feeling of deep personal responsibility that needed to be resolved and endowed with meaning, in order to mitigate grief. An appeal to history and reference to a historical context could be a means to that end, hence the urgency of contributing to history writing through the activity of commemoration.

At times editors and writers (especially of the parents' generation), however conformist, attest to their own anxieties that the Zionist dream may be turning sour – given certain Israeli realities of the 1950s (the decline of the pioneering ethos, party squabbles, corruption). They see the activity of commemoration, therefore, as a response to social ills that have developed: collective amnesia about the values on which the state was established, values for the sake of which they believe their sons have fallen. This complex of feelings is summed up by a telling metaphor – the 'sacrifice of Isaac by Abraham'. It was first used in a Zionist context in 1930 by the poet Yitzhak Lamdan to describe the pioneering effort, and was adopted by bereaved parents during the 1948 war. Through them it passed into current usage through the Yizkor books. In the Biblical story, both father and son agree to obey the order; and even in the post-Biblical Midrash commentary, only the father has some doubts (which he overcomes). Indeed, the 1948 war was not a controversial war, as the Yom Kippur and Lebanon wars would be. But gnawing doubts and anxieties remained; and certainly grief never disappeared, as all booklets testify. Healing is never assured.

Commemoration, it was hoped, might help to resolve this predicament within the context of the support group (family, friends, youth group, kibbutz, neighbours), which organized the commemoration and in a way stood for society at large – resolve somewhat, but never completely, particularly as far as parents were concerned. There was justification but no sign of real (or enduring) solace. Here is the testimony of a mother:

> It is difficult to acquiesce with this loss. Why is it that this being, so full of life and animation, lies still, his glowing eyes dimmed, his fresh body turning into earth? Why is it that there will be no more joy at my home, no worry for his future any more? I'll never hear his pals whistling for him. But why do I say this, I who have educated him to be a dedicated patriot, and even fight if necessary? Why do I say this, I who at your open grave declared that I am proud you fell for our homeland? Why?[5]

Why were 'books of commemoration' chosen to be, and why are they still, the main vehicle of commemoration? Is it just the mix of the individuality of the fallen and the collective ethos through the agency of a small, face-to-face community? Respect for learning, long cherished among Jews, certainly contributes to that predilection for books as artefacts of memory. Most of the 'special commemoration projects', such as libraries, were and are related to books and book learning.

Yet the phenomenon goes deeper than what is covered by the bland formula of 'people of the book'. It has roots in the Jewish tradition of commemoration, a tradition recently transformed and reinvented in the wake of the 1948 bloodletting.

These roots are to be found in the Yizkor (remembrance) books, which appeared in thirteenth-century Germany and later spread to Central and eastern Europe. They were chronicles of specific communities, updated from time to time by their notables, which depicted the history of the community: its major rabbis and prominent individuals, the persecutions it had suffered (especially since the First Crusade, that watershed of Jewish life in Christian Europe) and, most particularly, its list of martyrs, a list recited in synagogue four times a year within the framework of the special Yizkor prayer instituted in the early twelfth century. This prayer and the martyrs' names were the major motivation for the persistence of the literary genre and its conscientious updating. Historiography here was a sort of ancillary practice to ritual – that is, a way of conserving the collective memory by means of the perennial 'chain of martyrology', which was perceived as the Jewish people's lot in exile, the martyrs sacrificing themselves in obedience to the just demands of the Lord. Collective memory was thus conveyed in a religious interpretative mode, especially through sacred liturgical texts. Each new wave of persecutions was taken to be a re-enactment of former ones.

The growing secularization of the Jewish people in the nineteenth century filtered down in the early twentieth, in terms of elite historiography, to the level of collective memory, and reshaped the martyrology. It is not mere chance that this happened primarily in the two most lively centres of Jewish collective activity – eastern Europe and Palestine.

In eastern Europe the recasting of the tradition took place in the folk historical literature written in the 1920s under the impact of the pogroms that had taken place during the Russian civil war and the Russian–Polish war. The typical artefact is the community notebook (*pinkas*) which contains a description of the pogroms in a specific locality (Vilno, Pinsk, etc.), a list of the dead, the fluctuations of community life during the First World War, as well as a sketch of its life prior to 1914. These very sketches, sometimes quite long, reflected the change in outlook as compared to traditional Yizkor literature: in describing the community they did not limit themselves to rabbis and notables, but depicted all areas of social and economic activity and dwelt upon emigration to the New World.

Demographic transformations as well as pogroms are explained by this-worldly factors and not by a medieval-type theodicy.[6] This new, or rather reinvented, framework for collective memory created a new form of Yizkor book, in which European Jews, during the Second World War and much more intensively after it, would register their collective response to the Holocaust. Its artefacts constituted that spontaneous literature of Yizkor books and *pinkasim* commemorating communities that had been obliterated, and published by Landsmannschaften of the survivors not only in Europe, but also in North and South America as well as in Israel. Here the aim of the survivors, or of relatives amongst earlier immigrants, is to cope with their grief and make it into a tool for crystallizing a historical consciousness. There is very little theodicy, because of the secularized character of most Landsmannschaften. The stress is upon the detailed description of the pre-war community and the horrors of its extermination, so that both will leave their indelible mark on the collective memory. The identity offered to the survivors does not refer to the deity but to the dead – a historical relationship predicated upon the continuity of an ethnic, secular affiliation.

The centrepiece is the local community, and the individual is measured by his contribution to the latter. There is little trace of the ritualistic-liturgical context.

An analogous secularization of the Yizkor literature took place in the pre-1948 Jewish community in Palestine, starting with the Yizkor book to the memory of Second Aliyah members killed by Arabs (published in Jaffa in 1911), which produced numerous offshoots over subsequent years. As in eastern Europe, the thematic framework is that of a profane grief. Bereavement is integrated into a consciousness of historical continuity, but lacks a transcendental presence. The entity overarching the individuals is that of the nation, not the local shtetl. The individual 'martyrs', who are accorded in Palestine, from the very beginning, much more detailed attention than in the east European books (perhaps because of the smaller numbers involved), are measured by their contribution to the pioneering project of the nation.

Still, it is significant that these booklets were self-consciously given the title of Yizkor books and that they made ample use of the traditional martyrological discourse, reinterpreted according to the needs of the new ethos. Even modern societies, when facing war and the existential challenge of mass violent death, do need some anchoring in tradition. That this happened even in a revolutionary, future-oriented society such as the Yishuv only underscores this argument; all the more so as the 'commemoration literature' is suffused not only with secularism but also with agnosticism and atheism. God is absent from the great majority of these books. Emblematic of this profane state of mind is the poem written by a father addressing his dead son:

Standing before your closed bookshelves
as before the Ark of the Law [in synagogue];
Ark with no curtain.
Your father and mother shed tears there.
Tears with no prayers.[7]

The encounter with death presents the true mirror of a society. And here we have one which even in an existential crisis makes no appeal to religious transcendence; it does, however, feel an urge for tradition.

This new martyrological ethos subsumed by the Yizkor literature of the Yishuv puts its subject, those who died a violent death (usually at the hands of Arabs), in a special higher category among those who lost their lives for the sake of the Zionist endeavour (more 'sacred' than those who died of malaria, for instance). Here is the origin of the distinction still maintained by Israeli society between fallen soldiers and civilians killed by terrorist action.

The historical framework that endows their sacrifice with meaning is that of those who fell fighting for Jewish sovereignty, beginning with the Hashmoneans (second century BC), and those who rose in revolt against the Romans (first and second century AD), a tradition renewed, after a hiatus of nineteen centuries, with the First Aliyah. Jewish martyrology in the Diaspora is rarely, and at best erratically, mentioned. Unlike the traditional martyrology, which cherished passivity, accepting the fate laid down by the Lord, the Yishuv martyrology had a distinct activist edge. Even when commemorating those killed in the Arab attack on Tel Hai in 1920 – an event transformed into a General Custer-type 'epic of defeat' – the emphasis was on the 'last stand' as an inspiration to continue the struggle, to take the initiative, to imitate the model of a heroism that does not resign itself to Fate (whether imposed by Providence or by the nation's enemies). Heroism consists of revolting against Fate.

A traditionalist, religious (and passive) collectivist ethos was thus secularized first in eastern Europe, then in Palestine. As it underwent this metamorphosis, the effort – in both locations – absorbed a measure of individualism, another modernist ethos. In pre-twentieth century Yizkor books, only rabbis, notables or particularly heroic martyrs received such attention. The secular Yizkor and *pinkasim* literature of the 1920s or the post-Holocaust era concentrated on a wider gamut of prominent individuals (in culture, economics, social life) of an increasingly secularized shtetl. In Palestine, even when the numbers of dead during periods of riots were in the hundreds (1929, 1936–9), the 1911 formula was adhered to; a biography (usually accompanied by a photograph) of each of the dead, followed by testimonials, evaluations, memoirs, documents and literary or artistic bequests.

While the first initiatives were entirely due to the leadership of the labour movement and, above all, to its mentor, Berl Katznelson, the genre soon spawned a more spontaneous literature produced primarily in the kibbutzim, which possessed an institutional infrastructure such as a 'culture committee' and a stencilling machine.

The commemorative literature on the War of Independence represents not merely a quantitative leap – almost ten times as many booklets were published in the 1950s as in all the pre-state days; this was due to the scope of the casualties. What was still in Yishuv days to a large extent a semi-institutional literature, mostly beholden to the labour movement, now became a widespread social phenomenon, the product of a plethora of private initiatives.

Parents, friends, comrades-in-arms, neighbours, fellow residents and professionals created ad hoc grass-roots associations for publishing such books and booklets, side by side with kibbutzim, schools, etc.

The spread of the Yizkor literature as a socio-cultural mode of action had a direct impact upon what Roger Bastide calls the 'organization of memory'.[8] People remember as a part of a social group. Personal memories exist in relationship to the memories of other people who are relevant to the individual. Personal memories intermingle, influence each other and thus create a collective memory, feed it and maintain its continuity. A collective memory enables groups to attain a consciousness based upon a sort of 'network of complementarity'. Collective memory is, thus, not an abstract entity over and above individuals. It is the product of these exchange relationships to which each group member contributes his or her own memories. Obviously the weight of the various memories is not equal. The group's organizational structure moulds the organization of its memory. The contribution of elites carries more weight. Whoever articulates his or her memories in public leaves a deeper imprint than one who does it merely in private or not at all.[9]

If we apply these analytical tools to the Israeli case, we perceive immediately that the 'organization of memory' gave a distinct advantage to certain social groups in the early years of the state. For instance, a comparison of the distribution of the fallen commemorated in booklets shows that sabras are substantially over-represented among the commemorated (four out of ten as against three out of ten among the bulk of fallen soldiers of the 1948 war). The longer an immigrant was in Palestine the greater his chances of being commemorated. Soldiers who had come before the Second World War were over-represented; those who had come after 1940 were under-represented by half; those who had arrived during 1948 barely figured at all. This applies even more acutely to those who were given what one may term 'intensive' commemoration – that is, in a booklet as well as in a scholarship, grove or youth group, or who were the subject of an individual booklet rather than part of one consecrated to a whole group. Sabras and veteran immigrants had an even greater advantage. This inequitable commemoration is all the more noteworthy, given the fact that war casualties were evenly distributed among all social categories, a fact owing perhaps to conscription operating from the early months of the war.

What accounts for this commemorative imbalance? Social integration is crucial here. Commemoration is carried out above all by families, by friends, by fellow soldiers or by voluntary associations. Given that the median age of the fallen soldiers was twenty-two, if they had arrived in Palestine before the Second World War, they would have passed at least half their lives there, or at least had part of their schooling in Palestine. Moreover, those who had immigrated after 1945 were Holocaust survivors, and hence much more likely to arrive as orphans, without any other immediate relatives in Palestine.

As the poet Arieh Sivan, a veteran of the war, was to put it years later, writing about new immigrant soldiers:

We should try to remember them
but this is not easy . . .
In whose memory would a [newcomer] live?
He has no parents to visit his grave
through the seasons, and water his roots.
He has no room to fit his photo,
no friends to talk about him, no widow
to confer his name upon her son.[10]

While social integration is a major factor in the 'organization of memory' in what was (and still is) an immigrant society, it operates in tandem with the location of the individual in the gamut of articulation and social activism. The more educated the soldier, the greater the chances that his family, friends or fellow group members would have access to commemorative modes: a knowledge of Hebrew (there are virtually no booklets in other languages); a newspaper (likelier in a kibbutz, a youth group or a well-established neighbourhood); contacts with printers. No less crucial was the sheer fact of having relatives, friend or associates who could invest the time and who possessed the editorial capacity to collect (or write down) testimonials and memoirs. It is hardly surprising that the higher the educational standard of the fallen, the more he featured as the subject of a booklet. He was also more likely to be given 'intensive commemoration'. Being an officer was an extra advantage, as it presupposed a high level of education (the same is true of the sabras and veterans). The collective profile of the commemorated thus tends to be somewhat slanted in favour of elite groups.

This characteristic begins to change from the 1973 war onwards, as the immigrants of the 1950s or their offspring gained access to secondary education and became integrated into social networks (for instance, synagogues and sports clubs). Collectivity and its agencies still prime everything (or almost so), but the collectivity becomes more inclusive, more pluralistic and tolerant of differences, as evidenced in the rise (since the late 1960s) of an Oriental-traditionalist mode of commemoration, via synagogues. Yet even this old-new mode was still beholden to the collectivist ethos, hegemonic till at least the mid-1970s, if not beyond. The justification of giving one's life for the nation-state is never called into question. The best indicators are the protest letters that were sent by parents of fallen soldiers to Prime Minister and Defence Minister Ben-Gurion.[11]

They complain, quite bitterly, of insufficient financial support, obtuse civil service dealings with their problems, the state of their son's cemetery, etc. Yet the 1948 and 1956 wars (and the many raids in between and after) are for the bereaved and angry parents part of a 'good war', in the American sense – as applied to World War II – warfare enjoying a social consensus. The 1948 war, for instance, is for them a defensive war and one should be proud of what it accomplished, namely the State of Israel. A mother writes: 'My son was a brave fighter. He always fought against evil, for justice. He fought for the freedom of his nation and homeland. He could never fulfil the promise of his talents, as he threw caution to the winds, rushing to save the fatherland from mortal danger.' And she signs herself 'a mother who sacrificed everything in order to raise her son for the sake of the nation'. The father of another of the fallen writes that his son has 'a young brother whom we educate in the same spirit'.

In a public assembly of bereaved parents, raring to fight the Ministry of Defence over some urgent complaints, a leading militant declares: 'Nothing can compensate us parents for our loss, but the nation as a whole has received full recompense, there exists the State of Israel.'

Even the most bitter of the letters of complaint – sending back in protest the son's decorations or officer insignia – never question the collectivist ethos. One father, after describing the material destitution to which he had been reduced, writes:

Did you ask yourself how I and others of my ilk spend Independence Day? You would not relish knowing that. Yet I was among those who strove, craved for independence. Moreover, I am one of those who, if ever they had a moment of happiness in their life, experienced it when our pioneering endeavour finally succeeded.

We, his mother and father, who knew to educate our son in the pioneering spirit, in the spirit of sacrifice for the fatherland, we will also know how to preserve his memory to our last day. We and not others. And certainly, judging from your behaviour, not you.[12]

And more succinctly, another father, in an analogous context:

Our son fell for the fatherland and, despite the terrible pain, we understand that, without the casualties, our state could not have materialized. Fate decreed that our dear son would be among the fallen. This was inevitable and nobody wanted it to happen. Yet the fact that you, the government, condemned us to die of hunger, is unpardonable. Our dead son would not pardon you.[13]

The first significant breaking point of this collectivist ethos adulating the state (and the Zionist project it subsumes) is no doubt the Yom Kippur War, though, as we shall see, some cracks could be perceived even during the War of Attrition on the Suez Canal (1969–70). Those three weeks of intensive warfare in October 1973 – half victory, half defeat – elicited a multi-vocal chorus of commemoration, which launched the (still ongoing) debate within Israeli society about the meaning of that war and of sacrifice for the homeland.

One encounters there the whole universal gamut of reactions to sudden and violent death (guilt, anger, revenge). One likewise finds typical Israeli themes, such as the anxiety of the parents' generation (many of whom had fought in 1948) about whether their sons would stand the test of fire. This particular parents' generation, one must stress, was much larger than the one that existed in 1948, for almost all the war dead had at least one surviving parent, while in 1948 most immigrant-soldiers who had come after 1940 had no parent and few relatives in Palestine. And as the brunt of the 1973 war was borne by the regular army and young reservists aged 18 to 25, who accounted for 70 percent of casualties, parental doubts seemed to be assuaged. Furthermore, the share of the Israeli-born in the 1973 fallen generation was much higher than in the past, keeping pace with the changing make-up of the younger age-groups: two thirds of those killed were sabras.

However, the attitude of the 1973 parents' generation combines grief (as in previous wars) with particularly heavy guilt feelings. The lack of sufficient Israeli army preparedness made the parents, above all those who had served in 1948, feel responsible for the debacle of the early days of the war, particularly if they had perhaps served as role models for their sons and even motivated them directly to volunteer for combat service. Worse still, shaken in their confidence that society was worth defending on the battlefield, many parents began to wonder aloud whether there was any justification for death, let alone solace. Should the individual, must he, be sacrificed for the state?

The most salient thematic change consisted of the sombre reality of war casting its shadow upon this folk literature. Previous wars left in the Yizkor books matter-of-fact descriptions of the conditions of warfare in a manner that tended to work against militaristic glorification. Consider, for instance, the soldiers' conversations in *The Seventh Day*, published in the wake of the Six Day War. In Yizkor books of the 1950s and 1960s such descriptions were minimal and the sections dealing with the exact circumstances of their subjects' death tended to be laconic.

The post-1973 literature (including that of the Lebanon War) gives pride of place to descriptions of operations as well as of the circumstances of individual deaths. This is a virtually uniform phenomenon, all the more surprising given the spontaneity of this literature, but which could be accounted for, in part, by a 'demonstration effect'.

The 'operational' sections are fully documented. There are oral testimonies culled from comrades and commanders and from later visits of the parents to the particular sector of the front (at their initiative or with the army's help). The text is illustrated with sketches, operational maps are peppered with code names. It is documented often with the help of reports of military commissions of inquiry, appointed, at the pressing and much publicized demand of parents, to throw light upon controversial cases (e.g. the way the injured were evacuated from a certain battle).

Such reports never appear in the commemoration literature of the 1950s, because parents' protests, in this more conformist age, were channelled through correspondence with officials (including Ben-Gurion), and their none-too-frequent demands for inquiry were rarely satisfied anyway. The blow the Yom Kippur surprise dealt to the credibility of the army high command – till then basking in the glow of 1967 – and their political superiors is evident in the very multiplicity of such official reports after 1973. Moreover, such reports were now made public. Guilt feelings in high places combined here with the vociferous, no longer respectful and restrained, anguish of bereaved parents, backed up by the battle-bruised comrades who were so active in post-war protest movements.

Other documents that appear in the mid-1970s booklets concern men missing in action (MIA) and presumed dead. The MIA phenomenon was much broader than in any previous Israeli war, and adds a wrenching twist to bereavement, depriving it of the modest succour of the grave site. The dry language of such official reports barely covers the horror:

Tank Number xxx was the nearest to the Suez Canal. In it were found the bodies of two soldiers directly hit by Egyptian anti-tank missiles. The two other occupants, one of whom being your son . . . might have been thrown out of it or left it after it had been hit and might have been killed by enemy infantry.[14]

A stark note of finality is struck in the appendices of the booklets: technical ones such as the army official form 'List of Personal Objects and Documents Relating to an Injured Soldier': watch, key ring, purse, bus schedule, small coins. 'This is it,' says the document. 'He is no more.' Other appendices comprise letters written by parents to the son during the war in the days after his demise or disappearance and returned to them by military mail. All such letters have but one refrain: 'Please give a sign of life'.

This exposure to the horrors of war as well as the anguish of parents, wives and friends makes these booklets gloomier than those produced after previous wars. It could be argued that they render society even less likely to be infatuated by war. The anguish is illustrated by a multiplicity of details relating to the long wait for publication of lists of the dead (or MIAs or POWs); unpleasant contacts with insensitive army bureaucracy; the emotional ups and downs undergone by family and friends. All this is reported in a variety of styles, from the barely literate to the highly articulate. The deceased may be described warts and all, even in war. One mother recounts how her son reacted to the radio announcement on Yom Kippur 1973, at midday, that a war had broken out. 'You did not believe it. You said, "It's impossible; it's an electoral ploy." You lay down and fell asleep. You wanted to forget it all. I woke you up, confounded and depressed.' A tank commander named Jacob tells in a booklet commemorating his friend Danny, how they last met, a day before the latter would be killed:

On Sunday, 7 October, we came back to the Tassa camp [in Sinai] at seven. We ate breakfast and went through with tank maintenance. One of the guys told me: 'There was somebody here, with glasses, looking for you . . . He didn't say his name, must have gone to chow.' I rushed to the mess and here I see Danny, in unbuttoned overall, black undershirt, unshaven, Uzi slung on his shoulder, looked terrible. I said: 'Danny, how are you?'

Danny: 'Look, Jacob, it's horrible. We got wiped out yesterday. All my guys are gone.'

Jacob: 'Danny, do me a favour, don't tell me anything. Let's talk about now. We are alive. Let's get on with it.'

Danny: 'Jacob, you can't imagine what happened to me yesterday.'

And then he tells me how their tank got stuck last night. Nobody came to pull them out. They were told to fend for themselves. They fought their way out and joined our forces.

Jacob: 'Danny, listen, get a hold of yourself.

Danny: If I go, I will not come back.'

Jacob: 'Danny, enough is enough.'

I still tried to boost his morale, but in vain. We embraced . . . I accompanied him to his tank, he heaved himself into the turret . . . We waved to each other . . . I bit my fingernails. How did Danny get to such a state?, I thought. He was never a coward. I was desperate.[15]

Indeed, the commemoration literature changes its tropes: more of the realistic, less of the heroic. And as we shall see below, a third trope, the ironic, would creep in.

What makes the description of war horrors and those of its aftermath so traumatic is not just their exposure, but the wrath and outrage with which it is suffused. The commemoration literature of the 1950s was elegiac; the sense of loss somewhat mitigated by what was taken to be a worthy achievement, the state's birth and survival. The 1967 literature was immersed in a narcissistic, complacent and self-congratulatory tone: yes, war is horrible, but on the whole we kept our moral fibre and won – a tone which the 1973 generation would dub derisively 'shooting and crying'. The 1973 literature, on the other hand, is characterized by probing, merciless self-criticism, doubts as to the very justification for the slaughter. True, these were the dominant themes in the mid-1970s public sphere, expressed in the media and in protest movements. A 'feedback loop' operated here, manifest above all in the parents' and friends' conversations out of which the commemoration literature emerged. Yet the very fact that these themes were now expressed through a genre, the aim of which had been to cope with loss, shows how profound was the 'October Earthquake', privately and collectively. It was difficult even to look for some solace, whereas the failures, especially in the early part of the war, were too glaring to be eclipsed, in the eyes of the bereaved (as well as of most Israelis), by the victories of the later phase.

Criticism of the way operations were conducted was levelled by parents and comrades even in 1948, but, as we have seen above, not in public. Complaints were sent to the authorities, often to Ben-Gurion in person, through the proper channels. The tone was bitter but on the whole respectful; only in rare cases were medals sent back in protest or a commission of inquiry demanded (in vain). In 1973 the criticism is in the open – an indicator of a more transparent, less conformist society. That this criticism is to be found even in the Yizkor booklets gives it a particular weight. Here is an account of a reconnaissance unit going into battle in the Golan Heights:

> When I arrived at the base camp in the night following Yom Kippur it was three a.m. We found that our unit had fewer jeeps at its disposal than it was supposed to have by regulation. Some jeeps lacked machine guns. We had to 'steal' them from semi-armed vehicles in storage. No jeep was equipped with the regulation binoculars. We had to scrounge them. All this wasted a lot of time. Worst of all – we didn't find enough maps, and we are about to go into an area we didn't know at all . . . Driving up towards the southern part of the Golan Heights we met a horribly battered group of dozens of our soldiers going down by foot, like refugees, in torn clothes, most without arms. Some had fled from army positions, others had abandoned their tanks. They told us terrible stories.[16]

Another fellow soldier writes:

> For seven years we have lived the illusion of omnipotence. This led some of the IDF top command to recklessness, perhaps to corruption. We have been self-satisfied while the Arabs have drawn lessons from their debacle. How strange it was that they became the heroes of night warfare. We were frightened at night for they had night-vision instruments and we didn't.[17]

A scathing barrage of criticism targets the war strategy, for instance the wasteful tank battles of attrition. This sort of criticism was elicited in the past by only one botched battle, the Latrun battle of 1948. This is what one reserve soldier says of a tank battle in Sinai, which he had closely studied, in which his brother had been killed:

> What enrages me in particular is that his tank stopped dead twice during the operation. Is that what you call maintenance? The very fact that General Gorodish dispatched them against an iron wall of Egyptian tanks and infantry, not knowing really how effective the enemy missiles were, is infuriating. There were intelligence reports of these [shoulder-held] anti-tank rockets, but had they never caught his attention?[18]

The reservist goes on to lash out at the political leadership (for short-sightedness, avoiding a peace initiative before the war), yet he doesn't shun self-criticism and even finds some fault with his dead brother: 'One cannot lay all the blame upon the powers that be. They are an integral part of the people and each influences the other.' He points out that this very air of self-satisfaction can be found in his brother's letters, suffused with derogatory references to the Arabs and their culture. These twin factors greatly contributed to what happened in October 1973. Indeed, in one of the letters included in the Yizkor booklet, dating from 1969, the brother, then a teenager, reacts enthusiastically to an arrogant, militaristic speech delivered at his high school by General Ariel Sharon. He was sucked into the whirlpool of the state, that collective hegemony, and lost his individuality and later his individual life.

Exposure, openness and self-criticism are pushed even further in Yizkor booklets published by kibbutzim, which previously produced the more conformist specimens of the genre. Their publications now comprise letters of fallen soldiers complaining of the 'conservatism', 'mediocrity' and 'rot' of kibbutz society. Mutual support is found to be lacking, envy to reign supreme. The small-scale 'communities of memory' turn against the larger collectives.

Enveloped in such an air of crisis, it is hardly surprising that there is questioning of the justification for death in battle. This is certainly true of the secularist booklets that constitute the majority of the genre, though a somewhat smaller majority than in the previous two decades. For most parents and friends, even when facing such a terrible loss, invocation of the transcendental still has no place; sacred agencies are not their recourse, the profane dominates. God is absent from their (tape-recorded) conversations.

The secularist majority still accepted in the mid-1970s the basic justification for war as action taken in defence of the collective. The Egyptian-Syrian joint attack on Yom Kippur in 1973 helped most Israelis stick to this article of faith, which would be really shaken merely by the Lebanon war (1982–3). A tiny minority of the 1970s Yizkor books put the blame upon Israeli leadership for not offering political compromise in order to reduce Arab motivation to go to war. Many parents and friends said openly, however, that their own particular son/husband/comrade died in vain in the Yom Kippur war because of bad strategy/ tactics or sloppy training and maintenance. In the past it was unheard of to speak in this vein in the house of the bereaved or in such an intimate artefact as a Yizkor book, and, what's more, to do so before the end of the year of mourning. Many booklets used to end on a partly affirmative note: 'Our loss has meaning but there's no solace'. Now meaning – provided by the larger collectivity and by the many smaller ones that made it – was in doubt, solace virtually impossible.

Individualism emerges (or re-emerges, for it was there, only subdued) from this crisis of collectivism. The value of individual life per se is affirmed with a vengeance in the years following the Yom Kippur War, especially as later wars (Lebanon, the Intifada) were controversial to begin with. The small 'communities of memory' often turn out to be the spearhead of this new struggle.

A prefiguration of this new (and hitherto still developing) state of affairs can be detected in the protest outbursts of the Attrition war, which knocked off the 'security consensus'. In 'open letters' to the Prime Minister, later published in the press, some (regular and reserve) soldiers, as well as teenagers, asked whether this war was necessary. Hanoch Levin gave a particularly poignant voice to these questions and doubts in an acerbic cabaret play, *Queen of the Bathtub* (the said queen being the then Prime Minister, Golda Meir). The Tel Aviv theatre where it was staged was the object of angry and violent protests, led quite often by bereaved relatives who denounced it as sacrilegious. The show had to be taken off after two months. The cabaret number that enraged them most was a song where a fallen soldier talks to his father from his grave:

Dear Dad, when you stand at my grave,
Old, weary and very much childless,
And you see how they put my body into the earth
And you stand above me, Dad.

Don't stand so proud
Don't raise your head, Dad
We remained flesh against flesh
And it's time to cry, Dad.

So let your eyes cry over my eyes
Don't keep silent out of respect for me,
For something more important than Honour
Lies down at your feet, Dad.

And don't say you made such a sacrifice
For he who sacrificed was I,
And don't use high words any more
For I already lie very low, Dad.

Dear Dad, when you stand at my grave,
Old, weary and very much childless,
And you see how they put my body under the ground
. . . Ask for my forgiveness, Dad.[19]

The metaphor of the dramatic test of Abraham and Isaac was turned on its head in this most emblematic product of the early protest. Such a denunciation of the Bereaved Parent myth, pointing out that parents gained in social status and moral authority while sons rotted, was accepted in 1970 only by a young, mostly dissident audience. After 1973, one finds Yizkor books, notably in kibbutzim, where this sarcastic song had pride of place alongside the 'canonical' modern Hebrew poems on death and mourning. A hitherto marginal argument has moved into the very centre of public discourse and into that of its major audiences, the 'Family of Bereavement' – that Israeli term denoting the nebulous web of kin and adoptive kin (friends, comrades) that carries on the remembrance.

Furthermore, if in 1970 bereaved parents (in an improvised, voluntary, yet effective lobby) were the ones who contributed the most to the disruption and, later, the closing down of the *Queen of the Bathtub*, now you find them more and more at the vanguard of the challenge to the collectivist ethos, not in order to demolish it but to cut it down to size, dispute its hegemony and, in particular, to call in question its virtually overriding claim on resources, emotions and even individual life itself.

A group of reservist officers who had all fought in the Yom Kippur war (where some of them were wounded and/or decorated) wrote in April 1978 the famous public letter to Prime Minister Begin, urging him to promote the cause of peace with Egypt. The letter, which would launch the Peace Now movement, owed much of its echo to the moral claim (and urgency) the officers exuded and to the powerful collective 'memory trace' to which it referred.

The phenomenon rose to salience with the Lebanon war, which was controversial from the early days. A small yet prominent 'community of memory', the bereaved parents of soldiers killed in the conquest of the Castle of Beaufort, used various commemorative occasions and tools to fight against the continuing war, against the manipulation (by the Prime Minister and his ministers) of their sons' sacrifice for the purposes of public relations.[20]

Following them, the reservists of the IDF's number one commando unit (GHQ Commando) wrote to Defence Minister Ariel Sharon in September 1982 a letter protesting that the public had been hoodwinked by concealment of the real strategic goals of the Lebanon war (Beirut, not 'just 40 kilometres'). Then the army's youngest colonel, Eli Geva, himself a general's son, resigned rather than lead his men into battle in Beirut: the lives of Lebanese civilians and of Israeli tank crews were of greater concern to him than the state's strategic aims of 'reshaping the map of the Middle East'. The Beaufort example spawned many clones: 'Mothers Against

Silence' (during the Intifada), 'Four Mothers' (for the evacuation of South Lebanon), as also like-minded groups of serving soldiers' parents who refused the sacrifice of Abraham.

Other bereaved parents – often backed by their sons' comrades – would begin angry public fights for their rights to put their personal stamp upon the official commemoration of their sons, arguing that the latter are not state possessions, certainly not after their death. Such fights often moved into the courts and were usually decided by the High Court of Justice.[21] This vindication of individuality encompasses matters of litigation, including the right to add another (personal) line to those prescribed by the Ministry of Defence for the plates on the fallen soldier's tomb and the right to change the dates on the tombstone from the Jewish calendar to the Gregorian one.

'You, the state, cannot appropriate them now that they are dead,' they say, and others add, 'Actually, you had no right to appropriate them to begin with, when they were alive, definitely not for controversial, national-collectivist causes.' The moral status of the bereaved lends weight to this new turn in the public debate on collectivism (often given in Hebrew the telltale tag of 'Statism') vs. individualism. No wonder the term 'Sacrifice of Abraham' disappears from the rituals of commemoration (except in the national-religious, Gush-Emunim-inspired sector). Individualism continues to rise, but not without exacting a price. Shorn of 'healing metaphors' such as the Sacrifice of Abraham, lacking the support of social consensus about a Good War, facing the traumatic experience of combat against children and women (in Lebanon and in the Intifada), bereavement and commemoration have become more difficult than ever and the balance maintained by the bereaved more shaky. Nevertheless, the fact remains that the small 'communities of memory' are still the backbone of the voluntary commemoration, and not the state, exactly as they were when the pattern was set five decades ago.

Notes

1. Y. Amichai, *The Great Tranquillity*, translated by G. Abramson, New York, Harper and Row, 1983, p. 31.
2. Yizkor: Yigal Wilk, Jerusalem, privately printed, 1968, pp. 4–5.
3. R. Rosenthal, *Sayeret Beaufort*, Tel Aviv, privately printed, 1983, p. 41.
4. S. Avigur, *'Im Gur*, Tel Aviv, Am Oved, 1981, p. 181.
5. Micha Fisher, *Alim Le-zichro*, Tel Aviv, privately printed, 1952, p. 52.
6. See articles by N. Wachtel and L. Valensi in *History and Anthropology*, vol. 2, 1986.
7. E. Kalir, *Mikerev*, Tel Aviv, privately printed, 1950, p. 37.
8. R. Bastide, 'Mémoire collective', in *L'Année sociologique*, 1970, esp. pp. 76–96.
9. M. Douglas, *How Institutions Think*, London, Routledge, 1986, chs. 6 and 7.
10. *Ma'ariv*, 4 May 1981.
11. I.D.F. Archives, files 201–1551/5; 72/39–90; 1189–782/65.
12. ibid., file 377–580/56.
13. ibid., 28–60/62.
14. Yizkor: Ya'acov Kramersky, Kibbutz Mesilot, privately printed, 1974.
15. *Ner Zikaron le-Danny*, Jerusalem, privately printed, 1974. Both boys came from religious families.
16. *Havrei Ha-Goshrim*, Kibbutz ha-Goshrim: privately printed, 1975, pp. 11, 16.
17. ibid., p. 17.
18. *Ne'edar – Sihot Le-toch Ha-layla*, Tel Aviv, Eked, 1976, pp. 19, 31, 43, 70.
19. H. Levin, *Ma Ichpat La-tsipor*, Tel Aviv, Zemora-Bitan, 1987, p. 92.
20. See their Yizkor book, quoted in Note 2 above. However, the whole phenomenon discussed here never really touched the religious-nationalist sector.
21. High Court of Justice, Bar-Gur vs. Ministry of Defence (1996), Wexelbaum vs Ministry of Defence (1993), Ginossar vs. Ministry of Defence (1991). See Y. Haendel, *Har Ha-To'im* (1991), a novel about the day-to-day fight to institutionalize private commemoration patterns by parents visiting the graves in a military cemetery near Tel Aviv.

CHAPTER THIRTEEN

The Shift in Israeli Ideas Concerning the Individual and the Collective

Gadi Taub

For Israelis the fall from the age of ideologies to a post-modern world, from a seemingly coherent world to one that appeared to be fragmented and broken, was especially sudden. The slope was so steep because Zionism as an ideology, as a unifying social ethos, was such an immense success. Not only did it live to fulfil its main goals, it also retained vitality into a much later period than other nineteenth-century ideologies. When the whole of the industrial world was experiencing a wave of student uprising – a manifest expression of disappointment with the existing social systems and the ideologies they professed – Israel was still in the high noon of its post-Six Day War euphoria. But by the late 1980s we had already caught up with the rest of the west in its sense of fragmentation. We moved from one extreme to another with breathtaking speed: from a state of suffocating collectivity and an excessively ideological society to a feeling of collapse and disillusionment.

In the mid-1950s the literary avant-garde known as 'Young Poetry' fought to carve out a private space where it was permissible to say 'I', not only 'we'. When the poet Natan Zah wrote, in 1955, 'One moment of silence, please. Please, I want to say something,' he was trying to take a stance in opposition to what may be called the excessive recruiting force of Israeli society, and people then, under the suffocating collectivity of Israel, craved such a voice.

Within less than a generation, the kind of anxiety Israelis suffered from had completely changed. By the mid 1980s the dominant anxiety became a sense of lack of purpose and meaning, generated by the collapse of the collective sphere as a unifying force.

Yaakov Shabtai[1] was among the first to sense the change and gave it brilliant expression in his celebrated novel *Past Continuous* (1977). His protagonist, Goldman, grew up under the crushing weight of the ideologized Israel. His father, a fanatically devoted Zionist and socialist, a construction worker who saw his profession as a calling, would not put up with any deed or personal characteristic that did not conform with collective needs and ideology. For us, after we had become disillusioned with communist utopia, after the right had monopolized national sentiment, it is difficult to imagine this form of ardently patriotic leftism. But for Israelis in the late 1940s and early 1950s, it seemed natural. Goldman's father was not a stranger to our landscape.

Those who read the novel will not easily forget the powerful scene of the murder of Nuit Sombre, the neighbour's dog. It is worth quoting in some length, because it isn't just the portrait of a tyrant, but also an example, although extreme and horrifying, of something important with which Shabtai characterizes the generation of Goldman's parents. Its a vivid testimony to the power of a unifying, all-embracing ideology:

> Goldman's father refused to forgive [Kaminskaya, the neighbour], and he hated her and her ways and the songs she sang and the clothes she wore and her black dog, which she called Nuit Sombre and which stood quietly tied to the water pipe looking at Goldman's father, whose face was white as a sheet and tense with fright and wickedness.
>
> Nuit Sombre even wagged his tail, because of course he couldn't have guessed that Goldman's father was going to kill him in a couple of seconds, but Goldman's father approached him and suddenly pulled a builder's hammer out of his shirt and brought it down swiftly and furiously on his head, and Nuit Sombre made a queer moaning sound and swayed, and Goldman's father yelled at the top of his voice, 'Let him die! Let him die! He has to die!' and went on hitting the dog like a madman until he sank to the ground with his head all shattered and crushed. Nuit Sombre went on twitching for a little longer, making a feeble rattling sound in his throat, until he lay still, and the earth and leaves of the verbena and hibiscus bushes which were still in flower and the water pipe and walls of the house were spattered with splinters of

bone and blood and bits of brain, which remained there until the first rains fell and washed them away.

. . . there is no doubt that Goldman's father passed a sentence on Nuit Sombre for what seemed to him compelling reasons and killed him only after it had become clear that he had to die, and even if it had been his own dog he wouldn't have behaved any differently, because he was a Zionist and a Socialist and believed in plain living, hard work, morality and progress, in the most elementary sense of the words, and hated right-wing nationalists, people who got rich or wasted money on luxuries, and people who [slandered] Eretz Yisrael, and all this as part of a system of clear, fixed, uncompromising principles embracing every area of life and action, which he never doubted for an instant despite all the external changes and difficulties, and from which he saw no reason to deviate in the slightest degree.

He knew what was right and good, not only for himself but also for others, and could not tolerate error or sin, and for him every error . . . was a sin, and despite his own inherent generosity and even sentimentality he could not bring himself to forgive anyone, even his own family and friends, because his integrity verged on insanity and his sense of justice was dark and murky, and above all because he had a tyrannical, uncontrollable desire to impose his principles on the whole world, which went heedlessly along its different, lawless ways, leaving Goldman's father battling between disappointment and rage. There were always people who didn't know what was good for them and people made mistakes, [not to mention] those who actually sinned, often consciously, and in the end everyone violated the proper order of things, everyone, that is, except him, since he was the representative of this order, and accordingly he never knew a single hour of peace of mind, and his whole life, which was full of hostility and humiliation, passed in denunciations and accusations and arguments. Because of his principles he succeeded in quarrelling with almost all his friends and acquaintances, and those he did not quarrel with he ostracized and drove from the house – all except Joseph Leviatan, Avinoam and Sonia and Hanoch's father – surrounding himself with a protective wall of loneliness, but by virtue of these same principles he also succeeded in overcoming his loneliness and his disappointments and his despair when his daughter Naomi, Goldman's older sister, was killed in a traffic accident – according to one version – or committed suicide – according to another version.

It is hard to avoid the impression of the immense power ideology can command as a force unifying the whole of human experience and moulding it under a pattern of meaning. It is important to stress, however, that as Shabtai saw it, ideology does not necessarily assume the tyrannical character it had with Goldman's father. It does not necessarily turn into a frozen, rigid system of principles, and notwithstanding the fact that it is capable of arranging all details of life into a pattern of meaning, like a magnetic force-field, it does not lead necessarily to tyranny or lack of freedom. The high spirit that the ethos of the Zionist labour movement created in its adherents did not evade Shabtai's eye. Not in *Past Continuous* and not elsewhere. Even this book, which depicts Zionist socialism from the viewpoint of its decline, does not lack characters for whom idealism and the love of Zion were able to fill life with light and creativity.

But an ideologically charged atmosphere does invite types like Goldman's father Its decline, however, invites the Goldman-the-son types. When the unifying force of meaning recedes and shrinks, when life is confined to the private and loses the wider context, there may be an abundance of liberty, a freedom from the pressure of the collective, but another form of anxiety comes about, and it is no less grave – a sense of void, meaninglessness, a life that seems to lose all internal value.

Past Continuous is such an interesting example because it bears testimony to the rapid change Israel experienced in moving from one extreme to the other, from one form of anxiety to its opposite. In the transition from the world of one generation to that of its sons and daughters, a whole society moved from a suffocating ideological excess that threatened to erase the private sphere to a void where individuals float with hardly any collective attachment.

One cannot fail to notice the generational division in the book. For the older generation most hardships stem from an excess of ideology, while their sons suffer from something very different – an anxiety we can call, I think, post-modern: for Goldman the son, the world is fragmented and crumbled. Unlike his father who attached meaning to every single segment of human life, nothing in Goldman's life seams meaningful to him. He searches for meaning incessantly, frantically, but cannot evade a despairing feeling of banality: he translates an ancient book of astronomy, tries to repent and adopt religious belief, decides to devote himself to health and fitness, marries (and divorces three weeks later), but whatever he does, he can't escape his sense of inner emptiness.

This inner emptiness is clearly related to a lack of external convictions and the absence of a meaningful collective sphere and a unifying pattern of meaning. Goldman, like his peers, lives in the isolated bubble of the private. For him there is no collective bedrock on which meaningful ties to anything outside the self can be built. He has no link to anything larger than himself, to anything that unites human beings or ties them to a sense of order beyond the immediate. Shabtai's message and intention are clear: Goldman talks of almost nothing but philosophical questions regarding death, meaning, man's place in the cosmos, his despair in the face of chaos and arbitrariness. His sense of meaninglessness is so troubling that he is finally drawn to the only certainty he knows: death. He commits suicide.

***

It hardly needs much deciphering to see that the collapse of frameworks, not least the traditional formats of storytelling and that of language itself, is a central theme in the literature young Israelis write today: from the structural tricks employed by Etgar Keret, some of which are parodies of common literary genres, to the fuzzy hysteria that breaks all boundaries in Orly Kastel-Bloom's stories; from Yosef El-Dror's nonsense humour, all the way to the other side of the spectrum in Gafi Amir's careful, hurtful minimalism. The structure of story itself – as a frame through which to shed light on a segment of reality, to arrange a sequence in a meaningful order – seems to have turned into an instrument we cannot trust. In a reality that is seen as chaotic and arbitrary, the literary narrative cannot – does not even want to pretend to – force the real into a pattern that gives the elusion of order.

Such is the case in the explicit art-poetic stories that take the mechanism of the story as their overt subject, and equally among those writers for whom the weakening of narrative authority is a given to work with, not an interest in itself. In most of these writers the all-knowing narrator, such as was employed by Amos Oz, A. B. Joshoa or Meir Shalev, was replaced by something much more modest. This new narrator does not claim any higher authority than that of his or her characters and seldom indulges in an explicit attempt to explain or illuminate reality from a higher perspective. Accordingly, the language these writers use is what became known in Israel as 'thin language' – everyday speech, simple syntax, few metaphors, a tendency to refrain from what we would commonly associate with high literature. There are hardly any adornments and the majestic tone and sophisticated, multi-layered Hebrew associated with the writers of previous generations are stubbornly ignored.

Literary criticism in Israel often portrays the deliberate destruction of frameworks in these writings as a form of liberation, or, as it is commonly referred to now, 'subversion'. Such critics claim that Orly Kastel-Bloom releases us from the tyranny of hegemonic discourse. She deconstructs the Zionist narrative of colonialism, the discourse of male chauvinism and the tyranny of enlightenment and rationalism. She demolishes 'binary' world views and disturbs the slumbers of bourgeois society.

But such an interpretation seems to me somewhat contrived. Kastel-Bloom's horror world, far from being a merry liberation, is more of a lament for the loss of coherence. It is a frightening place, because it is fractured, violent, arbitrary and unpredictable. It lacks organizing patterns to support a sense of security. Fear, as Kastel-Bloom herself said, is the driving force of her writing. A fear that the world may spin into chaos, lose its meaning and direction, a fear that even the minimum stability that enables one to make modest plans for the future, to construct an approximate path into the void that lies ahead in time, does not exist.

The type of anxiety that led Goldman to suicide, the collapse of the sense of meaning and purpose, these are probably the most pervasive theme in the works of young writers. Keret and Amir, Yoav Katz, Uzi Weil, Yosef El-Dror and many others, all mourn in one way or another the loss of coherence. I will confine myself here to a single example – the story 'Ninety' from Keret's collection *Pipes*.

They said on TV that the court-martial sentenced the Arab who killed the female soldier to death, and they brought some people to talk about this, and that's why the news ended only at ten thirty and they cancelled 'Moonlighting'. Dad got mad at them and lit his stinking pipe at home, although it's forbidden because it stunts my growth. He shouted at mom that because of nuts like her, who voted Tehia,[2] the country is turning into another Iran, which is the country from which all the Persians came. And dad said that it will cost us dearly and that apart from the damage to our moral standing – I'm not sure I understood what that means – the Americans too will not overlook this.

The day after, they talked to us about it at school, and Tziyon Shemesh said that if you hang a man he gets a hard-on like in blue movies, so Tzila, the teacher threw him out, and she explained to us that on the subject of the death sentence people have different views and that it is a matter of the heart. And Tzahi, the dork, who had already had to repeat a school year, twice, not once, laughed and said that it is a matter for the heart of the Arabs, that they have to stop fucking or we'll hang them all by the neck, so the teacher threw him out too. And the teacher said that she will have no more stupid comments, and that she will go on with the lesson as usual and also punished us and gave us a lot of homework.

After school, the older kids argued about whether when you hang someone he dies of suffocation, or because his neck is broken. And then they made a bet for a carton of chocolate milk, caught a cat and hanged him from the basketball post, and the cat screamed a lot till in the end his neck really broke. But Miki, the miser, refused to buy the chocolate milk, because he said that Gabi pulled the cat's body hard on purpose, and that's why it happened and that he wants to see it again with a new cat. But everybody knew it was because he was such a miser, and they took his money by force. And then Nissim and Ziv wanted to beat Tziyon Shemesh, because that cat didn't even have a hard-on. And Michelle, who is maybe the prettiest girl in school, happened to pass by and she said we are all disgusting, and like animals, and I went over to the side and vomited, but not because of her.

It does not require an exhaustive interpretation to see that Keret's kid lives in a world that has spun out of control and lost all order, limit and norm, which is to say, it has lost all sense of coherent meaning. So much so that a feeling of vertigo makes him, finally, vomit. But Keret's kid does not vomit until the prettiest girl in school arrives on the scene. He does not vomit 'because of her', he tells us, and indeed it is not she who gives him a direct feeling of disgust. But in a sense, it is she who causes him to vomit. Because she introduces a scale. Because her very presence – such a contrast to the savagery all around – introduces a criterion alongside which all the rest is measured. From that viewpoint Keret's kid himself sees that 'we are all disgusting, and like animals'.

But I think the story provokes a larger question. In the absence of a meaningful collective sphere what do these young writers turn to in the hope of filling the void? The narrow answer is, I believe, in almost all of these writers, love. And this, it could be said without exaggeration, is true for Gafi Amir, Uzi Weil, Yosi Avni, Ronit Libermensh and many others. However, love here is not what it was for the counter-culture of the American 1960s. For the young student rebels of thirty years ago love was a weapon with which to challenge the social order and eventually change it. In these young writers love is not a instrument of change, it is a sanctuary. Not an attempt to change the world, but an attempt to find shelter from it. Gafi Amir's characters, in the international republic of soap opera viewers, seek redemption from the idleness of lying in bed in front of a TV screen, in sweat pants with a cigarette and a Coke, through man-to-woman relationships. As for many of her peers, it is finding a soul-mate, a lover, a partner, that constitutes the only hope they deem feasible. For them a sense of meaning, of a life worth living, is dependent on love, and by love, I do not mean only the breathtaking sensation of falling in love.

Predominantly in women writers of this generation (Orly Kastel-Bloom, Efrat Shtiglitz, Libermensh, Mizrahi, Amir), parenthood and marriage or at least a steady relationship are the main object of yearning. This deviates enormously from both the Romantic ideal and that of the 1960s. It is the bourgeois ideal itself – nuclear family, childrearing, a steady job – that is perceived as a 'haven in a heartless world', an escape from a world that is both banal and cruel. What Amir's female characters (usually in their twenties) long for is love that will transform itself into the stability and comfort of a family home. In Libermensh, Mizrahi, Irit Linur or Shtiglitz, stability becomes central enough to marginalize its origin in romantic love, and in Kastel-Bloom such an origin is missing altogether. Family is not portrayed as an indoctrinative arm of an oppressive bourgeois-capitalist order in the fashion of the 1960s rebellion. It is, for those writers, not an institution whose demolition is a precondition for a happy life. Rather, it is a vulnerable and precious arrangement, a small island of relative happiness that needs protection in a world that threatens constantly to destroy it.

But, notwithstanding the differences between the Romantic and the bourgeois ideal, there is a common denominator to these writers at a deeper level. What is the nature of this common denominator? In a narrow sense, love; more generally, the belief that a sense of meaning should be sought in the private sphere of life. If grand narratives have collapsed, if large frameworks of meaning have lost their ability to give value and purpose to life, we can only try and look for what we lost in the realm of the private. Meaning has been replaced by 'self-fulfilment'. Whether we look at Irit Linur's Yuppies, Amir's hurt bimbos, Keret's eternal 'Catcher in the Rye', Kastel-Bloom's neurotic mothers or Libermensh's aerobics instructors, they all pursue happiness – via career, love, relationship or parenthood – in the private sphere. The collective sphere, if it appears in these stories at all, only throws dangerously sharp splinters into private worlds. It is not an arena of coherence capable of anchoring individual lives in a larger context. It is a threat to the private. 'The Arab who killed the [female] soldier' (in Keret's *Ninety*), the map of Israel that Doli carves on her child's skin (in Kastel-Bloom's *Doli City*), the assassination of the Prime Minister in Uzi Weil's book (written long before the assassination of Rabin), the municipal draft drill in Yoav Katz's *Daniel Goes to the Army*, the Minister of Police in Kastel-Bloom's *Where I Am* or the son of the head of Mossad in Keret's *Pipes* – all of these bring the public into the private as a distant echo, devoid of context and significance.

There is of course nothing new in such a literary strategy. Literature as an instrument of political criticism has often used the private perspective to portray the political as a 'vanity fair', which loses its moral coherence when we come to evaluate the actual price individual participants pay. But it is hard, I think, to understand young Israeli authors solely through this perspective. This generation of writers does not depict ideology, politics, national symbols or mobilizing myths as frauds – first and foremost because all these have largely lost their force to mobilize. They have lost their power to signify or give meaning to life, even a fraudulent meaning. Fraudulent meaning presupposes at least a measure of inner coherence. We may agree or disagree about the coherence and force of Israel's collective symbolics, but as they appear in the work of young Israeli writers, they look more like a collection of fragmented historical debris than a dangerous disciplining apparatus. The ideological, the collective and social appear in these works more like broken pieces of old souvenirs that once served a purpose no one can now remember. Goldman's father is a total stranger in this world.

All this does not mean that the political has ceased to threaten the private. Symbols may have been rendered useless, but the political world itself can still be dangerous and violent. The head of Mossad in Keret's *The Head of the Mossad's Son* and the ritual examination of bullets in his Beretta gun; the Arab who is castrated by a Shabak interrogator in Keret's *Gaza Blues*; the Scud missiles of the Gulf War in Irit Linur's *Song of the Siren*; the memorial day following the Maalot bus hijacking in Amir's *The Most Handsome Soldier in the IDF* – all these are indicators of the menace of the collective that always looms in the background, of the unpredictable danger that threatens to burst into the private.

But there is a very important difference between the kind of threat the collective poses to the private in this generation's world and the kind of threat it posed to the Young Poetry generation in the 1950s and 1960s. In both cases the individual was placed at the centre and it was the collective that threatened him. But the Young Poetry rebels rose against an ideology that was too strong in its recruiting powers, against a collective sphere that crushed the private because it was so potent in harnessing individuals to collective purposes. The new prose writers point, I believe, to a very different threat. Not only is the collective sphere unable to draw the private into larger patterns of meaning; it is, in itself, so devoid of meaning and coherence, that it threatens to shatter whatever coherence may still survive in the private sphere. It is a disintegrating force, not an integrating one. The political world is a place where terrorists learn from the Syrians 'to shoot in the direction of the mobile radio antenna, because that's where the officer would be'. But the purpose of the war does not appear to be any clearer to the young soldier-narrator than 'some vague political interest' (Keret, *Kohi*). Keret's head of Mossad is frightening not because he is an oppressive ideologue, but precisely because it is never clear whether he has any moral commitments at all. What he does with his Beretta gun remains a mystery: 'There were days when the head of the Mossad would never leave home, and there were other days when he would come back really late. On those days when he arrived home, he would smile a weary smile to the son of the head of Mossad and his mother, and say, "Don't ask what kind of day I had today." And they wouldn't ask, just keep watching TV or doing homework for school. At any rate, if they did ask, he wouldn't answer.'

In the harsh reality of Israel – a reality of occupation, of endless, seemingly pointless war in Lebanon, of terrorist attacks, Intifada and violent nationalist cults – the private sphere has to erect a barrier against the collective, against the brutality that surrounds it, in order to create a living space for the self. But this barrier protects the self not from an excess of disciplining ideology but from the fragmenting force of chaos. The collapse of grand narratives threatens this self no less than over-powerful ideologies threatened it. This rallying around 'self-realization' or 'self-fulfilment' is therefore not an expression of hope, a source of new optimism. Rather it is an ad hoc solution, a default strategy stemming from the lack of other alternatives.

It is hard to say of these young writers that they portray the philosophy of 'self-fulfilment' in a very faltering light. On the contrary, they see it as a cul-de-sac. Taken together, the frightening chaotic world of Kastel-Bloom's fiction, Keret's ironic world of parodies, the sad and moving world of Amir's characters, all form a universe in which the search for meaning or even for a sense of meaning is bound to fail. The people they write about are lonely, usually frightened and covered by an invisible film of silent despair. I think one could say without risk of exaggeration that this generation of writers almost take for granted that fulfilment in the private sphere is a project doomed to failure. Because a world without a meaningful collective sphere, a common ground upon which webs of significance are woven to connect individuals, is, in the last analysis, a sad and confused world, often a brutal one. A world in which a sense of meaning is virtually impossible to achieve.

This should not be, of course, a surprising conclusion. When identity, meaning, ethos and culture are reduced to mere 'personal preference', as some current moral ideologies would have it, it is no wonder that they lose their force as anchors for a sense of purpose and meaning. Their very power is exclusively dependent on their being a common enterprise for the many. But self-realization, understood as an opposition to the very existence of the collective sphere, as a rebellion against it, undercuts the possibility of such unifying forces. This dichotomy between the individual and the collective, a sensibility that has become pervasive in Israel, turned out to be an obstacle to our sense of meaning and propose, not a way to promote it.

Part of the hostility to collectivity is surely a result of the pendulum swing from over-collectivizing to over-individualization. But such an observation should not obscure other influences. And the major source of influence, I believe, is American culture. We see it all around us, whether it is 'the American Dream' as it is reflected, say, in commercials and television game shows, or the shift from the work ethic of socialist Zionism to the no less stern, but very different in content, Yuppie careerism. But American influence does not stop at commercialization or Hollywood glitter and morality or the counter-culture revolution, which arrived in Israel somewhat late. In addition to all these we are witnessing a change in the form of moral argument within the elites. This form draws closer to the traditional moral rationale of conservativism in America, and rests on the idea of negative liberty. Contrary to mainstream Zionist socialism, we tend to see the individual as naturally in opposition to the collective. Much like the tradition of atomistic liberalism, from Locke to Mill and beyond, in modern America, the collective is seen as a necessary evil whose sole justification, apart from subsistence, is to protect the individual's liberty from infringement by the liberty of others. The collective is seen less and less as an arena for answering individual needs and more and more as an entity whose very existence threatens his autonomy. These assumptions are the foundation for works that attack institutional Zionism, such as those of as Idit Zartal or Yosef Grodzinsky, Tom Segev's criticism of Israeli identity, the opposition to the idea of the melting pot or, recently, the hypothesis of oppression-through-discourse, which is ubiquitous in post-modern thought.

We tend to view such criticism as a form of left-wing ideology aimed at right-wing nationalism. But this may be a misleading view. What motivates these critics is more a rebellion against the forces on which Israeli society was founded: Zionist socialism and its belief that social solidarity is a necessary dimension for a meaningful individual life. Radical autonomy, which serves as a basis for the criticism of the very idea of social solidarity, is a right-wing ideology. This is the heart and soul of right-wing liberalism. The portrait of the individual as agent of free choice – chooser of lifestyle and identity, values and ethos – is the flip side of the free-market economy. The so-called leftist radicalism is a major force in dismantling the collective sphere, in removing the moral obstacles on the way to privatization. It is no coincidence that this new form of moral argument is linked with the rise of

Reaganite economics and indeed it emerged at the time of Reagan's administration in the US. The left, in short, has adopted the moral world of the right, and mistakes it for its own. If it is to regain its own moral ground, it should rethink its attitude towards the legitimacy of a collective sphere.

Notes

1. Yaakov Shabtai, *Past Continuous*, translated by Dalya Bilu, New York, Schocken Books, 1985.
2. A right-wing Israeli party, no long in existence.

CHAPTER FOURTEEN

Observations Concerning the Individual in Arab Cinema

Ibrahim al-Aris

In the early creative days of Arab cinema, and specifically in the 1950s, when moral and oversimplified symbolism was in the ascendant, some individuals represented evil and others represented good, with all the implications and nuances that these carry with them. This eternal confrontation between good and evil, where good always triumphs, was the pillar of the realism that produced divers types of realities in the cinema.

After that, it was inevitable that the symbol increase in definition. Thus good and evil and all their related concepts became closely intertwined with social variables, which were subsequently to be given the appellation 'class conflicts'. Thus we moved from the cinema of realism to the cinema of the cause or causes. This transfer of interest was particularly evident in the period between the mid-1950s and the mid-1960s. It was the result of the triumph of radical forces in Egypt, of the entrenchment of the concepts introduced by the Revolution of Free Officers and of the changes witnessed by the other Arab countries from the Algerian war until the Iraqi revolution and the violent events in Lebanon. At the time this was called the period of Pan-Arab Nationalism, which culminated in and at the same time was curbed by the defeat of June 1967.

The agents of change who were most aware of the mood of the times realized the important role the cinema could play in this situation in stirring a desire for change among the masses. It was therefore natural for the cinema to abandon moral confrontation in favour of class/political/ideological confrontation. Examples of these early attempts are the films of Hussein Sidqi, with a Nasserite nationalist ring, those of Tawfiq Salih, with a clear note of rebelliousness and exhortation, and the early productions of Algerian cinema, idolizing the struggle against colonialism, emulating Gorky, Brecht and Cecil B. deMille at the same time.

We cannot deny here that the Arab cinema of the 1960s had begun to draw much inspiration from elsewhere, after its long period of development from a cinema of realism to being the cinema of causes. This change reached its culmination through a number of stages, which we can note here:

- The film *al-Usfur* (The Bird) by Yousif Shahin, which followed the film *al-Ard* (The Land), by the same director. It posed questions about freedom and the relationship between the authority of the state and the masses.
- The narrative films that dealt with the Palestinian issue: *al-Makhdu'un* (The Betrayed) by Tawfiq Salih and *Kafr Qasim* by Burhan Alawiyya.
- *Al-Jabal* (The Mountain) by Khalil Shawqi, which directed criticism at the Nasserite period and its top-down revolutionary achievements. Few paid attention to this film at the time of its release.
- The films of the New Egyptian Cinema group, especially *Ughniya 'ala al-Mamarr* (A Song in an Alley) by Ali Abdul-Khaliq and *Zilal 'ala al-Janib al-Akhar* (Shade on the Other Side) by Ghalib Shacth.
- *Al-Mumiya* (The Mummy) by Shadi Abdul-Salam and his work on revolutionizing the language of cinema itself by freeing it from the language of written narrative.
- A series of films that revealed some anger in dealing with sociological reality and the current crises: *Bas ya Bahr* (Enough of Sea) by the Kuwaiti Khalid al-Siddiq, *al-Hayat al-Yawmiyya fi Qarya Suriyya* (Daily Life in a Syrian Village) by the Syrian Umar Amiralay and lastly *al-Tuq wa al-Iswara* (The Necklace and the Bracelet) by the Egyptian Khayri Bishara.

With films like these, some of which at any rate are considered among the best productions in the history of the Arab cinema, we have moved from realism to the cause. However, at both ends of the spectrum the characters have remained symbolic. One of them carries the specific features of a class, which help one to see the whole film as 'metaphorical', a 'borrowing' for the expression of 'the struggles going on within our societies: national struggles against colonialism, reactionism and Zionism, closely interwoven with class struggles against the lackeys of colonialism and the parasitic classes, and the various forms of reactionism'.

This at least is how it was expressed at a meeting on alternative cinema in Damascus at the beginning of the 1970s – the language of ideological rhetoric, and at the same time the language of honest nationalist desires. Should not the film director play his role in the battle? As it was understood at that time, this battle had two aspects – backwardness and the iniquitous enemy, with his domestic and foreign lackeys – yet it was clear, as contemporary writers underlined, that the relationship between the two aspects was one of both cause and effect.

In these respects the cinema was at any rate more advanced than all the other arts. It was more aware of what was happening, even if it still had to wait for a time before discovering that, absorbed as it was in ideological discoveries and its search for means to elude the censors in the battle it was waging against the political authority, it had failed to notice that it had produced nothing different from what realist cinema had produced. The cinema of the cause had been nourished originally from the same material and believed that it had taken its place. Yet there was a lack of real change, giving rise to a constant feeling among the more discerning film-goers, that there was something still lacking. What was it?

It was inevitable that the root cause of the defeat of 1967 would be examined and be revealed not as a temporary reverse or simply a case of foreign betrayal. It was inevitable too that a series of repercussions would follow, from which resulted the disasters of the 1960s and 1970s, before the Arab film director would discover that, although he had pursued a bold, investigative course, nevertheless his path was not the only one possible. To reach the stage at which the director could pose a new type of question, the cinema would have to wait until the 1980s. It was only then that anyone would begin to tie together concepts like the 'other', the 'ego', 'authority', 'history', and the 'father'.

Before that, consideration of the ego had been forbidden, because of the view, inherited from the history of Arab thought, that the self must not be revealed. For this reason autobiographies are very rare in our Arab Islamic civilization. Where they are found, they are for purposes of justification (e.g. *The Sira of Ibn Sina*, written by al-Jurjani), to express repentance (e.g. *al-Munqidh min al-Dalal* (The Deliverer from Error by al-Ghazali) or they consist of an external portrait that makes no attempt to penetrate the person's inner life and dissect the self (as in *Ibn Khaldun and his Travels to East and West*). Even in our modern era, if we take a close look at the autobiographies of Taha Hussein or Muhammad Hussein Haykal or even Tawfiq al-Hakim, Ibrahim al-Mazini and others, we will see how superficial, and at the same time symbolic, the portrayals are. This is because the question of self can never be raised or exposed.

Because the self cannot exist, even in rudimentary fashion, without the presence of the other, the other has always been either an enemy or a marginal or marginalized figure. The enemy is everybody who is outside the House of Islam and belongs to the House of War. He is necessarily dissolute and deviant. In the best circumstances, the Muslim may treat him according to 'that which is better', thus seeking to win God's pleasure (e.g. the story of Saladin with Richard the Lionheart). The other within the society – leaving aside some controversial issues – is a marginal, a sexual pervert, an adulteress (not an adulterer of course), an outcast, a masturbater, a prostitute, a Jew, a Christian, etc.

It is true that a large number of Arab films contain characters who represent this other. However, what is really striking is that they are always presented as stereotypes (the Christian or the Jew), as caricatures (the sexual pervert or the adulteress) or as people who are sick and need to be isolated from healthy society (the outcast, the madman or the prostitute). The Christian is always the manager of the estate; the Jew is always a greedy merchant; the pervert is always depraved and hypocritical; the adulteress is always condemned, a sinner, the cause of the greatest misfortune. The outcast (like Qanadi in *Bab al-Hadid* (Door of Steel) by Yousif Shahin) always has a complex that eventually leads him into crime; the madman is either an object of mockery or a criminal; the prostitute is a woman who has departed from the way of righteousness and must pay the price for her wickedness (as in *Bidaya wa Nihaya* [A Beginning and an End] by Salah Abu Saif) or take the path of repentance, thanks to a sudden divine awakening (as in *al-Mar'a allati Ghalabat al-Shaytan* [The Woman who Overcame Satan]).

From Yousif Shahin's questions about identity in *al-Ikhtiyar* (The Choice) to Burhan Alawiyya's questions about the relationship of our history – not only our enemy – with our defeat in *Kafr Qasim*, many things changed in Arab cinema. Perhaps the clearest change was that it began to touch on and then openly deal with the concepts mentioned above. In *al-Sarab* (The Mirage), Anwar al-Shannawi raised some controversial sexual issues in unemotive language without any condemnation. The complexes that govern the personality of Ali Ru'ba Laz (*Nur al-Sharif*) and his twin compulsions to lust after his mother and to masturbate are not treated in this film as caricatures or in a condemnatory fashion. Anwar al-Shannawi thus took a big step in terms of the way directors deal with the texts of

Najib Mahfuz. For example, we notice that the director of the first part of the trilogy (*Hasan al-Imam*) totally ignores Kamal's lust for his sister 'A'isha. In the original story Mahfuz describes how Kamal sips water from the same cup from which his sister has drunk, placing his lips in the same place as she had placed hers. It is also noticeable how the director of *al-Shahhadh* totally ignores the interpretation of the story that attributes the whole crisis of Umar al-Hamzawi to his lust for his daughter. When he discovers her on the beach in Alexandria, he is struck by how much she has come to resemble her mother – she was 'like the mother was the day he met her'.

Although Anwar al-Shannawi dared to explore these matters in *al-Sarab*, the sexual issue in its entirety was not raised in its boldest form until Yousif Shahin began, in *Iskandariya Layh* (Why Alexandria), to excavate his own personal sexual history. The process reached its climax in *Iskandariya Kaman wa Kaman* (Alexandria Again and Again). In these films sexual perversion is no longer rooted in society but becomes a part of the history of the self, which it is acceptable to incorporate.

This history of the self is one of the basic innovations which was brought to Arab cinema by Yousif Shahin. The way he boldly probes his own personal depths is rare in our Arab culture and will give rise to a school composed of the best of his disciples: Muhammad Malas, Yusri Nasr Allah, Farid Bughadir, Nuri Buzayd and Khalid al-Hajar. If the Lebanese director Marun Baghdadi had been destined to live and complete his last film, *Zawaya* (Corners), he too would doubtless have been included in that list.

So too could some Moroccan productions that have also attempted autobiographies. However, their perspective is not too far distant from ideology (Sa'd al-Shuraybi's film *Ayyam min Hayat 'Adiyya* (Days from an Ordinary Life) and the film *Paris* by Jilali Farhati). This confrontation with the self was at any rate the key that allowed the Arab director to handle the other with a large degree of truthful sensitivity. With Ra'fat al-Mayhi and the Lebanese film directors, al-Akhdar Hamina in Algeria and Rida al-Bahi in Tunis, the Christian is no longer simply a stereotyped other whom we picture as a caricature and symbol of the group; rather, he has become an individual of flesh and blood, a distinctive cinema character with his own individual history. This treatment of the religious other was taken to its logical conclusion with Nuri Buzayd's portrayal of the Jewish grandfather in his film *Rih al-Sadd* (or *Rajul al-Ramad* (A Man of Ash). For this portrayal Nuri Buzayd received the criticism 'he deserved' – at the hands not only of Arab censors, but also of numerous Arab intellectuals and film directors, who could not stand seeing a Jew portrayed in an Arab film with this degree of affection and positiveness, even if he was, as in this case, an Arab Jew who was determined to remain Arab and to die in Tunis.

Excavating the self and excavating history

However, the portrayal of the Jew was not the only innovation in Nuri Buzayd's film *Rih al-Sadd*. This film alone contained almost all the various new elements that hit the Arab cinema in the 1980s: excavating the self, excavating individual and group history and, especially, a new view of authority.

In *Rih al-Sadd*, even though there is a great authority, which is repressive and omnipresent, its existence could not be logical and enduring were it not for the existence of smaller authorities on which the great authority rests and the parties that are directly involved in castrating individuals.

This proposition is based on the reality that in this world no dictator governs purely of his own whim or by force of arms. No rule or occupation or colonization can exist for a moment unless there exist internal elements on which it can rely for support. The German occupation of France during the Second World War would not have been possible if the majority of French politicians and more that 70 percent of the people had not supported the Nazis. The great dictator cannot exist without the tyrannical presence of the other dictators: in the village, in the quarter, in the workplace, in the school, but especially in the home. In this way Arab cinema went a short distance towards exploding the concept of the father (the elder brother, the school inspector, the employer).

Nuri Buzayd was one of the first, followed by Michel Khleife in *Urs al-Jalil* (Wedding in Galilee), Farid Bughadir in *Halfawin*, Osama Muhammad in *Nujum al-Nahar* (Stars of the Day) and Muhammad Malas in *Ahlam al-Madina* (City Dreams).

In the Arab cinema hitherto, the father had been holy and sacrosanct. In the worst case, he was a party in a generational struggle whose purpose was to win him over to the side of new ideas. It is true that the father was portrayed as harsh and violent in some Egyptian films of the 1950s (in the guise of Zaki Rustum and Abbas Ghalib). However, there he was a symbol of a class, not a father in the biological sense. Most of the time too he was paired with another father who was kind-hearted and reasonable (in the guise of Hussein Riyad, or even Hasan Fayiq, Shafiq Nur al-Din or Abdul-Warith Asar). As long as the father was a symbol and not a real father, everything was all right. However, suddenly the Arab cinema began to reveal another image of the father: the image of the lord and possessor of power, the individual whose fatherly position forces him to play the role of dictator in his home. The question was not 'How can we get rid of this father?' but rather 'How can we get rid of the dictator inside him?', 'How can we deliver him from his fatherly role and restore him to his humanity?'

In films like *Halfawin*, Farid Bughadir uses the technique of disgracing the father for his stupidity, while deifying the mother and enabling his child Nura to overcome him and his authority by revealing what he really is (as Oedipus overcame the Sphinx by revealing him as he really was in *Oedipus the King* by Pier Paolo Pasolini). In *Rih al-Sadd*, Nuri Buzayd presents the father in the form of employer in a carpenter's workshop: he rapes the young man Hashimi, which makes him unable to live a normal sexual life. In Michel Khleife's *'Urs al-Jalil*, the young man 'Adil represents the symbolic eunuch in the relationship between the father, who is the mukhtar (village chief), and the occupying authority, and reveals his castration and his impotence on the day of his wedding.

This overlap between the father and the political authority (and between the older brother and the political authority in Osama Muhammad's *Nujum al-Nahar*), and this mixture between dictatorship in a small place (house, work school, quarter) and dictatorship, as it is practised by the political authority, is the new discovery of the Arab cinema achieved in the 1970s. Of course, it is not enough to make the father simply a symbol of authority. Nor was the father used as a surrogate for the dictatorial authority: such a ploy would only led to brushes with the censors without clashing directly with them.

The fact is that the Arab film director was too mature to find a means of criticizing dictatorship in such an indirect technique. The father here is a real father, a father of flesh and blood, an affectionate and compassionate father. At the same time he is a father who lives behind a mask placed upon him by society, which imposes upon him his role, wiping out the little boy that lives deep within him and changing him into a little dictator who justifies and supports the existence of the big dictator, ascending to the pinnacle of authority. In this microcosm, unlike what must happen at the pinnacle of authority in the macrocosm, the physical extermination of the father is not required, through a coup, a revolution or a civil war or through an assassination. Such are the only possible ways of getting rid of the supreme authority in Arab societies, which have rarely experienced democratic elections that produce a president who represents the will of the electors. Rather it requires that the father be delivered from the fatherly role that has been assigned to him and that he be prevented from physically or figuratively castrating his son. This can only be done by restoring humanity to the father. Once so liberated, he ceases to play the role of the oppressor, separates himself from the great father and is no longer a justification for him, just as the cell of the family is no longer a justification for the great cell.

Will the father be restored by showing his behaviour as a child and as a teenager in a disgraceful light (as in *Halfawin*) or by opposing him (as in *Rih al-Sadd*) or by insisting on a humanitarian model of fatherhood (as in *Iskandariya Layh* and *al-'Usfur*) or by treating him as a child and seeking a grave for him, thus beginning a new generation in exile (as in the fourth part of *Risala min Zaman al-Manfa* (A Letter from the Time of Exile)), or through a determined desire to proclaim his death (as in *Hurub Saghira* (Small Wars) by Marun Baghdadi?

All methods are legitimate so long as the goal remains to explode the sanctity of the authority in the family cell in preparation for depriving the great dictator (the political authority) of its small, justificatory reflections.

However, the best way remains the establishment of the identity of the self face to face with the identity of the father. But how can the establishment of this identity happen when the act of castration has taken place and has made 'Adil (in *'Urs al-Jalil*), Hashimi (in *Rih al-Sadd*), and Jamal (the brother of Nuri in *Mercedes*) impotent? Is the ideal solution that practised by 'Adil's bride, when she compensates (in *'Urs al-Jalil*) for the castration of her bridegroom by carrying out 'Adil's role herself? Or is the best solution to withdraw outside the space completely – a withdrawal that will be shown to be futile in *Layh ya Banafsaj?* (Why, Banafsaj?) by Ridwan Kashif, and especially in *Sultan al-Madina* by Munsif Dhuwaib? Is there any sort of solution in geographical withdrawal (let us remember here that for Qasar, Kamal and even the French doctor in *al-Rajul al-Muhajjab*, by Marun Baghdadi, geographical removal gained nothing)?

The Lebanon war in the Paris métro

What the Arab cinema suggests varies according to the history carried on the shoulders of each director. The heroes of Burhan Alawiyya evoke the Lebanon war in the Paris Métro, and for the hero of *'Ubur*, by Mahmud bin Mahmud, even language and continual removals fail to produce a solution. In *Safa'ih min Dahab* (Sheets of Gold), by Nuri Buzayd, the oppression by the political power of the protagonist (reinforced by castrating him as well) does not lead to a deepening of the confrontation with it but to his being forced to confront himself and his history, which compels him to search for his identity.

Search for identity? Perhaps this is the best solution for arriving at a sort of balance within societies that work in every way they can against the individual, where the individual is almost obliterated on the altar of conceived group interests?

The search for identity is the search for a history – not the history of the archives, which has reached us through the perceptions of the authority (equally in the macrocosm and the microcosm) of itself, but the repressed history, the history of the individual; not the history of the castrated person, but the history that is still healthy, the history of the self, the history of the quarrelsome individual, the history that produced the values of individualism represented in the most beautiful artistic creations. Thus it is not by chance that the aesthetics dominant in films like *al-Mumiya'* (The Mummy), by Shadi Abdul-Salam, *al-Ha'imun* (The Wanderers) and *Tuq al-Hamama al-Mafqud* (The Dove's Lost Necklace), by Nasir Khamir and even in *Majnun Layla*, by al-Tayyib al-Wahshi, are really decisively ideological. Creation, whether it be of a pharaonic statue, an engraving in a mosque or an example of Arabic calligraphy, is an act of assertion against the rigidity and quiescence of society. Any recollection of the products of this individual creative genius as against the ideological recollection of moments of 'enlightening' history, in the political sense of the term, becomes an act of rebellion against the official history in favour of the history of the individual.

The search of the hero of *Tuq al-Hamama al-Mafqud* for the names of love, as he passes through the Andalus and reaches as far as Samarkand, and the absenting of the sexual identity of Aziz (the androgynous princess of Samarkand) are simply two aspects of one identity, the identity of the individual against the authority of the group.

The history of the individual remains castrated as long as the identity of the individual, the identity of the ego, remains tied to the image that society has formed of the father with his mask. This identity will remain the product of a castrated and castrating agglomeration as long as it continues to spring from the portrayal by the authority and the state of its history. When authority needed to be released from its image of itself and to be transformed from a father to an individual (thus authority became a means of administering society, not of repressing it), it was inevitable that the past would be recalled and delivered from its ideological associations, in other words, transformed from the history of the group to the history of the individual.

Such an operation, in the first place, demands a review of history. Numerous films have reviewed the father and his role and our view of the other, and have painted a history of creative forms, linking artistic products with the nature of the individual, not with the work of a group. Now the cinema has begun, albeit slowly and timidly, to paint history as the history of individuals, not the history of groups and classes. Thus the family cell, stripped of its sanctity (by Osama Muhammad in *Nujum al-Nahar* or Nuri Buzayd in *Rih al-Sadd* or Farid Bughadir in *Halfawin* or Yusri Nasr Allah in *Mercedes*) is the chief pillar of a healthy and cohesive society. The individual has gained a personal history. An individual with a dynamic rather than a static history is the basis of society – that is, if the existence of the group is unavoidable. In our view, this recollection of the history of the individual, at the expense of the history of the family cell, the social cell and the nation itself, represents a major revolution in the way Arab cinema directors have begun to present reality in new films.

Films like *Shayshakhan* by Mahmud bin Mahmud, *al-Bari'* (The Innocent) by Atif al-Tayyib, *al-Tahuna* (The Mill) by Ahmad Rashidi and *al-Bidaya* (The Beginning) by Salih Abu Sayf are able to pose the problem of the confrontation of the individual with his history and with authority from the perspective of ideological rhetoric. However, these films and numerous other ones mentioned above are innovative in portraying the nature of the identity of the individual, as an individual, as a self-supporting element, not defined by ideology or class. The innocent, in Atif al-Tayyib's film of the same name, and Nasr Allah in *Mercedes*, the personages of Sultan al-Madina, Yousif Shahin and those who act him in numerous introspective films, including Yahya in *Wid'an ya Bunabart* (Farewell, Bonaparte), the customer in Muhammad Khan's film of the same name, Faris in *Faris al-Madina*, and the hero of *Safa'ih min Dhahab*: these are all characters presented to us as if they had been born a moment before the beginning of the events of the film, springing from nothingness and hurrying off in search of their identity and their history. They are seeking in this way to belong to a society that accords with their ambitions, their desires and their individual history, not the society they inherited from their fathers.

In this sense, the characters of the new Arab cinema undertake a long night's journey to the day of the ego, searching for an identity that will link them with a history which is clearer and more energizing than the history that has been imposed. Overall, these films propose to us – not yet clearly, but with increasing clarity with every successive film – that the exodus of the ego from its prisons and from its direct inheritance (the mask of the father, which changes him into an executioner and a victim at the same time) is the best way of confronting the other taboo matters, such as the position of women, the other and the self. These taboos are what have shackled society and made it a means of imprisonment rather than a from a base from which the individual can take off (*Sultan al-Madina* and *Halfawin*).

It is not by chance that the majority of these film makers belong to the minority, whether within Arab societies or in their places of exile. Perhaps our concluding image should be the picture in the fourth and last part of the film *Risala min Zaman al-Manfa* (Letter from a Time of Exile), by Burhan Alawiyya, of the old man whom his son buries in exile in Strasbourg, France, far from Marjayun, his birthplace, in south Lebanon. Justifying his act, the son says that it is better for his father to be the first of his lineage to be buried here in exile, rather than the last to be buried in Marjayun. This sentiment serves as a symbol of a father whose role is finished and who is saved from his history. In death he is freed from his previous existence and his identity is reclaimed, as is his history as an individual, as he passes over into a society to which he is in no way related and which therefore cannot repress him.

Translated by Basil Hatim

CHAPTER FIFTEEN

Missed Opportunities: Me and my Gender

Mai Ghoussoub

It took me a long time to understand why my mother loved to tell the story of the doctor who delivered me. Whenever there was a willing audience, she would tell it. I must have heard it a thousand times.

For her story to make sense, you need to know that I am the second female born to my parents and that my sister and I are their only progeny.

'When Dr Razook left the delivery room, his face was tense and he walked past your father without looking at him. Your father was waiting anxiously for the baby to be delivered so that he could join me. (In those days, husbands were never allowed to witness the birth of their child.) The attitude of the doctor terrified your father, who thought that something terrible must have happened to me and to our baby. When he knew that I had given birth to a healthy baby girl, he was delighted. Dr Razook did not like to deliver girls, especially if the parents were his friends, and he felt his reputation as a gynaecologist was perturbed by every female he brought into the world. As for your dad and me, we did not care one way or the other, boy or girl.'

The story of my birth as told by my mother is a perfect metaphor for my country of origin. It is the story of juxtaposed values and contradictions. Yes, it is OK to be born a girl but the story never ends here. There is a 'but', a Mediterranean 'but' and a westernized OK that have to coexist, and modernized citizens somehow have to juggle and survive within the spaces of this coexistence. And they have to do it with grace and honour. My parents are from the generation of Middle Easterners who lived at the time of transition from the traditional values of large families to the westernized nuclear family with a maximum of two children, raised and educated in the best schools you could afford. They dreamt of bringing up free, responsible individuals – individuals who were nonetheless constantly reminded that they were the custodians of their family's honour, especially if they stood on the female side of the gender border; individuals who had to watch constantly for 'what the neighbours say' about them and their parents, their uncles, cousins and other relatives.

My story, the way I tried to live my life, is a desperate, not always unhappy, effort to reconcile at least two epochs, two modes of behaviour, two value systems that prevailed simultaneously and very concretely in pre-war Lebanon.

Let me come back to my mother. A clever woman, she was considered very marriageable thanks to her good looks and was consequently withdrawn from school, in the late 1940s, by her parents at the age of sixteen. She had loved her school and treasured the knowledge she had acquired there, mainly in the sciences. She had no say about her parents' decision and anyway she had fallen in love with my father. My father, a modern young man, cared very little about the difference in their religious confessions and courted her openly because he had 'good intentions'. They fell madly in love and married when she was seventeen and he twenty years old. They despised marriages of convenience or calculation, believed in true love and had the Hollywood movies, already triumphant over the screens of Beirut, to confirm the rightness of their romantic choice. There were a few couples like them in Lebanon in those days, but they were not the rule. Nine months after their wedding, they brought my older sister into this world. They were delighted; they adored her. One only has to look at the infinite number of pictures they took of her, and at the journal my mother kept, in which she recorded every smile, every tooth that appeared on the baby girl's face. It occurred to me once that the same Dr Razook had delivered my sister, and that he may have been as disappointed by his deed as he was when it was my turn to show up. But, for some unexplained reason, it was only my appearance that seemed to be a worthy story for my mother to narrate. The reason should have been obvious to me. It may not matter to the parents if the newborn is male or female, but in the wider society there is nothing to boast about when you bring only girls into this Middle Eastern world. You have to be very keen on bringing up a small, well-cared-for family to stop after the second child and not try for that special one that will perpetuate your name and speak for the virility of the father and the blessing of the mother.

Garçon manqué was the term I kept hearing about me. Tomboy. The French expression is more revealing. A boy missed. An opportunity missed. But the values that the post-industrial societies had introduced in our Levantine reality were tangible enough and no third child was to be expected. So my story meets that of my society. I am female, accepted as such but unconsciously or very silently wished different. The context in which I was born, the Lebanon of the 1950s, was a paradigm of this dichotomy. Some named the two poles in this combination modern and traditional, others used the labels east and west, now the term post-modern is frequently used.

I can think of a perfect metaphor: *un garçon manqué*, a missed boy, and *une opportunité manquée*, a missed opportunity. A country that has missed its democratic and tolerant potentialities. A happy alternative. But . . .

To go back to my gender and its implications: like any child who finds him/herself at the centre of attention, I started to play the role that made me successful among the members of my family and their friends. I started to behave as a tomboy. I wrote to Father Christmas asking him for a cowboy outfit. When I played with my dolls I did so discreetly, for the pleasure of mothering or dressing them was hampered by a sharp feeling of guilt and the fear of disappointing the grown-ups. I joined the boys in the courtyard after school to play football and all was free and fun until Sit Zalfa, an imposing old neighbour, saw me fighting physically over the score with one of the boys. She used to terrify us with her severe chignon and her Turkish and Italian vocabulary. 'Pronto,' she screamed, pointing her stick at me and then in the direction of my home. She visited my parents and told them that it was not 'right' for a nine-year-old girl to mix with the boys of the neighbourhood. That was the end of my street life. What the neighbours said proved more powerful than the cute image of a *garçon manqué*. The neighbours' opinion had a decisive influence on my parents, who still insisted that it did not matter to them if I were a girl or a boy. We were already in the early 1960s, and Lebanon enjoyed the rule of a functioning parliament; a coup d'état had been defeated and my mother as well as my aunts dressed in the latest Parisian fashion. My mixed school was preparing to separate the girls from the boys: yes, even the French Lycée adapted its rules to the Arab-Mediterranean reality of Lebanese society. Religion and religious teaching were not allowed inside the secular institution, but girls who were approaching puberty had to be separated from boys. A *garçon manqué* in a girls' school did not make much sense. A segregated secular lycée would have been an anomaly in France, but we were not in France, even though we spoke French and believed in the values of the Enlightenment.

I had heard my parents calling me a tomboy, and now I started hearing my mother asserting that I was very good in the sciences, the objective ones. Accordingly I became good at mathematics and physics. My grades in French literature, a subject I adored, did not impress my mother, whereas her face would beam with joy whenever she saw me resolving some geometry or calculus problem. This was a safer way of replacing the boy that was never to be born; safer than playing and fighting with the boys over a football kick. For sciences do not jeopardize virtue or reputation. At school, when I was not yet fourteen years old, I read *The Mandarins* by Simone de Beauvoir and heard of free love, but a concert by Johnny Halliday, the French pop star, was cancelled by the Minister of Interior, the 'progressive' Kamal Jumblatt, who believed that 'western degenerate images' did not suit our moral values and might be harmful to our youth. Along with all the citizens of the Lebanon in the 1960s, I learned to live with these conflicting attitudes and values. Jugglers we became: with more or less graciousness, sometimes over some broken eggs, we wove our way through mini skirts and scarves, chanting anti-imperialist slogans as well as the Beatles. The kitsch singer Taroub sang for an Arab public, while her sister Mayada set Arabic words to western pop songs. When a dance called the Hully Gully invaded the night-clubs of Lebanon, the famous Diva Sabah sang *Hully Dabke Yaba Of*:

> Hully Gully est connu chez tous les occidentaux,
> Hully Dabke Yaba Of est connu chez
> Les Orientaux, presque le même et tout le monde l'aime.

Neither we nor Sabah could have guessed that the Occident and the Orient were going to sing to totally different tunes. From Radio Cairo the mesmerizing voice of Umm Kulsum was asking for a rifle – A'tini Bunduqiya' – a rifle to liberate Arab land. We were reading Jean-Paul Sartre and starting to demonstrate for the liberation of Palestine.

By the early 1970s I was studying mathematics and French literature. Male and female subjects. Feminism was on the agenda: George Tarabishi translated Sheila Rowbotham, Germaine Greer's *The Female Eunuch* was available in the bookshops and Sonia Beiruti, a TV broadcaster, invited a few of us to her TV show to debate women's emancipation. Two scenes from that period keep recurring in my memory. First scene: on this TV show, I said I wanted to be a free woman and to be independent, to work so that I would not live off my father's or a future husband's money. My father, who was watching the programme, felt deeply humiliated. He took these words as an insult to his honour. Second scene: during a student demonstration, a few women jumped on the shoulders of their colleagues to lead and chant revolutionary slogans. Everybody in this demonstration had seen the pictures of May 1968 in France and the dynamic images of the women lifted above the crowds by their co-objectors. 'Scandalous,' screamed some passers-by, as well as a few demonstrators. The women were put down very quickly. We may have been influenced by May 1968 but we were not in the Latin Quarter of Paris; we were still on the shores of the Mediterranean.

We were a parliamentary democracy, we had no kings and no army generals ruling over us, but many of our politicians were the sons of landowners or sons of other politicians. They all spoke of democracy and we called for our right to independence as women while armed militias were being formed and operations to restore women's virginity were easily available. Somehow, I see a parallel between my studying mathematics at the American University and French literature at the Lebanese National University, between my gender that held me responsible for the family's reputation on one hand and my county's coexisting contradictions on the other.

Feminism was an obvious route to follow for somebody like me – a woman who had believed that men's spaces were not totally impermeable, nor mysterious or difficult to handle. You play with boys, enter their classrooms, obtain better grades than many of them and then you are asked to obey them or accept an inequality that places them above you? This was very difficult to swallow, especially if Simone de Beauvoir's *The Second Sex* has been widely read among your French-educated friends and her assertion that *'on ne naît pas une femme, on la devient'* (one is not born a woman, one becomes so) is a cool slogan to raise. Old feminism, that of the pioneers such as Hoda Sha'rawi or the active lawyer Laure Meghayzel, felt inadequate to our youthful impatience. We did not want only equality, the right to be professional while ensuring that we were first and foremost 'good mothers': we wanted to claim loudly and shamelessly that nothing could stop us from realizing our wishes and that our bodies belonged to us.

Engels, Reich and Alexandra Kollontai's teachings gave a social dimension to our belief that 'all is possible'. The country itself believed that its rise as the financial-tourism heaven of the Middle East and its enriched Gulf region was unstoppable, that the Palestinian resistance fighters were the local expression of the Vietnamese freedom fighters. We spoke out loudly against the hypocrisy of our society. We were getting more radicalized in our beliefs, and so were the contradictions and the conflicts in Lebanon.

A time came when, in the middle of the bloody and cruel sequences of the civil war, I started to miss the so-called hypocrisy of pre-war times. The feeling that 'I want everything and I want it now' dissipated. I looked with different eyes on the liberalism of my parents who had to bite on their Mediterranean wound and let me be. They tolerated my freedom of movement, even though my tomboy image was long dead and buried under the powerful influence of Sitt Zalfa and her ilk.

I moved to the other side of the Green Line, where I thought people would be free from the prejudices of my own milieu. There I found a reversed mirror detonating with the same kind of intolerance. What we called hypocrisy before the war was the best form of compromise people had found for living together. The taboo preventing one from spelling out one's dislike for the other had been a good discipline. Look around you and see how ugly it all becomes when people feel no inhibition in their intolerance. I am not calling for censorship, far from it. People have the right to express their feelings, however despicable we may think them, but this should not discourage us from doing all we can to relate hatred for the other's colour, race or sexual choice to the notion of bad, uncivilized and immoral and to link the violent expression of this hatred to legal judgment and action.

Yes, it took me a long time to realize why my mother loved to tell the story of Dr Razook and my birth. It took me longer to realize that the contradictions my parents had to live through opened great new spaces for me. And if they had not hoped for me to jump over the limiting fences my gender imposed on me, I may have been confined to living, all my life, on one side of the border(s) and I would have never learnt that we were all as human or as bad as 'the other' during the ugly years of our civil war. If my mother had not told this story, would I have had the confidence, some eighteen years ago, to face the London bank manager who was reluctant to deal with me as one of the directors of Saqi Books and 'would rather see my male boss'? Would I have had the courage to bend the long aluminium rod that holds my sculptures, would I have been capable to be 'the other', to integrate among the others without pain and often with plenty of fun? I may have been a missed opportunity for Dr Razook and others like him; I still believe that I am better off missing the narrowness of the choice that would have been my secure lot and instead taking the risk of following my individual routes.

Notes on Contributors

Muhammad Abi Samra is a Lebanese journalist, literary critic and writer. He is the author of two novels, *Pauline wa Atyafuha* (Pauline and her Ghosts), Beirut, 1990, and *al-Rajul al-Sabiq* (The Ex-man), Beirut, 1995. He has contributed to many Arabic publications, such as the Lebanese daily newspaper *al-Safir* and the Arabic daily *al-Hayat*. He works currently for the Lebanese *al-nahar* cultural supplement.

Hussein Ahmad Amin is the son of the eminent Egyptian Islamic historian Ahmad Amin. He worked as a diplomat and ambassador representing Egypt in different capitals. He advised the Egyptian Ministry of Culture and was Deputy Director of the Egyptian Institute of Diplomatic Studies. He has written many books on culture, history and political thought and translated many others, and has received two awards from Egypt and one from the former Federal Republic of Germany. Since retiring from the Egyptian diplomatic service he has served as an adviser to the International Committee of the Red Cross and taught at the American University of Cairo.

Ibrahim al-Aris is a Lebanese film critic and author of many books on cinema and culture. His books include *al-Sura wa al-Waqi'* (Image and Reality), Beirut, 1978; *al-Kitaba fi Zaman Mutaghayyir* (Writing in a Changing Time), Beirut, 1980; and *Marun Baghdadi: al-Hulm al-Mu'allaq* (Marun Baghdadi: The Hanged Dream), Beirut, 1994. He now heads the cinema section of the Arabic weekly *al-Wasat*.

Saleh Bechir is a Tunisian writer and journalist who since 1976 has worked for various Arab newspapers and magazines and published essays and articles (in Arabic and French, translated into English, Italian, Hebrew, among other languages) about cultural and political affairs. In 1999 he won, jointly with Hazim Saghie, the 'Search for Common Ground' award for journalism.

Murat Belge was born in Ankara and taught at Istanbul University between 1966 and 1981. He is now the head of the Department of Comparative Literature at Bilgi University, Istanbul. Between 1975 and 1980 he was editor of the independent monthly *Birikim*. Until 1988 he was editor of *Yeni Gundem*, a weekly political magazine. In 1990 he became one of the founders (in the Prague Assembly) of the Helsinki Citizens Assembly, an international non-governmental organization, and from 1993 onwards the chair of the Turkish Regional Branch.

Yaron Ezrahi is Professor of Political Science at the Hebrew University of Jerusalem and a senior fellow of the Israel Democracy Institute. Among his publications are *The Descent of Icarus: Science and the Transformation of Contemporary Democracy*, 1990, and *Rubber Bullets: Power and Conscience in Modern Israel*, 1997.

Mai Ghoussoub is a London-based artist and writer who was born and brought up in Beirut. She has written on questions of culture and Middle Eastern issues for international journals, and is the author of several books in Arabic as well as a memoir in English, *Leaving Beirut: Women and the Wars Within* (London, Saqi Books, 1998).

Iliya Harik is a Lebanese who has a doctorate from the University of Chicago and is now Professor of Political Science at Indiana University. He is the author of several books and articles on political sociology and political economy (in English and Arabic), with special reference to the Middle East and North Africa.

Ramin Jahanbegloo was born in Tehran and received his PhD in philosophy from the University of Sorbonne in Paris. He taught at the Academy of Philosophy in Tehran and worked as a researcher at the French Institute for Iranian Studies from 1994 to 1996. He was a visiting scholar at the University of Toronto and a Fellow at the Centre for Middle Eastern Studies at Harvard University. He is currently Adjunct Professor in Political Philosophy at the University of Toronto. He has published a number of books and many articles on political and philosophical themes for French, Indian and Iranian journals.

Khaled Mustafa is a Sudanese scholar and writer. He taught at the University of Khartoum, where he became Dean of the Institute of Music and Drama and Director of the university press. Between 1987 and 1990 he taught at Kuwait University. His political articles have been published in almost all the Arabic papers in London and others in Sudan and the United Arab Emirates. He has won two prizes for his plays and published five books in Arabic and English. His book *Turabi's Failed Revolution* is due out soon.

Hazim Saghie is a Lebanese columnist for the Arabic daily newspaper *al-Hayat* and editor of its weekly supplement, *Tayyarat*. He is the author of *al-Hawa duna Ahlihi, Um Kulthum Surat wa Nas* (Love without Lovers: Um Kulthum, The Image and the Text), Beirut, 1991; *Awwal al-'Urubah* (Early Arabism), Beirut, 1993; *Thaqafat al-Khomeinyyah: fi al-Istishraq* (The Cultures of Khomeinism: On Orientalism), Beirut, 1995; *Difa' an al-Salam* (In Defence of Peace), Beirut, 1998; and *Wida' al-'Urubah* (Farewell to Arabism), Beirut, 1998.

Sami Shourush is a Kurdish Iraqi writer and journalist who writes in both Kurdish and Arabic. He is the author of *Tanuu al-Akrad fi al-Iraq: Madkhal ila al-Siyasah* (Variations of the Kurds in Iraq: An Introduction to the Political Situation), Arbil, Iraqi Kurdistan, 2000. Some of his studies have been published in the Arabic cultural magazine *Abwab*.

Emmanual Sivan is Professor of History in the Faculty of Humanities at the Hebrew University of Jerusalem. His publications include: *Interpretations of Islam: Past and Present*, 1985; *Radical Islam: Medieval Theology and Modern Politics*, 1985; and *Mythes arabes politiques*, 1995. He has contributed many articles to Israeli and Arab newspapers.

Gadi Taub is an Israeli author of fiction and coeditor of *Micarov*, a social-democratic journal of literature and society. His book *A Dispirited Rebellion: Essays on Contemporary Israeli Culture* offers a panoramic view of the Israeli cultural landscape in the 1980s and 1990s. Taub wrote commentaries for the daily *Maariv* and for Channel One late night news. Having hosted various TV and radio shows in Israel he is now writing a PhD in American history at Rutgers University.

Els Van der Plas is a Dutch art historian, curator and art critic. She founded the Gate Foundation in Amsterdam (1987), an organization for international exchange, and since 1997 she has been Director of the Prince Claus Fund in The Hague. She lectures at various universities, including Cornell and Leiden, and writes for many national and international publications.

Index